THE VAL
OF TH
ENTERPRISE
CULTURE

The Moral Debate

Edited by

PAUL HEELAS and PAUL MORRIS

London and New York

First published 1992
by Routledge
11 New Fetter Lane, London EC4P 4EE

Simultaneously published in the USA and Canada
by Routledge
a division of Routledge, Chapman and Hall, Inc.
29 West 35th Street, New York, NY 10001

Printed and bound in Great Britain
by Mackays of Chatham PLC, Chatham, Kent

British Library Cataloguing in Publication Data
A catalogue record for this book is available
from the British Library.

Library of Congress Cataloging in Publication Data
A catalogue record for this book is available
from the Library of Congress.

ISBN 0–415–07614–5
ISBN 0–415–07615–3 (pbk)

Contents

Notes on the contributors

Ted Benton, Department of Sociology, University of Essex.

Anthony P. Cohen, Department of Social Anthropology, University of Edinburgh.

Paul Heelas, Department of Religious Studies, Lancaster University.

David Marquand, Department of Politics and Contemporary History, University of Salford.

Paul Morris, Department of Religious Studies, Lancaster University.

David Nicholls, Vicar of Littlemore, Oxford.

Harold Perkin, Department of History, Northwestern University, Illinois.

Raymond Plant, Department of Politics, Southampton University.

Barry Richards, Department of Sociology, Polytechnic of East London.

Nikolas Rose, Department of Human Sciences, Brunel University.

Sean Sayers, Philosophy, Darwin College, University of Kent.

Tony Skillen, Philosophy, Darwin College, University of Kent.

Marilyn Strathern, Department of Social Anthropology, Manchester University.

Alan Suggate, Department of Theology, University of Durham.

Kenneth Thompson, Faculty of Social Sciences, The Open University.

Lord Young of Graffham, Board of Directors of Cable and Wireless and of Salomon Brothers; previously Minister of Trade and Industry, and former Chairman of the Manpower Services Commission.

Preface

The 'enterprise culture' of contemporary Britain is about wealth creation and distribution; the producer and the consumer; even the 'active citizen'. Essentially, it is a programme of cultural reform, and one that has generated heated public debate. Bishops vie with opposition politicians to provide the most forceful critiques.

This volume derives from a conference organized by Lancaster University's Centre for the Study of Cultural Values as part of its 1988–90 research theme – 'The Values of the Enterprise Culture'. In contrast to much that has been published on the new conservatism, the focus here is very much on the moral significance of the enterprise culture. Taking their cue from the fact that the programme of reform is meant to have a profound bearing on cultural values, contributors draw on a range of academic disciplines to shed light on issues that concern all who reflect upon the wellbeing of the nation.

We have greatly benefited from many long discussions with the other two Centre members involved in running the conference, Russell Keat and Nick Abercombie. The volume that they have edited, deriving from seminar papers presented by members of the Centre at Lancaster, has now been published by Routledge (1991). *Enterprise Culture*, covering 'political representations of enterprise', 'enterprise culture in different contexts', and 'market values and consumer sovereignty', serves to complement the current focus on morality.

We would like to thank everybody who contributed to the conference. The Economic and Social Research Council provided a grant (W100261042) to help run the event, for which we are most grateful. Janice Parkes and Eileen Martin are thanked for typing several of the drafts.

PAUL HEELAS and PAUL MORRIS
Lancaster University, 1990

1 Enterprise culture: its values and value

PAUL HEELAS & PAUL MORRIS

> Our aim has always been more than just economic progress; it is to renew the spirit and solidarity of the nation (Thatcher, 1979).

Since coming to power in 1979, the Conservative government has been intent on constructing a 'New Britain', a Britain, in the words of Margaret Thatcher, that 'is free, prosperous, generous and secure' (1989). The new order is to be highly individualistic. What matters is giving 'individuals more and more control over their own lives' (Baker 1990), providing 'more choice and more opportunity to every member of our society – not just those who already have the means or the knowledge' (Howe 1989). The talk is of 'self-reliance' and 'self-respect'; of freedom from state control; of people drawing on their own resources to compete in the 'open' market, using the wealth they create to take responsibility for – and so exercise accountability over – their educational, housing and health requirements, rather than relying on the offices and organs of the state.

During the last decade, the word 'enterprise' has been elevated to a cultural status. The government has taken many steps – institutional, financial, educational, and other – designed to change the ways in which people make sense of and evaluate themselves and their activities. Strange as it may seem to those who think that 'enterprise' is simply to do with wealth creation and acquisition, the programme of enterprise reform lies at the very heart of the government's moral crusade. All the indicators are that this programme, albeit with increased social emphasis, will be continued in the new 'Majorite' regime, with its promise of 'cultural reform', the creation of a 'classless society' and a 'climate of opportunity', in the context of the open market (Major 1990, election speech).

It is true that the culture has a great deal to say about wealth creation; about the domain of production for the free or 'open' market. One aim is certainly to cultivate a distinctive 'economic culture' highlighting a set of values relating to autonomous enterprising selves and 'releasing the spirit of enterprise'. Lord Young defines the culture by writing of 'the sum of the talents of individuals who dare to use their initiative to supply their fellow-men with the goods and services they want' (see Chapter 2, p. 34). At the same time, he makes clear that enterprise is 'the key to prosperity'. The resurgence of capitalism and increased wealth creation are held to depend upon the culture taking root.

However, it is mistaken to suppose that the enterprise culture can be reduced to the economic realm of production. Advocates believe that the programme of enterprise reforms will serve to instil and nurture 'Thatcherite values' in other spheres of life, thereby elevating them to national status. The programme is designed to encourage the widespread cultural adoption of a distinctive way of allocating priorities and organizing activities beyond the market place as well as within it. It is designed to change how people think and what they value. Fundamentally, it is to do with changing how all of us understand ourselves.

As well as being enterprising producers, competing to create wealth rather than dissipating energies on non-productive forms of activity, people should also exercise their freedom of choice as enterprising consumers rather than being permissive, and should serve as active citizens, contributing to the public good rather than being selfish. Those who are unemployed should actively seek work, rather than taking refuge in the 'dependency culture' provided by the welfare state.

In more general terms, the culture is perhaps *the* vehicle in the attempt to establish a regime where the individual, rather than the state apparatus, can flourish. According to Thatcher, to cite her oft-quoted dictum, 'There is no such thing as society. There are individual men and women and there are families' (Thatcher 1987). The programme of enterprise reform, it appears, is vital if 'society' itself is to be abolished. 'Individuals', *themselves*, must acquire the values associated with the culture – generosity, responsibility, discipline, hard work – if selfish, indeed anarchical, forces are not to be unleashed when people are given the opportunity to take greater control over their lives.

With the exception of Lord Young, who writes as one of the chief architects of the reform programme, the contributors to this volume draw on a variety of academic traditions to subject it to critical scrutiny. To pave the way, we start here by portraying the culture itself in some detail. Attention is then given to the main criticisms that have been made by leading public figures. Finally, and with a shift of gear, we introduce a number of arguments made by academic commentators.

The official story

Since the enterprise culture is essentially an ongoing programme of reform, we feel justified in drawing on presentations made by its proponents. And, since the portrayal is designed for introductory purposes, we also feel justified in ignoring the fact that advocates do not always present it in identical fashion.

The culture of enterprise capitalism

Capitalism – minimally defined as production for a market by individuals or combines with the purpose of making a profit – never exists in isolation from other institutions, beliefs and values. It is contextualized, which is to say that it always belongs to an 'economic culture' (Berger 1987). Different societies have developed different forms of the genus 'capitalism'.

Pride of place in the culture of enterprise production is accorded to the assumption that wealth creation, the ultimate measure of success, is best obtained by a highly individualistic form of capitalism. The autonomous self is prioritized. Various specific personal virtues are greatly esteemed. Instead of resting on their laurels, producers should be ambitious and competitive, pitting their wits against the opposition, boldly setting goals and energetically 'going for it'. Producers should take the initiative, always being alert for opportunities: in particular, those provided by new consumer

requirements. They should be rugged, prepared to take on responsibilities, but not afraid to take calculated risks. They should
certainly be industrious. Such enterprising selves should act in
entrepreneurial or 'intrapreneurial' fashion.

Enterprise capitalism is thus very different from economic cultures which function in collectivist mode. Hierarchical – that is,
'command' – corporate cultures, where participants are not encouraged to act as independent agents ('what would my superior
think?') and where as much attention is paid to securing promotion as to grappling boldly with commercial challenges, are
far removed from the spirit of enterprise. Although both enterprising and corporatist selves might well be motivated by 'self
interest', the former never loses sight of the importance of wealth
creation. Enterprising selves work hard to obtain financial rewards;
more generally, to pursue a commercially envisaged mode of
self-development. In contrast, the work ethic of the corporatist self
typically owes much to the value accorded to status-improvement.

Enterprise and national culture

How is the enterprise culture supposed to take root and function
outside the traditional domain of industry and commerce? Exactly
what has it got to do with the citizen and the consumer; with new
Conservative values in general?

Much derives from the fact that the great goal is to encourage
as many as possible to use their talents to create wealth. As Peter
Morgan (Director General of the Institute of Directors) puts it, 'an
enterprise culture is one in which. . . *all* work for the success of
UK plc' (Morgan 1990: 2). Accordingly, steps have been taken
to introduce the market to those who have previously considered
themselves to be insulated from such forces. The assumption is that
those affected will be encouraged to become enterprising. Talk is
of 'the unleashed power of motivation by reward' and of people
being 'stimulated by market incentives'.

The market is entering 'professional' territories, be it education
or the National Health Service (NHS). The Secretary of State
for Education speaks of higher education as an 'industry', where
what matters is attending to 'production' to increase efficiency and
quality. The intention is that people will have to exercise initiative;

compete for 'consumers'; cost their activities and think of themselves as 'producers', if they are to prosper, let alone retain their jobs. In this fashion, the discipline and rigour of the market helps to construct a mode of selfhood defined in terms of the virtues of enterprise. Thus, the plan is that those running hospitals can no longer simply provide treatment without paying due attention to what it costs; without being properly accountable. They now have to think in terms of an economic culture that requires operations to be properly budgeted and 'sold' on the 'open' market.

The economic culture of enterprise is indeed *the* major weapon in the assault on those who have fallen foul of 'dependency culture', whether this is found among the middle classes, trade unionists, or the unemployed. Thinking of what Morgan calls the 'middle class salariat', namely those who 'don't have to worry about where the next pay cheque is coming from' (Morgan 1990: 7), the claim is that enterprise reforms effect a shift in consciousness – from simply relying on established positions and incomes to appreciating the fact, as Morgan puts it, that they now belong to a 'culture. . .in which every individual understands that the world *does not owe* him or her a living' (Morgan 1990: 2; cf. Wiener 1981, for a more comprehensive account of the supposedly deeply-rooted cultural distaste for capitalist endeavour). 'Empty suits' beware!

Clearly, enterprise reforms concerned with extending and intensifying the operation of market forces also mean that the 'consumer' has become an increasingly influential figure. Enterprising producers working in the world of commerce strive to capitalize on consumer desires; enterprising 'producers' working for organizations such as hospitals that have been opened up to the market have to compete for custom. Consumers belong to the enterprise culture by virtue of the fact that enterprise production is consumer-led.

Another reason for treating the sphere of consumption as integral to the culture is that the government clearly hopes that ever-increasing numbers will become enterprising consumers. Enterprising selves as producers appreciate the value of wealth creation and have acquired the virtues to pursue this goal. This ethic, the argument goes, should also inform their activities as consumers. Among other things, they should have learnt the importance of responsibility, moderation, or discipline. They should not want to fritter away their hard-earned income on frivolous, hedonistic, non-remunerative consumer activities. Their aim is to save, then to invest in commodities which, if managed properly by means of enterprising skills, become a remunerative asset.

In fact, the government has encouraged enterprise in the sphere of consumption by a variety of strategies. Of first importance, measures have been taken to jolt 'passive' consumers out of their apathy. People who have been relying on state provision have been encouraged to take a more active role, buying their council house, investing in private pensions and health insurance, etc. Another measure has been to encourage the wider ownership of shares. Yet more steps – for example, vouchers to be used to buy educational provision – are on the agenda (MacGregor 1990). Whatever the method, the outcome, it is hoped, is that consumption becomes a business-like activity, people shopping around for the best or most cost-effective forms of education, health care and so forth. 'Thatcherite values' in general are nurtured, the then Prime Minister stating:

> We can only build a responsible, independent community with responsible, independent people. That is why Conservative policies have given more of them the chance to buy homes, build up capital and acquire shares in their companies (Thatcher 1988a).

In particular, that cardinal value – freedom of choice – is catered for. And this freedom encourages the spirit of enterprise among those who provide the consumer-purchasable products. Producers must produce the right goods at the right cost if they are to compete successfully.

The enterprise culture is also portrayed as generating, and in that sense encompassing, another kind of activity: that is, 'active citizenship'. Thus consumers can increasingly 'vote' when they spend money or – looking to the future – use their 'vouchers'. 'Consumer democracy' should ensure that inefficient universities and NHS hospitals, for example, have a challenging future. In addition those who have been well-educated as enterprising capitalists are naturally prompted to act for the public good. Or so it is claimed. In the words of Lord Young (see Chapter 2, p. 42):

The individualism of the enterprise culture, that we are seeking to promote, will not just exhaust its energies in work and the pursuit of material reward. I believe it will bubble over into other activities. Now that our companies are becoming more profitable, we are now witnessing closer involvement with the community, and a greater willingness to second employees and put money into voluntary projects.

And, in the words of Thatcher herself:

> As prosperity has increased, so the fundamental generosity of our people has prompted far more personal giving. Of course, there will always be a minority whose sole concern is themselves. But those who care, and they are the great majority of us, now have the means to give. And they are giving in full measure. . . The fact is that prosperity has created not the selfish society, but the generous society (Thatcher 1988a).

Overall, then, although the programme of developing an enterprise culture may be primarily focused on the domain of the producer, its advocates nevertheless clearly believe that it has a much greater contribution to make to 'the spirit and solidarity of the nation' than merely rejuvenating capitalism. Advocates believe that the programme is also bound up with nurturing enterprising and responsible consumers together with active citizens. The cultivation of 'popular capitalism' (ownership of small businesses, houses, and shares), together with other institutional and financial reforms, should do much to ensure that the enterprise culture dislodges its rivals on the national scene. As Thatcher puts it, 'Economics are the method. The object is to change the soul' (Thatcher 1988b).

The so-called 'dependency culture' is clearly a primary target. Enthused by the economic culture of enterprise, and having to confront reforms that have brought the consumer-driven market to bear, many organizations (including those that were once nationalized) can no longer afford to provide sinecures or 'nests' for the unenterprising. Those who are unemployed (not least those who supposedly belong to the 'underclass') and others who have acquired the custom of relying on the state for welfare, housing and educational provision, can no longer remain so content with their lot. In addition nothing short of a 'short sharp shock' is required to shift the more 'unenterprising'. Furthermore, the unemployed learn that they have to show enterprise (in particular, the kind of self-help and self-responsibility advocated by 'get on your bike'), or suffer the consequences of the erosion of state provision. Those with jobs, who do not heed the possibilities opened up by enterprising producers (such as apparently better education or health care), have only themselves to blame if they do not bother to set about improving their circumstances.

However, the role of the enterprise culture in reforming 'the soul of the nation' does not stop here. That the rigours of individualistic wealth creation (and high interest rates!) are held to instil a sense of discipline – if only to invest for the future – and encourage hard work means that the culture is a powerful weapon in the battle against the 'permissive society'. Enterprising producers should not have the time to go on more than the odd binge; enterprising consumers should not be inclined to waste money on activities that are pleasurable but not financially rewarding. Hedonistic activities should neither sap the energies and commitments of producers nor undermine the moral fabric of the nation.

Enterprise and the 'moral economy'

Critical assessments of the enterprise culture have to take into account the claims that have been summarized: that the enterprise culture encourages people to *value* economic activity; that it addresses the evils threatening 'the soul of the nation'; and that it encourages the 'right' kind of values–cum–selfhood in general. Crucially, however, moral assessments have to take into account the way advocates attempt to justify the programme of reform by insisting that it provides a just 'moral economy' for the population at large. The key to the matter is the promise, as Thatcher puts it, that 'wider distribution of wealth' will result. The population will become better off all round.

Advocates argue for the 'trickle-down effect'. The general idea, as the Bishop of Liverpool, David Sheppard, formulates the claim of right-wing thinkers, is that:

The poor can only be helped towards prosperity by making the nation wealthier. Once the economy is free, the advance can speed up, with the wealthiest in front like the leading ranks of marching soldiers in a regiment. The faster they go, the further will those in the following ranks advance, including those at the rear (Sheppard 1989).

Successful entrepreneurs create work for others, either directly by way of employment or indirectly by way of their role as business consumers. Wealth creation is also justified by a claim which concerns another kind of 'trickle-down': that is, that those who are successful producers will quite naturally exercise their 'generosity'. Quoting John Wesley – 'Gain all you can, save all you can, give all you can' – Thatcher continues, 'Those words remain true today, and the British people remain true to them' (Thatcher 1988c). In addition, the prioritization of wealth creation is justified by the 'safety net' argument: 'Help will always be at hand for those who cannot help themselves' (Thatcher 1989).

In other words, welfare provision is required; and, in turn, this depends upon revenue. As Young puts it, 'our public goods and services depend on the health of our economy, which, of course, depends on enterprise and the success of our free market system' (see Chapter 2, p. 38). In a speech in 1988, Thatcher spoke of the highest ever level of social services (Thatcher 1988a). In another, she made the point that 'tax cuts are the incentive to create the wealth which pays for higher benefits' (Thatcher 1988c). She went on to quote Abraham Lincoln: 'You cannot strengthen the weak by weakening the strong'. Neither should it be forgotten that the enterprise culture supposedly contributes to the wider distribution of wealth by providing opportunities for the less well off to 'better themselves'.

Overall, the culture of enterprise is treated as primary to the task of 'putting the "Great" back into Britain'. The nation, it appears, is to be transformed into UK plc, and a prosperous business at that. But this rejuvenation of capitalism is also held to have a powerful bearing on moral rejuvenation. Those intent on propagating the culture have much to say about how life *ought* to be led. Rather paradoxically, however, the claim concerning the 'wider distribution of wealth' – which does so much to legitimize the project – smacks of a value that is not much in evidence among advocates of enterprise, that is, egalitarianism. For the economic culture of <u>enterprise</u> is informed by the assumption that competition – <u>generating winners and losers</u> – is vital.

Contesting enterprise values

The government's vision of the 'New Britain', with enterprise reforms leading the way forward, has stirred up a hornet's nest. Given that the intention is to introduce a new order – pertaining to the self, the economy, the government, and their interrelationships – it is hardly surprising that 'state of the nation' issues are widely contested. And, given that deeply embedded values are at stake, nor is it surprising to find that bishops have to compete with members of the Labour opposition in providing the most forceful criticisms of the 'conviction' politics of Conservative politicians. We now summarize the ways in which the enterprise programme has been criticized by leading public figures.

The egalitarian critique

The majority of criticisms are of this variety. The most obvious – and common – objection is that inequality is enhanced: a growing gulf between the rich and the poor; the perpetuation, indeed growth, of a victimized 'underclass'. In May 1990, the all-party Social Services Committee in the House of Commons announced that government figures, supposedly showing that the poor are becoming better off at twice the rate of those on average income, were based on miscalculations. In actual fact the income of the poorest 10 per cent had risen by 2.6 per cent compared with an average of 5.4 per cent. Labour leaders made much of this, claiming that it entirely discredited the notion that extra revenue generated by the enterprise culture 'trickles down'.

The work ethic of the enterprise culture clearly owes much to the idea that money is a great motivator. The culture is competitive. Because motivation is held to owe much to financial reward, inequalities are needed in order to maximize production. There must be winners and losers. Whether it be by way of rewarding those who have demonstrated their productive prowess by pay rises or by way of tax cuts (especially for those who had previously been heavily taxed for their 'success'), money is put to work. Perhaps these incentives are justified if the 'trickle down' really operates. But if it does not, those with enterprising skills simply become more wealthy.

Advocates of the culture can, of course, respond by claiming that increasing prosperity actually 'prompts far more personal giving'. Wealth distribution is thus in the hands of active, charitable citizens who do not simply devote themselves to becoming ever more prosperous. However, many have criticized the implausibility of Thatcher's famous claim, made to the General Assembly of the Church of Scotland, that 'it is not the creation of wealth that is wrong but love of money for its own sake' (cited by Raban 1989: 13). One of the reasons why charitable giving appears not to have increased as much as it should in terms of the advocated dynamic of the enterprise culture (and increased business profits) is that people committed to wealth creation are only too likely to become attached to what they earn. An economic culture that values independence, that requires competition, and that holds that those who work hard and productively are *entitled* to monetary rewards, is not exactly a favourable environment for the charitable version of 'trickle down'. Consuming becomes more important than caring. And, as the Bishop of Durham states, 'the rewards system does vividly put a premium on indecent and obscene greed' (Jenkins 1987).

Another major strand to the egalitarian critique is to argue that welfare provisions are being eroded. Advocates of the enterprise culture argue that young, unemployed and healthy people, for example, who have learnt to rely on state 'handouts' rather than joining Britain plc, must be made to realize that the world does not owe them a living (cf. Thatcher, citing St Paul's 'If a man will not work he shall not eat' with obvious approval (Raban 1989: 12)). Welfare provision is changed to get them to mend their ways. Critics object: fine, but what if there are no job vacancies in the vicinity of these people's homes? The enterprise culture is supposed to generate more opportunities, but unemployment figures are high and the number of small businesses has not increased to the extent that enterprise-talk might lead us to expect. This is only to be

expected, critics continue, given that the culture has much to
do with 'the survival of the fittest'. Certainly, there will always
be losers.

A related objection is that measures taken to get people to
stand on their own feet can only too readily have a 'blanket
effect', harming those who *cannot* join the enterprise culture. This
is the kind of objection that has prompted attacks such as the
Bishop of Durham's famous Easter Day 1988 accusation that
the government's restructuring of social security was 'wicked'
(Jenkins 1988).

Overall, then, these critics claim that the culture does not provide
a just, market-led form of wealth distribution and neither does it
operate satisfactorily to generate wealth creation among the poor.
Dr Runcie, when Archbishop of Canterbury, claimed that the
Church of England had a moral duty to oppose the 'use of the
taxation system to reward success, rather than to meet social needs
which are urgent and crying' (Runcie 1988a). Measures taken to
encourage enterprise weaken the welfare state but do not provide
a proper alternative.

The quality of life critique

A different, though not unrelated, kind of criticism has focused on
how the culture affects the quality of personal life. The constant
refrain is that it becomes impoverished. Much hinges on the claim
that those who have adopted the values of enterprise try to live
their lives as though they were 'small businesses', dedicating their
skills and effort, their very being, to maximizing their personal
wealth. Those working in the jungle of the individualized and
competitive 'open' market (so the objection goes) tend to become
obsessed with a limited version of what life has to offer. In the
words of John Paterson of the Church of Scotland 'an exclusive
concentration [on wealth creation] endangers an understanding of
the true meaning of life' (Paterson 1988). Indeed, it is commonly
argued that such people acquire unsavoury characteristics.

Not without good reason, the last decade has frequently been
described as 'the workaholic 1980s'. To value competitiveness; the
constant display of energy and initiative; the setting of material
goals; and so forth, is to live in a world where life becomes a

perpetual endeavour; where stress, guilt and fear of failure are likely to loom large; where the workaholic ethic threatens familial and personal relationships and leisure pursuits; where companionship in the workplace is constantly threatened by rivalry and suspicion; where the emphasis on responsibility and accountability exacts its toll. The subjection of human activity to the verdict of the market does not exactly encourage such human values as loyalty and integrity. The ethic of wealth creation is far removed from what Runcie (1986) describes as the 'worth ethic'. Indeed, the culture often generates a 'fear ethic'. Certainly no one can be *contented* in a world that asserts that one's 'best' efforts can always be bettered.

Turning to the domain of the consumer, it is claimed that, rather than encouraging the exercise of enterprising virtues (such as responsibility and discipline), the culture encourages people to spend their money, in the words of a well-known song, on 'living in the material world'. When wealth creation and making a profit become the yardstick to measure the self in its central role as a producer, it is highly tempting to display success by way of conspicuous consumption. The cultural emphasis on competition in the realm of production readily gets transferred into competition in the realm of consumption. Furthermore, the government itself has done much to encourage consumption – for example, by relaxing credit controls during the earlier 1980s – in some measure to help encourage the development of consumer-led capitalism. In addition, it is surely no coincidence that those who work at the heart of 'enterprise', city boys and yuppies, exemplify the adoption of undesirable, hedonistic, consumer attributes: attributes, it can be noted, that do not accord with those of the ideal enterprising self.

Runcie (1988a) speaks of 'the excessive pre-occupation with prosperity and success and of monochrome values in our society'; he also speaks of 'the self-interest society'; of 'greed, hedonism and the lust for power' (Runcie 1988b). Neil Kinnock has long been speaking of 'the materialistic, "loadsamoney" society'; of the 'uncaring "me-now"' world in which we live. Others speak of the 'born to shop' mentality; of the self defined in terms of consumer accessories. Although these sins are not always laid directly at the door of the enterprise culture, the point remains that values, which advocates say are nurtured by the enterprise culture, are apparently vitiated by it. How can there be personal restraint and generosity in a society that is increasingly dominated and motivated by the ethic of acquisition?

Enterprise reforms have also been subjected to what can be called 'the philistine critique'. Attempts to treat the professions as though they were consumer-led commercial enterprises are held to have a 'lowest common denominator' effect. Deregulation measures (for example, those aimed at commercial television) encourage consumers to exercise their power and 'vote' for trash. Those providing TV programmes find it increasingly difficult to maintain their 'Reithian standards', offering cultural-cum-educational services. Urged to 'commodify' knowledge, so that it becomes a 'product' which helps prepare student 'consumers' for careers in commerce, universities find it increasingly difficult to improve the quality of life by performing their traditional, humanistic role. Arguing the case that education had come to be seen primarily as a commodity in the market-place, Runcie (1990) continues, 'We end up with minds as sharp as razors and about as broad'.

Two other criticisms can be mentioned. First, it is claimed that the culture contributes to crime. On the one hand, there is the glorification of wealth creation; on the other, there are the losers. Accordingly, the unemployed experience relative deprivation. Some are tempted to be enterprising in the wrong sort of way, applying their skills to commit crimes in order to succeed. Similar points are also made by those who see the City as exercising a corrupting influence. And, second, it is claimed that the culture contributes to the destruction of the environment (and thereby to its own long-term decline). As Jenkins puts it, 'the current enterprise culture and rampant free market are simply not sustainable. The ecology of the world will not stand constant expansion of our present types of consumption' (Jenkins 1987; cf. Runcie 1988b).

The wealth creation critique

Despite the fact that the enterprise programme is more difficult to criticize in terms of its role as a vehicle for wealth creation, it can be argued that it does not provide a satisfactory way of increasing the national 'cake'. Moral justification of the exercise – especially the fact that it provides the best way of 'respond[ing] to the many calls for help' (Thatcher, quoted in Raban 1989: 13) – is thereby undermined.

Some draw attention to the success of Japanese capitalism operating in terms of an economic culture far removed from individualistic enterprise. Some point to the German success story, attributing this to an economic culture that also deviates, albeit less significantly , from that provided by the culture of enterprise in Britain. Some point to the situation in 1979 and ask, are things really any better today?

Could it be the case that certain unintended consequences of the enterprise culture have required governmental responses, responses that are currently leading the country into recession? Those who answer in the affirmative argue that rampant consumerism, fuelled by the culture of enterprise and the credit boom, has had an adverse effect on the balance of payments. Furthermore, the culture of consumption, together with the ethos of enterprise, is now translating into high wage demands. The outcome is high inflation – and high interest rates. That great enterprise unit, Britain, suffers accordingly.

Fundamental issues

Having seen how the enterprise culture has fuelled controversy in the public realm, we now consider several of the same issues in their somewhat broader historical and theoretical contexts. The 1970s saw a political and cultural counter-revolution in much of the Western world. The studies of Rawls (1973) and Nozick (1974), and the reinterpretation of aspects of the doctrines of classical liberalism (see King 1987, and Green 1987), re-opened some of the most basic political questions, announcing a new era in political philosophy. The electoral successes of particular evolutes of the major 'right-wing' parties in a number of Western democracies, including Mrs Thatcher's Conservatives,[1] marked the transition of marginal voices and 'think-tanks'[2] from the theoretical periphery to the political centre, challenging the cherished 'truths' of the post-Second World War consensus of Keynesian macro-economic interventionism, social welfare provision, and the nationalization

of key industries, as methods designed to limit the negative consequences of the capitalist market.

In Britain the debate appears to have been primarily concerned
with the appropriate means of the distribution of resources and
has involved the questioning of fundamental conceptions, such
as the legitimate limits and extents of government; the nature
of individual liberty; and the place of the market. The Keynesian
model collapsed under the urgency of the weight of its perceived
failure to account for 'stagflation' (high inflation and high unemployment), enhanced by the 1973–4 oil crisis; the sheer escalation
of government spending; the end of a period of sustained economic
growth; and demographic class shifts (Beer 1982).

The consensus was to be replaced by a new individualism; a
stress on competition; the sovereignty of the consumer; monetarist
and supply-side economic policies and a wholesale re-evaluation of
government-directed attempts at egalitarian redistribution.

This counter-revolution has led to the rejection of Keynesianism
by all the major political parties in Britain and their acceptance of
significant elements of the enterprise culture, including a greatly
enhanced place for the market, underwriting the importance of
understanding the nature of this culture and heralding a new
framework for British political and cultural life.

Although many of the theoretical underpinnings of the enterprise
culture are not in themselves new, it is unhelpful to see these as
mere revivals of classical liberalism, traditional conservatism, or
some unstable combination of these, as they are to be found in new
post-consensus contexts and in novel configurations. The specific
counter-revolutionary context of the enterprise culture is the vital
component in understanding its nature and the terms of the debates
in which its proponents have been engaged.

Although it is clear that thinkers such as Hayek and Friedman
have greatly influenced the arguments of the advocates of the
enterprise culture, these have tended to be couched in terms of
the specific British political context, strengthened and supported
by the economic difficulties in recent British history, and framed
in the light of a particular reading of that history – the economic
decline of Britain, especially since 1945.[3] In a sense, the so-called
'crisis of the left' has led to this re-examination of fundamentals
being a somewhat one-sided affair, with a historical gap between

the claims of the 'enterprisers' and the 'received wisdom' of the positions of their opponents.

Attempts have been made both to dismantle elements of consensus Britain – as in privatization and deregulation policies – and to create new political realities – as in the development of a property-owning and share-owning democracy and in consumer choice in areas such as health and education.

Whilst *The Right Approach* (Conservative Political Centre 1976), one of the foundational documents of the enterprise culture, contends that what is being proposed is but 'common sense' and that 'the facts of life invariably turn out to be Tory', elsewhere the positions have been carefully argued against the consensus view.

These debates have been understood by some commentators as essentially economic – as the transition from demand-based government fiscal policies to monetarist and supply-side government economic policies. But, as the penetrating insight of one commentator puts it, 'behind the . . . monetarist controversy . . . lies a much more serious argument between rival views of human society . . .' (Brittain 1983: 256). In what follows, our intention is not to review the extensive literature on a number of core moral debates generated by the enterprise culture counter-revolution but rather to highlight two related yet somewhat artificially separated, significant areas of moral concern.

Liberty and equality

Although there is little disagreement concerning the centrality of the moral value of the freedom of the individual, the nature of this liberty has been the subject of considerable debate. The equation of the right to individual liberty with the right to material resources (minimally an absence of poverty) and other forms of empowerment, as found in Tawney's classic study, *Equality* (Tawney [1931] 1964: 164 ff), became progressively enshrined as an egalitarian 'orthodoxy' ('social justice' programmes), particularly in post-1945 welfare and education policies funded by a redistributive system of taxation.

Hayek (1944, 1960) rejects this equation – 'the characteristic confusion of freedom with power' (Hayek 1944: 19) – which he considers to be a feature of all forms of socialism, and calls for a return to an earlier conception of liberty, a notion referred to by Isaiah Berlin (1969) as 'negative freedom'.[4] Hayek defines freedom as the absence of coercion by other persons and, although coercion cannot be entirely eliminated, his focus is on the conditions of its minimization (Hayek 1960: 11–13). These are the conditions which allow for individual invention and enterprise – the wellsprings of civilization and progress. He understands coercion to be a relationship between persons where one is *intentionally* coerced 'to serve the ends of another' (Hayek 1960: 20).

Drawing heavily on Hayek (and Friedman 1962), Keith Joseph, one of the intellectual architects of the enterprise culture, offers a sustained attack on the Tawney–consensus equation (Joseph and Sumption 1979). Joseph argues that there is no real connection between liberty and equality, the link being forged as moral legitimation for the growth of postwar welfarist wealth redistribution, and that the legitimate 'choice is between equality' – which can only be pursued by means of coercion – 'and liberty' – which necessarily entails inequality (Joseph and Sumption 1979: 47; Hayek 1960: 17). Following Hayek (1967: 70), Joseph insists that coercion must be intentional. Accepting that the market does generate inequalities, including relative poverty, as these are not the result of the action of any agent but merely the result of thousands of discrete individual decisions, they cannot be held to be coercive. In the section entitled, 'Poverty is not Unfreedom', he contends:

> A person who cannot afford to buy food may well have a justifiable grievance which ought to be rectified politically, but it would be misleading to describe his grievance as lack of freedom (Joseph and Sumption 1979: 49).

Joseph argues that such political rectification is not an issue of liberty and should take the form of minimum support, determined on an absolute not relative basis (Joseph 1976: 75). Even equality of opportunity is understood solely in terms of freedom from coercion (p. 27). He further contends that inequality is not only a fact of life and a consequence of individual liberties but is both necessary and desirable in order to ensure competition, the creation of wealth and progress (cf. Hayek 1960; Friedman 1962: 9).

Policies designed to effect more equal distribution of resources, Joseph claims, are not only coercive and threaten individual liberty but are counter-productive and give rise to a series of negative consequences (economic, psychological, moral and political; cf. Hayek 1967: 24–5). Liberty is primarily to be exercised by the self-interested consumer in the market place, including the political, educational and medical 'markets'.

Accepted by many enterprisers, the disjunction between equality and liberty on moral grounds has been widely contested by opponents, many of whom advocate on equally moral grounds some notion of 'positive freedom'.

Plant (1984), while recognizing the necessity of 'negative rights' (pp. 4–6), argues that individuals require positive resources in order for there to be 'equal liberty (that is) equal for all citizens' (p. 8). Macpherson (1973) rejects the limitation of democratic liberty to freedom from coercion and develops a classification of 'impediments' to the use of 'men's powers' – 'their potential for using and developing their uniquely human capabilities' – including the lack and/or scarcity of the adequate means of life, means of labour and physical security (pp. 39–76). So, for example, a man's power to undertake productive work is impeded by the lack of his access to the means of labour. These are require-ments for the realization of 'democracy' - essentially a 'social' form of organization – and the political task is to minimize these impediments.

Likewise, Rawls (1983), albeit from a very different perspective, holds that the disparities of property ownership and wealth result in liberty having a differential value dependent upon means (p. 204), and that finally these levels of inequality are 'incompatible' with political liberty and threaten to undermine existing political freedoms (pp. 225–7).

The morality of the market

Debates about the 'morality of the market' go back at least to the securing by merchants of a degree of autonomy for their markets from the state. Aristotle, for example, distinguishes between 'natural' wealth and 'wealth-getting'. Natural wealth refers to the 'necessary' art of acquisition as an integral part of the economy of the household, such as in the 'provision of food', while wealth-getting is deemed 'unnecessary' and refers to trade where the aim is to use money and goods merely to acquire further money and goods. He considers wealth-getting to be unjust for a number of reasons, including: that advantages are taken of others in exchange; that wealth-getting becomes an end in itself as opposed to utilizing exchange as a means of securing goods and services necessary for the 'good life' and that there is no limit to such wealth-acquisition (Aristotle, in McKeon 1941: 1135–41).

There is a long tradition in western literature concerning doctrines of just price and 'distributive justice', which have sought to limit the importance of the sphere of the market and viewed it, often negatively, as a part of a much larger and often static political/theological/social whole. Macpherson (1978) has examined what he calls 'the economic penetration of political theory' that accompanied the rise of mercantile culture and led to the dominant position of the economic.

The rise of the Keynesian consensus was very much based on what were taken to be the lessons of the Depression of the 1930s. The inherent instability of the market system was to be corrected by macro-economic policies and the moral (distributive) limitations of the market corrected by social provision.

Enterprisers contend that the market is a better system than government directed redistribution, both morally and in terms of the efficiency of the distribution of goods and services. They further maintain that it is vastly superior in terms of its overall wealth-creating potential.

Hayek, as part of his argument concerning liberty, considers that, although we understand little of the precise nature of market mechanisms, we can be sure that the market brings 'good' and is the great engine of civilization and progress. The negative consequences for individuals cannot be held to be unjust as there is no agent of the impersonal market-system of distribution and results are unforeseeable and unpredictable. For Hayek, it is merely contingent that the market *appears* to reward the virtuous (Hayek, 1960). Plant, however, maintains that, like the weather, there are in fact patterns, a degree of predictability, even if there is no responsible agent – 'the impersonal market does not distribute its benefits and burdens in a wholly random way' (Plant 1984:

6) – those who enter the market with greater resources reap greater benefit. But the moral question, he insists, is how we respond to the effects of the market or of a 'maldistribution' of resources. Do we act on this 'knowledge' by ensuring social provision?

There are a number of claims for the morality of the market. Most of these are based on default, in that it is a claim for the *relative* moral superiority of the market system when compared with systems of government allocation. For example, the literature of the dependency theorists (see Plant and Hoover 1990: 70 ff) argues that for some members of society welfare is actually counter-productive and reduces rather than increases their ability to enter the market.

A second set of arguments is based on the threat of loss of liberty and democratic values due to the coercion of state economic redistribution over market allocation. Friedman (1980) and Novak (1982) link democratic values to the market both in terms of their mutual occurrence and argue that a capitalist market is a necessary condition for democracy. It might be noted that the advocates of some type of positive freedom argue that democracy without correctives to market outcomes is itself under threat (Rawls 1973; Macpherson 1973; Plant 1984). It is also claimed that the market reinforces 'moral' virtues such as effort, thrift, honesty, self-reliance, independence and risk-taking.

The major claim for the morality of the market is, of course, that all, including the poor, will benefit from a general increase in economic growth – the trickle-down effect. It is not asserted that an overall increase in wealth will result in wealth differentials being lessened or a progression towards 'uniformity' or 'equality', but that the whole scale will move upwards (Joseph 1976: 32). The trickle-down effect is the enterprise culture's version of 'egalitarianism'.

Samuel Brittain, a keen supporter of the market, insists that it is still too early 'to expect any evidence of "trickle down" to those at the bottom' (Brittain 1989: 34), but he is worried that the 'least well-off have fared so badly'. He cites official government figures (*Social Trends*, 1988 and 1989, quoted in Brittain 1989) to conclude that those at the bottom did poorly in relation to the past and in relation to others, and even in absolute terms 'made only modest gains' (Brittain 1989: 35). Brittain recommends an attack on middle-class welfare.

The proponents of enterprise culture have sought to redefine liberty, excluding consensus 'social rights', and continue to advocate further reductions in the sphere of public 'enterprises' and government spending on services, as they redefine the limits and extents of government in light of the new dominance of the market. Can enterprise and the market be extended to replace the plethora of government institutions? The enterprise culture offers 'rival views of human society' to those of consensus Britain.

This book is divided into four parts. Part 1, 'Enterprise culture: then and now', begins with a forceful statement of the virtues of the culture in Britain today. Other papers in Part 1 place the contemporary Conservative version in historical context, comparing it with various forms of economic cultures and exploring some of the different ways in which it is possible to speak of 'enterprise'. Part 2, 'The morality of enterprise values', is focused on 'the market'. A central issue is whether there are legitimate boundaries to the market or whether market forces should be introduced into walks of life previously protected from them.

Part 3, 'The ethics of the enterprising self', addresses the culture in terms of how it serves as a vehicle for self-understanding. Contributors adopt very different approaches, from the psychoanalytic to the existential, subjecting the enterprising self to critical scrutiny. In Part 4, 'Religion and enterprise', the moral implications of the culture are highlighted. Contributors attend to the various ways in which it is legitimated by – indeed, incorporates – Christian teachings.

Various claims are made concerning the significance of the enterprise culture in daily life, ranging from the view that it is merely a propaganda device to the claim that it is making a significant impact. From an explicitly evaluative perspective, several contributors favour the view that the culture is nothing more than a 'selfish philosophy'. Others, however, are by no means so negative. Several argue in favour of a more 'humanistic' version of the culture: a version that emphasizes many of the virtues of being enterprising but that does not attach primacy to life in the realm of the market.

Notes: Chapter 1

1   Cf. Nigel Lawson's claim that in 1979 the Tories differed radically from all post-1945 governments, Labour *and* Conservative (Lawson 1980).
2   See Morris (1991).
3   Elements of what is often referred to as the 'Wiener thesis' (Wiener 1981), have been widely accepted by proponents of the enterprise culture. The sentiments of Keith Joseph – 'Britain never really internalized capitalist values . . .' (Joseph 1975: 61) – is widely echoed in the literature of the enterprisers (for example, Lawson 1988). The reversal of the decline of the British economy is a primary impetus underlying enterprise programmes, and as the principal causes of this decline are 'cultural', remedial 'cultural engineering' is required. For a critical historical appraisal of the thesis, see Raven (1989).
4   For a critique of Berlin's classification of types of freedom, see Macpherson (1973: 95–119).

References: Chapter 1

Aristotle: see McKeon, R. 1941.
Baker, K. 1990. No return to stifling socialism. *The Times*, 14 March 1990.
Beer, S. 1982. *Britain against Itself*. New York: Norton.
Berger, P. 1987. *The Capitalist Revolution*. Aldershot: Wildwood House.
Berlin, I. 1969. Two Concepts of Liberty. In I. Berlin, *Four Essays on Liberty*. Oxford: Oxford University Press.
Brittain, S. 1983. *The Role and Limits of Government*. London: Temple Smith.
Brittain, S. 1989. The Government's economic policy. In D. Kavanagh and A. Seldon (eds), *The Thatcher Effect*. Oxford: Oxford University Press, pp. 1–37.
Conservative Political Centre. 1976. *The Right Approach*. London: Conservative Political Centre.
Friedman, M. 1962. *Capitalism and Freedom*. Chicago: Chicago University Press.
Friedman, M., and R. Friedman 1980. *Free to Choose* (London: Secker and Warburg).
Green, D. 1987. *The New Right*. Brighton: Wheatsheaf.
Hayek, F. A. 1944. *The Road to Serfdom*. London: Routledge.
Hayek, F. A. 1960. *The Constitution of Liberty*. London: Routledge.
Hayek, F. A. 1967. The road to serfdom after twelve years. In Hayek, F. A., *Studies in Philosophy Politics and Economics*. London: Routledge.
Howe, G. 1989. Annual Disraeli Lecture, London, reported in *The Daily Telegraph*, 28 April 1989.

Jenkins, D. 1987. God, bishops, Tories and the election. *The Times*, 5 June 1987.

Jenkins, D. 1988. Radio 4 interview, reported in *The Daily Telegraph*, 4 April 1988.

Joseph, K. 1975. *Reversing the Trend*. London: Rose Books.

Joseph, K. 1976. *Stranded on the Middle Ground*. London: Centre for Policy Studies.

Joseph, K. and Sumption J. 1979. *Equality*. London: Murray.

King, D. 1987. *The New Right*. London: Macmillan.

Lawson, N. 1980. *The New Conservatism*. London: Centre for Policy Studies.

Lawson, N. 1988. *The New Britain*. London: Centre for Policy Studies.

MacGregor, J. 1990. Reported in 'Vouchers for schools on Tory agenda', *The Daily Telegraph*, 15 October 1990.

McKeon, R. (ed.). 1941. *The Basic Works of Aristotle*. New York: Random House. (*Note* pp. 1135–41 are *Politica*, sec. 1255–8.)

Macpherson, C. B. 1973. *Democratic Theory: Essays in Retrieval*. Oxford: Oxford University Press.

Macpherson, C. B. 1978. The economic penetration of political theory: some hypotheses. *Journal of the History of Ideas*, 39.

Morgan, P. 1990. Address to the Annual Convention of the Institute of Directors. London: Institute of Directors.

Morris, P. 1991. Freeing the spirit of enterprise: the genesis and development of the concept of enterprise culture. In R. Keat and N. Abercrombie (eds), *Enterprise Culture*. London: Routledge (pp. 21–37).

Novak, M. 1982. *The Spirit of Democratic Capitalism*. New York: Simon & Schuster.

Nozick, R. 1974. *Anarchy, State and Utopia*. Oxford: Blackwell.

Paterson, J. 1988. Cited in *The Daily Telegraph*, 25 May 1988.

Plant, R. 1984. *Equality, Markets, and the State*. Fabian Society Tract 494. London: Fabian Society.

Plant, R. and K. Hoover. 1990. *Conservative Capitalism*. London: Routledge.

Raban, J. 1989. *God, Man and Mrs Thatcher*. London: Chatto & Windus.

Raven, J. 1989. British History and the Enterprise Culture. *Past and Present* (May): 178–204.

Rawls, J. 1973. *A Theory of Justice*. Oxford: Oxford University Press.

Runcie, R. 1986. Sermon for a special Industry Service Year, St Paul's Cathedral, reported in *The Daily Telegraph*, 8 May 1986.

Runcie, R. 1988a. Panorama interview, cited by F. Mount. 'Runcie's coloured views on the "monochrome society"'. *The Daily Telegraph*, 1 April 1988.

Runcie, R. 1988b. Speech to the Global Survival Conference, Oxford, reported in *The Daily Telegraph*, 12 April 1988.

Runcie, R. 1990. Speech to the Headmasters' Conference, Aberdeen, reported in *The Daily Telegraph*, 19 September 1990.

Sheppard, D. 1989. Joint lecture with Derek Worlock, at La Sainte Union College, Southampton, reported in *The Daily Telegraph*, 11 May 1989.

Tawney, R. H. [1931] 1964. *Equality*. London: George Allen and Unwin.

Thatcher, M. 1979. Address to Conservative summer school.

Thatcher, M. 1987. Interview in *Woman's Own*, October 1987.

Thatcher, M. 1988a. Address to the 10th Conservative Party Conference, reported in *The Daily Telegraph*, 15 October 1990.

Thatcher, M. 1988b. Quoted in *The Sunday Times*, 7 May 1988.

Thatcher, M. 1988c. Annual speech to Tory women in London, reported in *The Daily Telegraph*, 26 May 1988.

Thatcher, M. 1989. New year message for 1990, reported in *The Sunday Times*, 31 December 1989.

Wiener, M. 1981. *English Culture and the Decline of the Industrial Spirit 1850–1980*. Cambridge: Cambridge University Press.

PART 1

Enterprise culture: then and now

2 Enterprise regained
LORD YOUNG of GRAFFHAM

I hold strong views on enterprise, its values and its value. Although the relative decline of the British economy started a long time ago, during the late nineteenth century, it became most visible after the Second World War. By the 1960s and 1970s the decline of enterprise – for that is what is at issue – had become a major problem. This was one of the main reasons why I entered politics.

The two pillars of enterprise are openness of markets and the initiative of individuals. The basis of the enterprise culture lies with the restoration of the age of the individual. Individuals must be given the scope to develop their skills, take on responsibility, and use their personal initiative. In a centrally controlled economy the value and values of enterprise are thwarted. In addition the welfare state stifles enterprise by generating dependency and creating poverty traps, which are most difficult to break out of. Although I recognize the need for safety nets for those at the bottom, there must also be the possibility of ladders available for those displaying enterprise. Who could say that they want to hold back, rather than free, the enterprise of individuals?

Morality and the market

Some oppose an enterprise economy because they associate enterprise and free markets with a lack of morality. But is it greedy for parents to want to provide for their children? Is it virtuous to hand over responsibility to the state? Personal responsibility is vital – individuals must carry the consequences of their actions. This very responsibility is essential for the operation of the market economy. As Brian Griffiths has argued, the market economy has to be supported by moral values. Trust between individuals is needed, otherwise it cannot function. Furthermore, the market must have a just set of rules to ensure that competition is fair. The market of the enterprise culture is not to be equated with the nineteenth-century laissez-faire economy. It is not a jungle without rules.

Materialism

Some argue that enterprise and the market are just about material goods for material rewards. Such criticism ignores two things. First, our public goods and services depend on the health of our economy, which, of course, depends on enterprise and the success of our free open market system. If it did not produce sufficient national wealth we would not be able to afford desirable public support for health, education and other services. The cake must be created before it is divided up. Failure to do so has dire consequences. Thus, with the best of intentions, the Labour Government during the economic crisis of the 1970s had to cut the real pay of nurses, and did so in four years out of five. But in the enterprise economy of the last decade nurses' pay has risen by nearly a third in real terms.

Secondly, public *and* private goods are equally materialistic. The decision to provide either health care or subsidies to the arts involves real resources, in terms of capital and in terms of labour, being allocated to those areas. Public goods are just as materialistic as private goods. The difference is that decisions on purchasing public goods are not taken by the individuals who receive them but by a government bureaucracy working under the rules laid down by a minister – who in turn is answerable to Parliament. The extent to which they meet the real needs of the individuals for whom they are provided, or the extent to which they are actually taken up, is very variable.

Government and the limits of market freedom

Is the enterprise culture to be understood as it has been by its opponents: that is, as a free-for-all? When there are no checks or controls on the operation of the market, large companies readily override the interests of consumers and smaller companies and people can be treated unfairly. But our belief is in *open*, not *free* markets. Thus Government intervenes to act against monopolies and ensure competition – to establish ground rules so that people can be confident about markets, their health and safety, and to provide information to protect individuals working in those markets. The government, therefore, has a vital role in enforcing minimum standards and helping to set the rules required for the market to work efficiently. This role is restricted to ensuring the efficiency of the market, leaving the individual free to make decisions. In short, enterprise needs government, but of a limited kind.

The efficiency of the enterprise economy

My basic assumption is that the market economy is the most efficient way to provide people with the goods and services they seek. In accordance with the tradition that runs from Adam Smith to Milton Friedman, it is now generally accepted that the market is the most efficient mode of organization. The market system that produces economic order out of the chaos of millions of individual decisions is truly amazing. Quite simply, the market outperforms state-directed economies. Obviously, the range of goods in the High Street and of services made available by the operation of the market is vastly superior to the range provided by state-run economies. A neighbour of mine married a German girl. When she returned to see her family, as recently as the early 1980s, she would bring fresh fruit as a gift – her family lived in East Germany! Before the Second World War the economies of Switzerland and Czechoslovakia were in much the same shape, but today the differences are there for all to see (although it is to be expected that the newly unleashed spirit of enterprise in Czechoslovakia will now work to close the gap). The recent political changes in Eastern Europe have most cruelly exposed the gross inefficiencies of state-controlled systems. And just as state-controlled economies distort the workings of the market and threaten its principle of the voluntary exchange of goods and services at freely determined prices, so state-controlled bureaucracies result in similar distortions and inefficiencies, with regard, for example, to the provision of health care.

Enterprise culture is also vital in private enterprise

Until recently, private businesses, particularly the large companies, have developed managerial structures of the corporatist variety. These have eroded enterprise *within* the company. Many of the workforce have become remote from decision-making, unable to exercise responsibility and initiative. Symptomatic of this elitist corporatism has been the failure of management to invest in developing the skills of employees. In such companies, it is only too easy for middle management and the like to take the easy way out, resting secure in their nests while passing risky but potentially profitable decisions to others elsewhere in the system. Much the same inefficiencies arise as in the sphere of the state-run sector. Corporatism, the development of the corporate state, has been just as much a failure on the part of private business as it has been in public affairs.

Employee involvement is a key feature of the enterprise culture. That is why small firms are important and that is why individuals are treated as such, and are encouraged to act as 'intrapreneurs' – exercising initiative themselves. Some companies have already learnt from the Japanese of the advantages of direct communication with employees, and devices such as quality circles to involve the employee directly in the improvement of productivity and efficiency. The displacement of individual responsibility must be prevented. The efficiency of enterprise culture is built upon the liberation of the enterprise of the individual.

Values

Thus, over the decades, individual responsibilities have been displaced: both by government and by private enterprise. It is ironic that Beveridge, the architect of the welfare state, should have attached such immense importance to personal responsibility; should have been so acutely aware of the dangers of welfarism. We must ensure that individual enterprise (the virtues of responsibility, initiative, competitiveness and risk-taking, and industrious effort) are fostered and rewarded in order to ensure that both private businesses and state services flourish.

So far I have discussed the absolute importance of individual enterprise for both the public and private spheres. Some ask whether this stress on individualism leads to a lack of concern for other people in the community. However, it is far from the case that capitalism and private enterprise prevent community responsibility and voluntary work. I was struck by the comment of the Director General of the St John's Ambulance Brigade. He said: 'Voluntary work is not the antithesis of popular capitalism; on the contrary, the same spirit of individualism moves both.' The individualism of the enterprise culture, that we are seeking to promote, will not just exhaust its energies in work and the pursuit of material reward. I believe it will bubble over into other activities. Now that our companies are becoming more profitable, we are witnessing closer involvement with the community, and a greater willingness to second employees and put money into voluntary projects. I emphasize two strands in private enterprise. First, a concern with efficiency and market forces, which will maximize the wealth creation potential of our economy. Secondly, the stress on individual success and development, which will spill over into communal activity. Our expectation is that these two strands will fuse together to regain enterprise and build the enterprise culture.

Enterprise regained

The numbers of the self-employed have increased annually since 1979, the total increase being in excess of one million. In contrast, during the 1970s numbers declined by 100,000. Today, there are more than three million self-employed – the largest-ever number. Another indication of the success of the enterprise culture is that we have witnessed a record rate of business start-ups during the period 1979–87. The net increase in new businesses has averaged more than 500 a week during this period, nearly 900 a week in 1987 and 1,200 extra a week in 1988.

The Enterprise Allowance Scheme, in just under three years to July 1989, has enabled more than 450,000 people to set up their own businesses. This has provided a ladder for unemployed people, who in years past would not have expected the opportunity to start their own businesses. Additionally the Enterprise Initiative has considered more than 30,000 applications for consultancy support, 90 per cent of which have been from firms with under one hundred employees, and a third from firms with fewer than ten.

Enterprise: a strategy for our future

The restoration of enterprise in Britain has played a major role in the revival of growth, employment, and prosperity. Further encouragement of the instinct for enterprise in the British people will be, I believe, the spur to still greater economic success. Enterprise is not a mere collective abstraction. It is the sum of the talents of individuals who dare to use their initiative to supply their fellow-men with the goods and services they want. In the past, there was an unfortunate and unnecessary bias against enterprise in British culture. In future, that bias must be overcome. Individual entrepreneurs need positive encouragement to take an active part in the creation of prosperity. We must strive to bring schools, universities, and other educational institutions to a closer understanding of the needs and hopes of the enterprises in which their pupils and students will one day work. We also must bring businesses into the schools to play their part in education.

One of the characteristics of the enterprising spirit is that it can never be satisfied (unfortunately, governments only too easily can!). Individuals will always set themselves new goals and challenges. An increasing number of individuals will come to see that the responsibility and choice that are the hallmark of private enterprise are not a burden but an opportunity to develop. That, indeed, is the answer to all those people who believe that private enterprise will lead only to a materialistic society in which the spiritual values of people will be ignored.

But my pressing concern is to make sure that private enterprise has the necessary competitive incentives to produce an efficient economy. After all, private enterprise is the *key* to prosperity. And only with such an economy can we afford the public services that we rightly should provide for our citizens. At the same time, the enterprise culture ensures that we do not blunt the responsibility of our citizens. We must encourage their individual talents rather than use the wealth created by enterprise to perpetuate the sins of the past. We *must* have an enterprise culture, not a dependency culture. Although enterprise is vital in encouraging the individual skills of people working within the economy, it also has a crucial role to play within the community. I urge it to do just that: to work for the public good.

3 The enterprise culture in historical perspective: birth, life, death – and resurrection?

HAROLD PERKIN

'The enterprise culture', as one would expect in an age when the advertising man is king, is a propaganda device – a highly successful propaganda device, but a propaganda device all the same. Born in the Renaissance and Reformation, it reached maturity in the Victorian age to boost the self-image of the self-made man. It has been revived in the late twentieth century to boost the self-image of the corporate business man. It has the great advantage for its protagonists of implying that its opponents are lazy and supine dependants on the 'nanny state' and that other cultures and earlier ages were anything but enterprising.

In historical fact, there has always been enterprise and there have always been entrepreneurs. Who could be more enterprising, in the sense of changing the world and the way people lived, than Julius Caesar, Saint Paul, Mohammed, William the Conqueror, Gengis Khan, Columbus, or Isaac Newton? Even in Schumpeter's narrower economic sense of a man who introduces a new good, a new method of production, a new market, a new source of raw material, or a new organization of industry (Schumpeter 1961: 66), entrepreneurs began with the first user of fire, the first planter of seed, the inventor of the wheel. In Charles Wilson's sense of a man with 'a sense of market opportunity, combined with the capacity to exploit it' (Wilson 1957: 103), it would include Jason and the Argonauts who sought the golden fleece with which the Colchians sieved the river's gold; William the Marshall under Henry III, who gained a great estate and noble titles by winning tournaments and holding rich nobles to ransom; or Alderman Sir William Cokayne, the Jacobean Lord Mayor of London who tried to monopolize the cloth-finishing trade and wrench it from the Flemings; and all the 'undertakers' (the original Anglo-Saxon for entrepreneurs) of that rapacious age.

Alan Macfarlane, in *The Origins of English Individualism*, believes that the English were enterprising individuals as far back as we can find evidence:

> the majority of ordinary people in England from at least the 13th century were rampant individualists, highly mobile both geo-graphically and socially, economically 'rational', market-oriented and acquisitive, ego-centred in kinship and social life (Macfarlane 1978: 163).

So they were: we have only to read John Ball on idle gentlemen, William Langland on grasping priests, or Geoffrey Chaucer on the tricks of mercenary knights, millers, monks and other deceivers to be convinced of that. But that is why there was manorial, royal and canon law to hold greed, lechery and covetousness in check. Men do not make laws to ban nonexistent conduct. Medieval England was no altruistic Utopia. But neither was it a Thatcherite heaven in which 'looking after number one' was the supreme virtue and self-love the state religion.

The difference with the later enterprise culture was that it no longer recognized the moral restraints placed on ambitious profitmakers in past ages. Merchants and manufacturers were regarded as a low form of life, good servants but bad masters, at best necessary evils to be kept in subordination to higher ideals: the service of God, king, feudal honour, courtly love, even military conquest. The enterprise culture was not the creation of something new but the shedding of many things old, including the just price, the just wage, the ban on usury, and all the elements of the moral economy. Instead of taming the 'old Adam' in all of us, it threw away the restraints of religion, morality and political authority on economic conduct and made enterprise 'free'.

Max Weber (1930) attributed this change to the rise of Prot-estantism, which made 'labouring in one's vocation' a nobler way of praising God than fruitless prayer and meditation. R. H. Tawney ([1926] 1938) took this further and showed how Puritan concern for individual salvation through work and the 'postponement of pleasure principle' could lead to worldly success and acquisitive individualism. But the argument is tenuous and ignores the many medieval merchants and bankers, including post-Reformation Catholic ones who were just as acquisitive as any Puritan. Jacob Burckhardt with a sounder instinct saw how the Renaissance, 'the mother and source of modern man,' of 'excessive individualism' and 'victorious egoism,' dropped the religious basis of ethics and introduced a new morality, the Machiavellian ethic of enlightened self-interest. (Burckhardt 1960, esp. pp. viii, 302–21). The Machiavellian moment (with apologies to John Pocock, 1975) is as good a date as we shall find for the gestation of the enterprise culture.

I am not, of course, saying that medieval people were all saints and paragons of virtue. On the contrary, they harboured some of the greatest sinners who ever lived. William the Conqueror and his sons were monsters of wickedness, and the Crusaders who raped and looted Constantinople and put thousands of Moslem prisoners to a horrifying death in Palestine were precursors of Hitler and Stalin. The point is that they knew that they were wicked, and could expect divine wrath and everlasting torment for their sins. When you believe in a supernatural ethic you can be more wicked, knowing that you challenge God and defy His laws. When you believe in enlightened self-interest, the end soon justifies the means, and success and riches become proof of God's blessing – if indeed you still need any other kind of blessing than success itself. The Renaissance, then, rather than the Reformation (which originated in moral revulsion from the sins and extortions of the medieval church) was – appropriately enough, with its art and architecture paid for by the corrupt dealings of a venal clergy – the mother of the enterprise culture.

It took a couple of centuries, however, for the infant to grow to manhood and dominate society. Tawney shows how strong the resistance against it was from Puritan sages such as John Bunyan and Richard Baxter, who were more severe on usurers who charged excessive interest, enclosers of common lands, grasping tradesmen, and oppressors of the poor than their Catholic predecessors. It took the whole of the seventeenth century, a Civil War and a Revolution for the new outlook to capture the hearts and minds of the majority of thinking people. Tawney saw the passage of the generations and the triumph of political over moral economy in the transition from Praise-God Barebones, the godly disciplinarian who gave his name to a Cromwellian Parliament and the Rule of the Saints, to his son Nicholas Barbon, pioneer of fire insurance in this world, who wrote a notably secular *Discourse on Trade* in 1690. The cool eighteenth-century belief in having your cake and eating it was anticipated by Richard Steele in 1684: 'Prudence and Piety were always very good friends. . . You may gain enough of both worlds if you would mind each in its place.'[1] We are not far away in spirit from Victoria's first Prime Minister, Lord Melbourne: 'Things have come to a pretty pass when religion is allowed to invade the sphere of private life' (quoted by Russell, 1903, Ch. 6).

Changes in opinion, however, are 'merely academic', as lay people say scornfully, unless they have practical consequences. What practical difference did the rise of enlightened self-interest, acquisitive individualism, in modern terms the enterprise culture, make to life in Britain, and eventually in Europe and its offshoots? All the difference in the world, is the short answer. The Industrial Revolution, the spread of capitalism from the supposed centre to the periphery, the enormous increase in human productivity and, therefore, in income and wealth per head (however badly distributed by class and continent), the explosive growth of national and world population, its concentration in huge sprawling cities, the shrinking of the planet by rail, steamship, air transport and telecommunications, the race into space, the waste of the earth's mineral resources and fossil fuels, the destruction of the forests, the extinction of whole species of wildlife, the pollution of the atmosphere, aquafers and seas, the puncturing of the ozone layer, the greenhouse effect, the threat of nuclear holocaust – all the blessings and ills that flesh and grass are heir to in this brilliantly technocratic world can be traced to the invisible hand of enlightened, or not so enlightened, self-interest and the enterprise culture.

This practical revolution in attitudes took place in three major transitions, which made a difference not just to the way people thought but to the way they behaved towards each other: in the attitude to usury and credit; in the meaning of property; and in what Sir Henry Maine called the movement in all modern societies from status to contract (Maine 1874: 170). Credit was transformed from a last resort in disaster – a bad harvest for the peasant, the loss of a ship and its cargo for the merchant, a cathedral's collapse for a bishop, a desperate war for a king or baron – into an instrument of productive investment. Usury, therefore, was no longer a sin, the exploitation for gain of a neighbour's dire need, but a fruitful participation in the creation of wealth, especially where it enabled larger capitals to be assembled to tackle large-sale projects like overseas trading expeditions to India, China and the Americas, great works like the Carron Ironworks, the London Plate Glass Company, or the Quaker Lead Company, or the numerous river navigations and canals of the eighteenth century. Lending was only harmful if it was 'excessive', defined by an Act of 1624 as over 6 per cent and limited by the eighteenth century to 5 per cent, a rate which fortunately coincided with the cheap money of the early Industrial Revolution and enabled entrepreneurs to borrow cheaply. Though the legalization of usury did not by itself cause cheap money, the new attitude behind it played a large part in the onset of industrialism.

It also introduced the first of the paradoxes of individualism: that invested credit worked best if it were collective, on the joint-stock principle. It enabled men to sink deeper mines, build bigger works, make bigger roads and canals, send out larger ships and fleets, and generally to do greater things than they could do as individuals. This might not be what the later apostles of individualism had in mind when they opposed collectivism, although John Stuart Mill believed that if joint-stock enterprise went beyond a certain point it might as well be state enterprise, and Karl Marx thought that joint-stock organization was preparing the way for state socialism. It is a reminder, nevertheless, that individualism still requires the cooperation of many individuals, and that the only real individualist was Robinson Crusoe. It was collective investment, usually but not always by the bourgeoisie, that awoke, in Marx's phrase, the enormous forces of production slumbering in the lap of social labour.

The change in the meaning of property was even more radical. Medieval property was limited and contingent, a temporary loan from God, subject in this world to the parallel claims of the church, the king, the superior feudal lord, the rights of the occupying peasants, and of charity to the poor. No one owned the land, except in remote theory the king. Each tenant in the hierarchy owned an estate upon the land, a bundle of claims to a share in the produce: rent in cash, kind or labour, tithes, feudal dues, the husbandman's residue of the harvest after all these claims were met, and so on. The manorial lord was only one tenant on the ladder: he owned the serf but not the land itself, only his circumscribed rights to dues and labour services. It was the evolution from contingent to absolute property that turned lordship into ownership and made the manorial lord the absolute owner of the land. That evolution took three centuries, from the Black Death and the emancipation of the serfs to the abolition of feudal tenures at the Civil War and Restoration, during which the landlords defeated the claims of the church, the peasants, and finally the king, to emerge as freeholders, real owners of the land, able to do with it as they pleased (see Perkin, 1969: 52–5).

Thus the English landlords, not the merchants and industrialists, were the real begetters of the enterprise culture. They used their new-found freedom to 'do what they would with their own' to become entrepreneurs: to enclose the common fields and pastures, introduce new crop rotations, and increase the yield of the soil; to open coal and other mines, and develop ironworks, brickyards, and other resource-based enterprises; build docks, roads, canals, and sometimes even factories; and to let land for any purpose that would yield a rent. They did not always wish to do these things themselves, but they were always willing to lease land for the purpose to capitalists who would undertake the development. More important, as parliamentary legislators they paved the way for every kind of economic development by passing acts for enclosures (forbidden under the old regime in favour of keeping population on the land for defence against invasion and rebellion and to discourage discontent), for roads, canals, and later docks and railways, for joint-stock banks and later for limited companies of all kinds. The legislative framework of the Industrial Revolution was provided by the enlightened and self-interested landlords.

This brings us to the second paradox of the enterprise culture, that it took the state to create the conditions for its emergence. It was parliament that confirmed the changes in the law of property, culminating in the Act of 1660, which exchanged feudal dues for an excise on beer. It was parliament that in the early seventeenth century ceased to pass laws against enclosure and later in the century began to pass enclosure acts. It was parliament that passed the acts for roads, canals, railways, and docks, enabling private companies, among other things, to force individuals to sell them land by compulsory purchase. In the final analysis, it was only the state that could create the free market in land as in everything else, and only the state that could guarantee freedom from intervention by itself.

The third and final major change was the movement from status to contract, from the just price and the just wage to the contractual price, from the moral economy to the free market, in goods and labour as well as land. Just as there have always been entrepreneurs, there have always been markets. But there was, and is, no such thing as a perfectly free market. A market requires accepted laws of ownership and contract, protection against theft, fraud and violence, and usually a set time and place where the bargaining can occur. To the endless question for medieval historians about the military or commercial origin of towns and their markets, the best answer is both: men came to town to trade under the protection of a powerful lord in his castle, abbot in his monastery, or saint in his shrine. The lord or abbot soon discovered that protection could charge a rent: hence the *firma burgi*, the market charter, market tolls, 'pie powder' courts, the merchant guild to pay the rents and tolls, craft guilds to resist the squeeze by the merchants and the invasion of rivals and so on. Thus the market came to be hedged about with taxes and restrictions, which became increasingly burdensome. In the later middle ages, kings got into the act and the market and its taxes and restrictions were nationalized, with staples, customs duties, grants of monopoly, and the like – a period which Adam Smith (1776), somewhat unfairly perhaps since it was the last thing merchants wanted, stigmatized as the mercantile system, which reached its zenith under the Tudors and early Stuarts.

It was not surprising, therefore, that merchants and their customers and parliament itself began to complain under those impecunious monarchs, James I and Charles I, about the burdens of arbitrary taxation and the hidden tax of private monopolies. The worst of the private monopolies were abolished in 1624, and in 1641, on the eve of the Civil War, Charles I agreed to abolish the Star Chamber and the prerogative courts through which the crown had enforced its disputed rights and taxes. From the Restoration onwards the king could no longer raise taxes except with the consent of parliament, which meant that in effect he could not arbitrarily interfere with the internal trade of the country – though with that consent king-in-parliament continued to levy excise duties on a vast range of goods and services, from windows and male servants to soap and home-produced cottons. In short, from 1660, and certainly from 1689, there was in effect internal free trade in England, and from 1707 throughout Britain, which became the largest common market in Europe. In contrast to France, where Colbert's system of minute regulation of manufacturing survived down to the Revolution, state intervention in Britain operated only with regard to foreign trade. Adam Smith's call for free trade came in a country where the internal market had been virtually free for more than a century. His principle, that the division of labour was limited only by the size of the market, enjoyed full development and helped to create that prosperity which he celebrated in *The Wealth of Nations* ([1776] 1905).

Meanwhile, the other restrictions on the market, and so the moral economy itself, were withering away. The guild system became moribund, and workers were able to engage in any craft of their choice. The fixing of prices and wages by the magistrates became routine, with the same rates being fixed every Easter for year after year in the eighteenth century until they were abandoned altogether, so that when hard times came again in the Revolutionary Wars the justices of the peace had almost forgotten that it had ever been done, and began to fix a bread scale of poor relief, the Speenhamland system, instead.

The moral economy, abandoned by their masters, lived on only in the minds of Edward Thompson's protesting crowds, the food rioters and forest dwellers, who demanded the just prices and customary rights that the authorities had abandoned (Thompson 1971, 1975). When in the early nineteenth century craftsmen tried to appeal to the old statutes protecting wages, prices and exclusive employment, parliament responded by repealing these laws in 1813–14. The attack on the old poor law, culminating in the

New Poor Law of 1834, completed the demolition of the moral economy and finally established the free market in labour. This response was 'the abdication on the part of the governors' that Carlyle condemned (1840, Ch. 6; cf. Perkin 1969: 183–95). Long before the classical economists came along to theorize it out of existence, the moral economy had declined and been replaced by the free market in all but foreign trade. And, by the third paradox of the enterprise culture, it was the state that had produced it.

By the end of the eighteenth century, then, the new outlook had succeeded in all three ways, in the credit system, in the meaning of property, and in the evolution of the internal free market. The morality of enlightened self-interest was expressed gracefully by Alexander Pope (1734, Epistle IV, line 396), 'That true self-love and social are the same'; more cynically by Bernard de Mandeville ([1714], 1924): 'Private vices, public benefits'; and as a complete blueprint for the wealth of nations by Adam Smith: 'self-love' was 'the governing principle in the intercourse of human society', by means of which 'every individual necessarily labours to render the annual revenue of the society as great as he can', and is 'led by an invisible hand to promote an end which was no part of his intention' (Smith [1776] 1905, Vol. 1: 15, 456, and in index under 'self-love').

It is true that merchants and manufacturers were still regarded, even by Adam Smith, as 'an order of men, whose interest is never exactly the same with that of the public, who generally have an interest to deceive and even to oppress the public, and who accordingly have, upon many occasions, both deceived and oppressed it':

> People of the same trade seldom meet together, even for merriment and diversion, but the conversation ends in a conspiracy against the public, or in some contrivance to raise prices.

> Masters are always and everywhere in a sort of tacit, but constant and uniform, conspiracy, not to raise wages above their actual rate (Smith [1776] 1905: 265, 134).

To this extent, even as late as 1776, the very eve of the Industrial Revolution, the entrepreneur was still regarded with suspicion and the enterprise culture was still not fully accepted.

It was the classical economists, Ricardo, James Mill, Nassau Senior, J. R. McCulloch, and company, who finally gave the coup de grace to the moral economy (see Perkin 1969: 221–30). Their belief that in the market 'things will always find their own level' – what Coleridge called 'the psychological description of a storm' – and that no amount of state interference or moral exhortation could alter the outcome except for the worse, effectively destroyed the need by the economically powerful to think of the consequences of their actions. There was no just price: according to Say's law, one half of the goods in the market bought the other half, and that determined the price. Thus, there could be no such thing as a glut or a depression – in the midst of some of the worst slumps in history! There was no just wage: there was a limited 'wages fund', and to fix wages higher than their 'natural' level led only to unemployment for other workers. According to Malthus, Nature said to the poor man, 'there is no room at my table'. If the poor starved, it was no concern of the rich: to offer them public relief or even private charity except under the strictest conditions encouraged them only to breed and produce more paupers and so make the problem worse. The market was king, and punished unmercifully, with starvation and death, any interference with its inexorable operation.

The demise of the moral economy – some would say the euthanasia of an already expiring patient – ushered in the golden age of the enterprise culture. The ideal of the entrepreneur, based on capital and competition – active capital managed by the owner himself, whose abilities were tested in the market place – challenged the aristocratic ideal of the old society, based on property and patronage – passive property providing rent for a leisured life, and patronage jobs for the boys from the public purse, which the new ideal called 'Old Corruption' – and steadily defeated it. Privilege in church and state, in the civil service and municipal government, in the armed forces and the universities, was gradually swept away, taxation reduced, and free trade enforced by corn-law repeal (1846) and the Cobden Treaty with France (1860).

The entrepreneurial ideal was symbolized by Samuel Smiles's self-made man, the noble soul who raised himself from obscurity to affluence by introducing some useful product or device to benefit the welfare of mankind: James Watt of the steam engine, Thomas

Telford of the roads and canals, George Stephenson of the railway, Sir William Armstrong of the machine tools and big guns, Thomas Holloway of the patent medicines, even the Harmsworth brothers of the popular press. It is true that Smiles's *Self-Help* (1859) is an encomium to more than the industrial entrepreneur: to painters such as Gainsborough, son of a clothworker, scientists such as Faraday, son of a blacksmith, and poets such as Keats, son of a stableman, and to many others who did not strike it rich. But most Victorians loved a nouveau riche: even Victoria and Albert opened their doors to self-made men like George Hudson, the 'Railway King' – until they found that other people's money had been embezzled in their making.[2]

What most did not notice was that for every self-made man there were perhaps a hundred who failed to make it, and a great number who were unmade by the competition. Some, however, rejoiced in the competition, which they regarded as nature's way of weeding out the failures and those unfit to survive. Poor Darwin has had his name taken in vain in the label social Darwinism, the economic struggle for survival not in savage nature but in civil society. Malthus had shown the way, but the real progenitor of this theory was Herbert Spencer, a (Lamarckian) evolutionist before Darwin, and inventor of the phrase 'the survival of the fittest', who contemplated with equanimity the extinction of the unfit, even where he admitted they were objects of pity. He extended the blessings of evolution from the jungle of the carnivores to the civilized garden of human society:

> Pervading all nature we may see at work a stern discipline, which is a little cruel that it may be kind. That state of universal warfare maintained throughout the lower creation . . . is at bottom the most merciful provision which the circumstances admit of (Spencer 1951).

In the same way that carnivores weed out the old, sickly and malformed among the lower creatures, human predators perform a benevolent function in civil society:

> It is in the human race that the consummation is to be accomplished. . . [T]he well-being of existing humanity and the

unfolding of that perfection, are both secured by that beneficent, though severe discipline to which the animate creation at large is subject: a discipline which is pitiless in the working out of good: a felicity-producing law which never swerves for the avoidance of partial and temporary suffering. The poverty of the incapable, the distresses that come upon the imprudent, the starvation of the idle, and those shoulderings aside of the weak by the strong, which leave so many 'in shallows and in miseries', are decrees of a large, far-seeing benevolence. It seems hard that an unskilfulness which with all his efforts he can not overcome, should entail hunger upon the artizan. It seems hard that a labourer incapacitated by sickness from competing with his stronger fellows, should have to bear the resulting privations. It seems hard that widows and orphans should be left to struggle for life and death. Nevertheless, when regarded not separately but in connection with the interests of universal humanity, these harsh fatalities are seen to be full of the highest beneficence – the same beneficence which brings to early graves the children of diseased parents, and singles out the intemperate and debilitated as the victims of an epidemic (Spencer 1851).

This far-reaching benevolence was endorsed, Spencer claimed, by Christianity:

The command 'if any would not work neither should he eat', is simply a Christian enunciation of that universal law of Nature under which life has reached its present height – the law that a creature not energetic enough to maintain itself must die. . . (Spencer 1851: 322–3).

Spencer's benevolent law of nature was simply the dark side of the enterprise culture, and even he began to fear that its reign was slipping. By 1884, in *The Man versus the State*, he was unrepentant – 'the lapse of a third of a century . . . has brought me no reason for retreating from the position' – but more pessimistic about the survival of his pet philosophy. 'The old, strong, wise Liberalism, based on contract and voluntary cooperation, was being undermined by the "New Toryism" of state regulation' which was preparing the way for 'the coming slavery of Socialism' (Spencer

1884: 17, 34, 68). He was right: at the zenith of its success the enterprise culture began to decline. With remarkable foresight, Spencer saw it coming.

It was not just that socialism was in the air in the 1880s, with the founding of Hyndman's Social Democratic Federation, William Morris's Socialist League, and the Fabian Society. The tide had already turned in the very heart of politics, in law and public opinion. A. V. Dicey, the Victorian analyst of law and opinion, dated the hegemony of collectivism from 1865, and by 1898 in his lectures at Harvard he was bewailing the long decline of Individualism. In his book, published in 1905, he added a chapter on 'the debt of Collectivism to Benthamism' – 'the greatest happiness of the greatest number' could lead just as easily to state intervention as to laissez-faire – and he traced the beginnings of collectivism to the factory acts, poor-law reform, educational grants, and so on, of the 1930s, the very start of his epoch of Individualism (Dicey [1905] 1952: 64, Lecture IX).

I have tried to show elsewhere that individualism versus collectivism is a false antithesis, and that the earlier forms of collectivism were merely attempts at providing a framework of law for individualism: the inspection of factories, poor relief, public health, and so on, provided a form of policing those individuals who behaved in anti-social ways, which fell short of collectivist provision (Perkin 1981). This intervention was provoked not by paternalist or socialist ideologues but by the intolerable consequences of the free market, the unintended effects of allowing entrepreneurs to do as they pleased, in the overworking of factory children, slum housing, cholera epidemics, food and drug adulteration, acid rain, unsafe mines, railway accidents, coffin ships, and the like.

Some historians, such as Kitson Clark and Oliver MacDonagh, have seen in this merely 'the pressure of facts', the reaction by public opinion, politicians and civil servants to what they saw as intolerable social problems. Their critics, like Henry Parris and Jennifer Hart, have seen an evolution in the opinion formers themselves, particularly the Benthamites, from a belief in non-intervention to collectivist remedies for the same social problems (see Perkin 1981: 69 for a bibliography of this controversy). Both, of course, are right: some reformers, such as Michael Thomas Sadler or Lord Ashley, reacted instinctively to the horrors they saw around them; others, such as Edwin Chadwick and Kay-Shuttleworth, with a systematic application of the Benthamite programme of 'inquiry, report, legislation, execution, inspection'. Whatever the provenance of collectivist reform, however, the free market was under attack from the moment of its triumph. As Arthur Taylor (1972) has argued, there never was a moment of complete laissez-faire: state intervention in social policy began before the achievement of free trade in the economic sphere, and has continued ever since.

Similarly, Martin Wiener (1981) has traced 'the decline of the industrial spirit' back to 1850, when the enterprise of the industrialists, he argues, began to decelerate as soon, it seems, as it got into top gear. Wiener's thesis has been somewhat mangled by his critics, on numerous grounds: that there were lots of successful entrepreneurs after his chosen date, from Northcliffe, Leverhulme and Nuffield to Marks and Spencer and the Sainsburys; that most other industrial countries, including America, Germany and France, had their anti-industrial cultural critics without losing economic momentum, and that the values preached by them were not old aristocratic and pre-industrial ones (aristocrats were often money-making entrepreneurs and would marry anybody for her money) but new professional ones, the values of the masters and dons at the reformed public schools and universities, who put public service before what they called mere money-making. He is right, however, that many Victorians never accepted the enterprise culture, and were opposed to it from the start.

This raises the whole question of what in fact 'Victorian values', now so fashionable in some quarters, were. Were they the values of the entrepreneurial ideal, the enterprising individual, standing on his own feet without state aid, and thriving on competition and the struggle for wealth? Or were they the values of his critics, the reformers and public servants who tried to regulate and limit his activities? Even the classical economists, as that great revivalist of the free market Lionel Robbins has shown, came to doubt whether laissez-faire could be applied to children, women workers, and others who could not compete on equal terms in the market (Robbins 1978: 101–2). John Stuart Mill, though he thought that 'letting alone should be the general practice' and that the burden of argument for intervention should lie on the intervenors, led the way in undermining laissez-faire as a universal principle (Mill [1848] 1904: 573), and his followers, J. E. Cairnes (1873), T. E. C. Leslie (1879), and Stanley Jevons (1882) learned, in Jevons's phrase, 'to judge each case upon its merits'. Mill himself and his wife Harriet Taylor made the complete transition from Benthamite individualism to Benthamite collectivism and came to call themselves 'socialists', by which they meant supporters of state intervention in the treatment of specific social problems beyond the competence of individuals (Mill [1873] 1958: 196).

If the middle generation of Victorian thinkers were in doubt about laissez-faire, how much more so were the late Victorian economists and philosophers. By the 1880s, when Spencer began to worry about the encroaching threat to economic and personal liberty, both the older universities were teaching doctrines of public service and social responsibility to a generation of young men who would go out into the world to study social problems and help the less fortunate, if necessary by government intervention. At Oxford, T. H. Green was preaching 'the politics of conscience' and positive in place of negative freedom:

> It was the business of the state, not indeed directly to promote moral goodness, for that, from the very nature of moral goodness, it cannot do, but to maintain the conditions without which a free exercise of the human faculties is impossible (Green 1885–88, Vol. 3: 374).

His pupil Arnold Toynbee went further, arguing:

> First, that where the individual rights conflict with the interests of the community, there the state ought to interfere; and, second, that where the people are unable to provide a thing for themselves, and that thing is of primary social importance, then again the State should interfere and provide it for them (Toynbee 1883: 233–4).

At Cambridge, Alfred Marshall, the leading neo-classical economist of the day, said in his inaugural lecture in 1885:

> it will be my cherished ambition, my highest endeavour . . . to increase the numbers of those, whom Cambridge, the mother

of strong men, sends out into the world with cool heads and warm hearts willing to give some at least of their best powers to grappling with the social suffering around them; resolved not to rest content until they have done what in them lies to discover how far it is possible to open all the material means for a refined and noble life (see Pigou 1925: 174).

His pupil and successor, A. C. Pigou, the pioneer of welfare economics, declared in 1914:

The position from which I start is this. It is the duty of a civilized state to lay down certain minimum conditions in every department of life, below which it refuses to allow any of its free citizens to fall. There must be a minimum standard of conditions in factories, a minimum standard . . . of leisure, a minimum standard of education, of medical treatment in case of illness, and of wholesome food and clothing. . . The standards must be upheld all along the line, and any man or family which fails to attain independently to any one of them must be regarded as a proper subject for state action (Rowntree and Pigou 1914: 36).

Green and Marshall and their colleagues did send out strong men with cool heads and warm hearts to study social problems and evolve systematic remedies for them – men such as Beveridge and Keynes, Morant and Llewellyn Smith, Tawney and Clement Attlee, whose analyses of poverty, unemployment and education played a central role in the origins of the welfare state. The protagonists of the free market will say – have said – that this is where the rot set in, where the 'industrial spirit' began to decay, where Britain lost its enterprise and drive, where its long twentieth-century economic decline began. They blame it on the values taught in the public schools and universities, values which might be described not in terms of the new socialism of the Fabians and the Independent Labour Party but in those of Spencer's 'New Toryism', a paternalistic concern with the welfare of the people for the purposes of national efficiency and social justice. But the very stridency of their criticism and the near-disappearance of opposing values by the Second World War, when all political parties were united on the need for a universal welfare state, is proof that they believed that the enterprise culture was dead and in need of resurrection.[3]

What had killed it? The free marketeers would no doubt say a mushy, sentimental, misplaced humanitarianism that mistook public charity for kindness and undermined the real foundations of prosperity and economic growth, the energy and resourcefulness released by the individual's responsibility for his own survival and need to compete in the market. The real cause, however, was much more positive than that. The common thread uniting the reformers, most of whom were professional men educated for careers in the public service, was what I have called the professional social ideal. That ideal was based on their own situation in society, on the priority they gave to expertise and merit, measured by the standards not of the market but of their professional peers, on the need for social justice and national efficiency, and not on the law of the jungle but on a civilized society, where professional services were valued and rewarded and supplied to all who needed them.

The professional ideal had been the ally of the entrepreneurial ideal in the early stages, working together to end the idleness and corruption of the old pre-industrial society. Competition as an antidote to privilege had united them for much of the nineteenth century, but for the one it meant competition in the market place while for the other it meant competition in the examination room, for the best jobs in government and in the professions. When the market failed to provide the conditions of a civilized social life and instead generated social problems requiring professional remedies, the two parted company and began to oppose each other. By the early twentieth century, as Dicey and others nostalgic for the old individualism complained, the professional supporters of collectivism had won the battle for the mind and were coming out on top.

It would take too long to explore all the connections between the professional social ideal and the welfare state. Suffice it to say that the welfare state is the practical expression in social policy of the professional ideal. From its point of view, social problems such as poverty, disease, unemployment, slums, and lack of education are by-products of the market, which exist to be solved by professional analysis and administration. They are examples of inefficiency and waste – waste of material resources and human talent which, even

if you believe in competition and the market, frustrate the efforts
of individuals to create wealth and prosperity. Their remedies
require cool heads rather than warm hearts: national insurance,
employment exchanges, panel doctors, slum clearance and town
planning, state secondary education and university scholarships,
and the like – all, incidentally, providing more jobs for public
professionals. As Richard Titmuss remarked in 1960, the welfare
state seemed to exist as much for the welfare professionals as for
their 'clients' (Titmuss 1960: 10–11, 13–14). Be that as it may, the
professional ideal and the welfare state represented a revival of the
moral economy, a reverse movement from contract to status, to a
single status that T. H. Marshall in 1950 called social citizenship,
a status that gives every member of society a claim upon all the
rest for help and support in the contingencies of life (Marshall
1950: 34).

How then do we account for the resurgence in the last fifteen years or so of the enterprise culture, the revival of the free
market, the backlash against professional society, the return to
'Victorian values' that the Victorians themselves were in process
of repudiating? Is it a cyclical reaction, an example of what Albert
Hirschman has described as the long cycle of shifting involvement
between private interest and public action and expenditure, the
inevitable swing of the pendulum that results from the revulsion, first, from the intolerable social problems that accompany
unfettered enterprise and, secondly, from the intolerable public
expenditure and taxation produced by state provision (Hirschman
1982: 6). Has the welfare state become so successful that its supporters have become complacent and think that they can do without
it? Or is it the effect of propaganda by the free enterprise lobby,
harnessing the discontent with the high costs of welfare, at last
getting its message across after years in the wilderness?

The answer is all and none of these things. All three have
made a contribution, but to a much more major development
in world history, the transition from industrial to post-industrial
society. What we have seen in the twentieth century, not only
in Britain but in all advanced countries, is a profound change in
the nature and structure of society, of which the welfare state, a
near-universal phenomenon, is just one symptom. In terms of long
historical change it is the third phase of what Colin Clark (1940)

once called Petty's law, the tendency of all societies to move with economic growth from agriculture to industry to services.[4]

What is now happening to industry in the third phase of Petty's law is what happened to agriculture in the second: just as it then took a smaller percentage of the workforce to grow the food for everyone else, it now takes a smaller percentage to make the consumer goods for everybody. The rest are released for the expert services that people increasingly demand: medicine, education, entertainment, holidays, yes, even government, especially welfare, and even law and order and defence. These provide work not only for public-sector professionals but also for a vast range of private-sector ones: in finance, insurance, leisure services, and a great deal more. In Britain, while the manual working class shrank from about 75 per cent of the workforce in 1911 to about 58 per cent in 1971, and entrepreneurs (employers and proprietors) from about 6.7 per cent to 5.2 per cent, the class of 'higher professionals' and 'managers and administrators' grew from 4.4 per cent to 16 per cent. About a quarter of these in 1950 and still, despite privatization, in 1986 were public-sector professionals, employed by the state. The rest were employed increasingly by a shrinking number of large corporations.[5]

This phase of development I have called in a recent book (Perkin 1989) the rise of professional society. It is obvious enough on the side of the public sector, where the professionals have played a large part in the expansion of the twentieth-century social service state. But the real test of professional society is the professionalization of private enterprise itself. There are still large numbers of entrepreneurs of the old-fashioned Victorian kind about – 27,000 in 1963, in firms employing ten or fewer workers – but most of these are subcontractors, sales outlets and franchisees of the big firms. In 1909 the 100 largest manufacturing firms produced 15 per cent of total output; by 1930 26 per cent; by 1971 45 per cent. Today, the largest 200 firms produce 85 per cent. The same is true of the service industries: witness the 'big four' high-street banks and the half-dozen supermarket chains that, according to the Ministry of Agriculture, Fisheries and Food, distribute 66 per cent of the food. Between 1957 and 1976 the stock market valuation of the 100 largest public companies rose from about 60 per cent of the total to more than 90 per cent, and the current takeover boom suggests that it has not stopped there. Meanwhile, such firms are no longer controlled by their owners, who are too numerous to count, but by professional career managers, often appointed by other corporations. As long ago as 1963 less than a third (29 per cent) of the largest 116 companies were headed by such owners; a third (32 per cent) were headed by career managers, and the rest (39 per cent) by 'coordinator controllers', that is, professional managers appointed by holding companies and the like. Even where founders' kin were still in the chair, they were usually themselves principally managers of other people's capital. In 1969 the chairmen of the largest 100 companies owned on average 2.5 per cent of the equity, the whole board of directors only 7.5 per cent.[6]

In other words, British industry has undergone a managerial revolution. These private sector professionals brought with them their own version of the professional ideal: expertise based on specialized training, equality of opportunity, appointment and promotion by merit, and even their own notion of single status. It was the employers, represented by the Industrial Society, not the trade unions or the government, that as long ago as the 1960s suggested that all workers should be treated alike, and that manual workers should have the same conditions of work, periods of notice, holidays with pay, paid sick leave, pension rights, and so on.[7] Not all employers have followed suit, but the trend is in that direction – or was until the recent revival of free market attitudes. Single status in industry is to the private sector what the welfare state is to the public-sector professional: a means to share with the working class some of the benefits of a professional career. In some ways, the private sector has done more for the 'professionalization of the working class' than has the welfare state.

These two versions of the professional ideal have not prevented the two professional groups from quarrelling. On the contrary, the main social conflict in this new professional society is the struggle for income, status and power between the public-sector employees, who want higher public spending at least on their own particular service, and the private-sector managers, who want reduced public spending and lower taxation. The second blame the first for the enormous growth of the state during the twentieth century, for the rampant and accelerating inflation of the last two decades, which they see as mainly due to government overspending and mismanagement of the economy, and also for Britain's economic decline, which they attribute to the steering of investment towards 'unproductive' investment in state enterprises, including social security, hospitals, education, and the like, and away from production in the private sector. Although this analysis is grossly oversimplified, in that public spending, particularly on education to create the human capital for productive industry, on the health service to maintain an efficient workforce, and even on unemployment insurance to preserve a reserve of labour, can be productive, and that a large part of the private sector, especially the defence industries, pharmaceuticals, electronics, and so on, is dependent on government spending, the perception, which is what matters, is of a continuing power-struggle between the two rival groups of professionals.

It is not surprising, therefore, that the private sector professionals should be attracted by the free market ideology and the enterprise culture. Although it was finally put into theoretical form in the days of Ricardo and Marx for the small-scale individual capitalism of early industrialism, and for an economy infinitely less productive than our own, it has many advantages for the professional managers who run the much more organized and sophisticated corporate capitalism of post-industrial society. It makes them the heroes of the struggle for 'liberty', the guardians of the citizen from the overmighty state, the protectors of the consumer against the interfering planner, the saviours of the taxpayer from the pilfering bureaucrat. For the corporate manager himself, moving from a nationalized industry to a privatized corporation, it offers a change from a situation in which his salary is a 'cost' to be criticized by politicians and taxpayers to one in which it is a 'proof' of his merit and success. Ironically, it appeals to competition as the best determinant of merit and the fairest allocator of income and rewards, at the very time when the giant corporation is swallowing up more and more of its competitors. It has no conception of a threat to freedom from the overmighty corporation, which is now so large that it outweighs the Gross National Product of many countries and can undermine whole communities and even national economies by exporting investment and jobs elsewhere. It calls attention to the threat from Big Brother, the state, while diverting attention from the more insidious embrace of Big Sister, the giant corporation.

Despite the protestations of the free enterprise lobby, which insists that the state still has the upper hand through the legal control of armed force, the struggle is more evenly matched than might be expected. The giant multinational corporation is now part of an international corporate network, a neo-feudal system in which corporate barons hold allegiance to higher and lower corporate lords in a complex hierarchy of interdependence. The corporations, either individually or collectively, can bring influence to bear on the politicians and bureaucrats, who cannot afford to ignore their wishes, and can, with supreme irony, capture the state itself for their ideology and so use it to ensure freedom from state intervention. Indeed, cynics might say that the propaganda of the free enterprise lobby is directed to that very end, not to freeing the market but to persuading governments to allow the corporate managers to control it in their own interests.

On the other hand, the corporations have an ambivalent attitude towards the state, and do not wish it to withdraw from the market altogether. They need it not only to maintain the environment in which they operate, but also as their insurer of last resort: when all else fails, they can always appeal to the state for subsidies to bail them out. Like all elites before them, the landed aristocrats of pre-industrial society and the individual entrepreneurs of the Victorian age, they like to have their cake and eat it too – the protection and support of the state without suffering its adverse interference in their corporate affairs.

What, then, in all this is left of the enterprise culture? Enterprise still exists, certainly, for professionals of all kinds exist to perform expert services and justify their status and rewards by 'doing their own thing', which includes creating new products and services, whether they work for the government or the corporations. In fact, there is still individual competition within the large organization, between professionals who compete for promotion, higher salaries, and the respect and admiration of their peers. Entrepreneurs, as Schumpeter pointed out half a century ago, do not have to be owner-managing capitalists: they can be Tsarist Russian bureaucrats, Japanese samurai, or even Christian missionaries digging wells in the Sahel. It may be that corporate capitalism, which controls and limits competition and, therrefore, the duplication and waste of effort involved in multiple failure, is a more efficient way of promoting enterprise and economic development than the completely free market. Certainly, the rate of economic growth has (until recently) been greater since the Second World War under corporate capitalism than it was under the free-for-all small-scale capitalism of Victorian Britain.

It has also without undue strain – whatever the critics say – been able to support an unprecedentedly generous welfare state, a great experiment in social responsibility which has taken the age-old anxiety out of life not only for the working class but also for the middle class, who have probably benefited from it even more. To have achieved both record living standards for the great majority and a moral economy which guarantees security and opportunity for all – as far as they can be guaranteed in this uncertain world – is surely a great and unprecedented achievement. But the enterprise culture, if by that is meant the values of the individual owner-managing capitalist who dominated, though not for long or without challenge, Victorian Britain, is as dead as Queen Victoria. I doubt whether, despite Margaret Thatcher and her free marketeers, it will ever see the resurrection.

Notes: Chapter 3

1   N. B. [Nicholas Barbon], *A Discourse on Trade* (1690), and Richard Steele, *The Tradesman's Calling* (1684), cited by Tawney ([1926] 1938: 245–6, 243).
2   George Robb of Northwestern University is completing a PhD on white-collar crime in nineteenth-century England, which reveals the enormous opportunities for embezzlement opened up by the development of company organization and the free market.
3   Cf., inter alia, the publications of Hayek, from *The Road to Serfdom* (1944) to *Law, Legislation and Liberty* (1982), and those of the Institute of Economic Affairs.
4   See Colin Clark, *Conditions of Economic Progress* (1940); the 1960 and later editions drop 'Petty's Law' and refer to 'a wide, simple and far-reaching generalization'.
5   For the statistics in this paragraph, see Goldthorpe (1980: 60–1), Halsey (1972: 113), and *Social Trends*, Central Statistical Office (1986).

6 For the statistics in this paragraph, see Hannah (1976: 85, 89–91, 96, 216), Prais (1976: 10–13), Barratt Brown (1968), and Bannock (1973: 2).

7 Cf., inter alia, *Status Differences and Moves towards Single Status* (Industrial Society, 1970); and Alice Russell, 'The quest for security: the changing working conditions and status of the British working class in the 20th century', Lancaster University PhD, 1982, Ch. 6.

References: Chapter 3

Bannock, G. 1973. *The Juggernauts: the Age of the Big Corporation.* Harmondsworth: Penguin.

Barratt Brown, M. 1968. The controllers of British industry. In K. Coates (ed.), *Can Workers Run Industry*. London: Sphere.

Burckhardt, J. 1960. *The Civilization of the Renaissance in Italy.* New York: New American Library.

Cairnes, J. E. 1873. *Essays in Political Economy*. London: Macmillan.

Carlyle, T. 1840. *Chartism*. London: James Fraser.

Clark, C. 1940. *Conditions of Economic Progress*. London: Macmillan.

Dicey, A. V. [1905] 1952. *Law and Opinion in England during the 19th Century*. London: Macmillan.

Goldthorpe, J. H. 1980. *Social Mobility and Class Structure in Modern Britain.* Oxford: Clarendon Press.

Green, T. H. 1885–88. *Works of T. H. Green* (edited by R. L. Nettleship). London: Longman.

Halsey, A. H. 1972. *Social Trends in British Society*. London: Macmillan.

Hannah, L. 1976. *The Rise of the Corporate Economy*. London: Methuen.

Hayek, F. A. 1944. *The Road to Serfdom*. London: Routledge and Kegan Paul.

Hayek, F. A. 1982. *Law, Legislation and Liberty*. London: Routledge and Kegan Paul.

Hirschman, A. 1982. *Shifting Involvements: Private Interest and Public Action.* Princeton, NJ: Princeton University Press.

Jevons, W. S. 1882. *The State in relation to Labour*. London: Macmillan.

Leslie, T. E. C. 1879. *Essays in Political and Moral Philosophy*. Dublin: Hodges, Foster and Figris.

Macfarlane, A. 1978. *The Origins of English Individualism*. Oxford: Blackwell.

Maine, H. 1874. *Ancient Law*. London: John Murray.

Mandeville, B. de. [1714] 1924. *Fable of the Bees*. Oxford: Clarendon Press.

Marshall, T. H. 1950. *Citizenship and Social Class*. Cambridge: Cambridge University Press.

Mill, J. S. [1848] 1904. *Principles of Political Economy*. London: Longman.

Mill, J. S. [1873] 1958. *Autobiography*. Oxford: Oxford University Press.

Perkins, H. 1969. *The Origins of Modern English Society*. London: Routledge and Kegan Paul.

Perkins, H. 1981. *The Structured Crowd: Essays in English Social History*. Hemel Hempstead: Harvester Press.

Perkins, H. 1989. *The Rise of Professional Society: England since 1880*. London: Routledge.

Pigou, A. C. (ed.). 1925. *Memorials of Alfred Marshall*. London: Macmillan.

Pocock, J. G. A. 1975. *The Machiavellian Moment: Florentine Political Thought and the Atlantic Tradition*. Princeton, NJ: Princeton University Press.

Pope, A. 1734. *An Essay on Man*. Dublin: George Faulkner.

Prais, S. J. 1976. *The Evolution of Giant Firms, 1901–70*. Cambridge: Cambridge University Press.

Robbins, L. 1978. *The Theory of Economic Policy in English Classical Political Economy*. London: Macmillan.

Rowntree, B. S. and Pigou, A. C. 1914. *Lectures on Housing*. Manchester: Manchester University Press.

Russell, G. W. E. 1903. *Collections and Recollections*. London: Nelson.

Schumpeter, J. A. 1961. *The Theory of Economic Development*. Oxford: Oxford University Press.

Smiles, S. 1859. *Self-Help*. London: John Murray.

Smith, A. [1776] (1905). *The Wealth of Nations*, Vol. 1. London: G. Bell.

Social Trends (1986), (London: Central Statistical Office, HMSO).

Spencer, H. 1851. *Social Statistics*. London: John Chapman.

Spencer, H. 1884. *The Man versus the State*. London: Williams and Norgate.

Tawney, R. H. 1921. *The Acquisitive Society*. London: G. Bell.

Tawney, R. H. [1926] 1938. *Religion and the Rise of Capitalism*. Harmondsworth: Penguin.

Taylor, A. J. 1972. *Laissez-Faire and State Intervention in 19th-Century Britain*. London: Macmillan.

Thompson, E. P. 1971. The moral economy of the English crowd in the 18th-century. *Past and Present*, 50 (February): 76–136.

Thompson, E. P. 1975. *Whigs and Hunters: The Origins of the Black Act*. London: Allen Lane.

Titmuss, R. M. 1960. *The Irresponsible Society*. London: Fabian Society.

Toynbee, A. 1883. *Progress and Poverty*. London: Kegan Paul.

Weber, M. 1930. *The Protestant Ethic and the Spirit of Capitalism*. London: Allen & Unwin.

Wiener, M. 1981. *English Culture and the Decline of the Industrial Spirit, 1850–1980*. Cambridge: Cambridge University Press.

Wilson, C. 1957. The entrepreneur in the industrial revolution in Britain. *History*, 42: 101–17.

4 *The enterprise culture: old wine in new bottles?*

DAVID MARQUAND

The enterprise culture has been variously seen – as a slogan, as an ideology, as a dream and as a nightmare. I shall treat it as an aspiration: as an aspiration implied (though not logically entailed) by an exceedingly complex – indeed, in some respects internally contradictory – exercise in *statecraft*, some elements of which are ideological in character while others are not. I shall argue that the aspiration is unlikely to be achieved in full. But I believe that it may be, indeed that it has already been, achieved in part. I also believe that, whether it is achieved or not, the attempt to achieve it is likely to have profound consequences for our political economy and our political, cultural and moral lives. I shall focus principally on the nature, antecedents, rationale and implications of the aspiration, but I also want to speculate a little on the possible consequences of pursuing it.

Unfortunately, this is easier said than done. The term is heavily loaded with emotion, both favourable and unfavourable; like many such terms, it is also swathed in confusion. Therefore, I shall begin by making certain distinctions. In the first place, I distinguish between an (or the) enterprise culture and the existence within a given society of enterprising people. This may seem an obvious distinction, but it is nevertheless an important one. Advocates of the enterprise culture often suggest that it is only in such a culture that enterprising people are to be found, or at any rate that such a culture is uniquely hospitable to enterprising people. Since most of us like to think we are enterprising, that suggestion is a powerful rhetorical weapon. But if the term is defined in such a way, it ceases to be of any analytical value, and there is no point in discussing it any further. Enterprising people exist and have existed in a huge range of societies; to judge by the decorations in the tombs of the Valley of the Kings, there were plenty of them in Pharaonic Egypt, and the most cursory reading of the *Iliad* shows that they equally plentiful in Homeric Greece. But it would obviously be ludicrous to suggest that these were enterprise cultures.

Secondly, I distinguish between the enterprise culture and the competitive market. I do so because advocates of the enterprise culture often seem to take it for granted that it is an indispensable prerequisite of a market economy; indeed, they sometimes use the two terms almost interchangeably. This seems to me a dangerous oversimplification. Whatever else it may or may not be, today's enterprise culture is plainly an echo or a replica of the early-nineteenth-century 'entrepreneurial ideal' which Harold Perkin (1972) so memorably described some years ago. And, as Perkin has himself argued, markets antedated the entrepreneurial ideal by centuries, if not by millennia. But it is not necessary to go back to the dawn of human society to see that the bundle of ideas associated with the word 'market' and the bundle associated with the word 'enterprise' belong in two different compartments. In the mixed economies that have been characteristic of the developed western world since the Second World War, resources have been largely allocated by the market. But the mixed economies of the postwar period were not sustained by enterprise cultures, and in certain crucial respects the governing philosophies of those who managed them ran counter to the principles underlying what is now advocated as the enterprise culture. Indeed, advocates of the enterprise culture were (and are) fiercely critical of the mixed economy on precisely those grounds. To put the point at its simplest and crudest, while it may be true that an enterprise culture cannot exist without a market economy, the converse does not hold.

Thirdly, I distinguish between the enterprise culture and the wave of change that has swept through the world economy in the last fifteen or twenty years, and which, in the opinion of many observers, is replacing the 'organized capitalism' of the postwar period with a new kind of 'disorganized capitalism'. All over the western world, this school of thought argues, the last fifteen years have been marked by a switch from 'Fordist' to 'post-Fordist' industrial processes; by the decline of traditional mass-production in favour of new forms of 'flexible specialization'; indeed, by the emergence of a new 'techno-economic paradigm' based on custom-ized products made for specialized markets, small production runs, decentralized decision-making and a new kind of craftsmanship. At the same time, disillusion with 1960s-style 'heroic' planning has encouraged a shift away from the 'macro-corporatism' that often underpinned that form of planning. Irrespective of ideology, government after government has sought to give freer rein to market forces; everywhere 'de-regulation' has been the order of the day (cf. Lash and Urry 1987). British advocates of the enterprise culture have spotted these trends, and have sought to assimilate them into their argument. It is because Britain is moving towards an enterprise culture, they claim, that these changes have taken place; the fact that they are taking place proves that the enterprise culture runs with the grain of the times. Unfortunately for that argument, such changes have appeared throughout the western world; indeed, it is at least arguable that they have gone further in parts of continental Europe than they have here (cf. Hirst and Zeitlin 1989). But it is only in the United Kingdom (and perhaps in the United States) that governments have also sought to create an enterprise culture.

Hence, to take one of the most obvious recent examples, consider the battle currently taking place over the so-called 'social dimension' of the European Community's 1992 project. As is well known, the 1992 project involves a massive exercise in deregulation, designed to set market forces free and, in doing so, to promote higher investment and more rapid growth. As such, it fits the paradigm of 'disorganized capitalism' rather well. In the view of the Brussels Commission and of most Community member governments, a necessary corollary is a social programme designed partly to ensure that deregulation does not lead to what the Germans call 'social dumping' or a 'race for the bottom' and partly to maintain a social and political consensus in favour of the project. Mrs Thatcher and her colleagues approved of deregulation, but they violently opposed the proposition that its effects should be mitigated by social policies at the European level. Indeed, they attacked the Commission's Social Charter as 'corporatist' and even as 'Marxist'

– in other words, as incompatible with their version of the enterprise culture. But most continental governments (including the Christian Democratic Government of West Germany) support it, because to them it is axiomatic that social partnership and a social consensus are prerequisites of a successful programme of deregulation and perhaps also of a successful market economy.

Behind this difference of opinion, there lies, I believe, a much more fundamental difference of approach, which in turn reflects an even deeper difference of culture and tradition. The British Government, supported by British advocates of the enterprise culture *à l'anglaise* or *à l'Américaine*, holds, in effect, that economic change and adjustment to economic change come and can only come through the market: in Albert Hirschman's suggestive language, through Exit and the threat of Exit (Hirschman 1979). The undistorted, competitive market rewards economic agents who adjust and punishes those who fail to adjust; thus, the enterprising and adaptable prosper, while the unenterprising and unadaptable fall by the wayside. Interference with market forces, whether by the state or by the intermediate voluntary associations of civil society, can only slow down the adjustment process. The continental tradition embodied in the Brussels Commission's Social Charter sees the processes of change and adjustment in a more complex way. It does not deny that Exit and the threat of Exit have a part to play. But it holds that Exit can and should be supplemented by what Hirschman called Voice: that economic agents are influenced, not only by the hope of reward and the fear of punishment, but by persuasion, negotiation and mutual education.

Hand in hand with this difference goes a more subtle one. Economic change produces losers as well as gainers. Central to the politics of change is the question of how to deal with losers and potential losers. As John Zysman (1983) has argued, if change is to take place, losers and potential losers must either be bought off, or swept aside. Implicit in the tradition of Anglo-Saxon economic liberalism is the assumption that losers must be swept aside – most obviously by the market, but also by the state, whose role is to ensure that market forces are not impeded and that market outcomes are not interfered with. In the continental tradition, losers are bought off (as, for example, in the commonn agricultural policy): a degree of strict allocative economic efficiency is sacrificed for the sake of social peace and political consensus. Not the least of the implications of the Social Charter and the divergent responses to it is that these differences of tradition and assumption have survived the huge techno-economic shifts of the late-twentieth century; that 'post-Fordist' 'disorganized capitalism' (if that is indeed what we are seeing) can perfectly well co-exist with an economic culture quite different from the enterprise culture of present-day Britain and the United States.

Finally, I distinguish between the enterprise culture and what Samuel Beer (1982) has called the 'romantic revolt'. By this, Beer meant the complex shift of mood and sensibility that seems to have taken place in many, if not all, advanced industrial societies in the 1960s and 1970s. Central to this shift, in Beer's view, was a new assertion of the 'romantic' values of authenticity, spontaneity and individuality and a corresponding rejection of hierarchy, bureaucracy and externally imposed classifications and identities. This 'romantic revolt', he thought, had undermined the collectivist polity of the postwar period, because it had facilitated class decomposition and eroded the authority both of corporatist producer groups and of the old, elitist political class. All this had made necessary a switch to a new populism reminiscent of that of the United States.

The extent – even the existence – of such a romantic revolt is clearly debatable. Personally, I think Beer spotted something. I also think there is a connection between his romantic revolt and the enterprise culture of the Thatcherites. In particular, I think that the rhetoric of the enterprise culture – the rhetoric of 'choice', 'freedom', 'individualism', 'initiative' and the rest – appeals because it strikes chords that the romantic revolt has brought into existence. In spite of all this, however, I still believe that the enterprise culture and the romantic revolt must be distinguished from each other. In the first place, the range of identities legitimized by the enterprise culture is very limited. It gives increased scope for one's identity as a consumer, but not for other identities. Indeed, it is positively hostile to identity-choices that threaten the authority of the entrepreneur and the supremacy of entrepreneurial values. You can be a heretic ranging the supermarket shelves, but you must be a conformist everywhere else – necessarily, since it is of the essence of the enterprise culture that it gives pride of place to entrepreneurial values and to the entrepreneurial character type. (This is another reason why the enterprise culture should be distinguished from the market economy: the market is morally neutral, but the enterprise culture extols particular moral values at the expense of others.) More important still, the romantic revolt is essentially anti-hierarchical: the values of authenticity and individuality run against the values of order, discipline and obedience. Despite its individualistic rhetoric, however, the enterprise culture, at least as understood by its most enthusiastic advocates, is, in one crucially important respect, profoundly hierarchical. The modern free market, it is important to remember, is a place where hierarchically organized firms compete for custom: part of the point of the enterprise culture is to empower the consumer in the market, but part is to legitimize hierarchy in the firm.

Having spent some time describing what the enterprise culture is not, I now want to discuss what it is, or at least what it may be. Here I agree with Harold Perkin. What is under discussion, it seems to me, is a latter-day version of the nineteenth-century entrepreneurial ideal: an attempt to realize Sir Keith Joseph's 1975 aim to resume 'the forward march of *embourgeoisement* which went so far in Victorian times' (Joseph 1975: 57). I also agree with Perkin that this involves a kind of historiographical conjuring trick, which it is important to see through. The trick, of course, is to equate the modern, bureaucratic, hierarchical, professionally managed firm with the individualistic owner-manager of early capitalism. Advocates of the enterprise culture seek to justify the power and rewards of private-sector corporate managers and of the outcomes of market competition between the corporations they manage, just as supporters of the nineteenth-century entrepreneurial ideal sought to justify the social claims of the individualistic owner-managers of that period. Moreover, the justification offered by the former is essentially the same as that once offered by the latter. Just as the nineteenth-century entrepreneurial ideal depicted the owner-manager as a Promethean hero who, by his abstinence, enterprise and willingness to take risks, created the wealth that the whole society enjoyed, so the advocates of the enterprise culture depict the professional managers of today's private-sector corporations as the wealth creators on whose enterprise and dedication the prosperity of the rest of us depends (cf. Morgan 1990). But there the similarity ends. Despite the obvious special pleading of its advocates, the entrepreneurial ideal of the nineteenth century referred to a recognizable social reality. The owner-manager it celebrated was not, of course, a Promethean hero to everyone – that depended on one's point of view – but he did at least exist and he was at least an entrepreneur. He did risk his own capital, and he did have to survive in a fiercely competitive market. However enterprising they may be in the ordinary sense of the word, today's corporate managers are not, in that sense, entrepreneurs. They risk other people's capital, not their own. And although the giant firms they run still compete with each other, the market in which they do so is a quite different creature from the atomistic market of 150 years ago.

This leads on to one of the most puzzling features of the whole subject. To put it simply, why should any justification be necessary? Supporters of the free market often imply that markets are in some profound sense natural and that institutions or practices that 'distort' it are in some sense unnatural. Then why not simply eliminate such 'distortions', accept market outcomes and leave morality out of it? On market-liberal assumptions, the rewards produced by the undistorted market are, by definition, just. The notion that they might be unjust is based on a fallacy. If a successful corporate manager is worth $500,000 a year in the market-place, and requires a battery of managerial powers and privileges to enable his firm to function successfully in the market-place, then it is right for him to receive $500,000 a year and to be given the powers and privileges he needs. Then why bother to legitimize them? Surely, the market is itself the source of legitimacy?

The answer, I believe, is twofold: one, so to speak, internal to the enterprise-culture camp, and the other external to it. The 'internal' answer has been put best by F. A. Hayek in Volume 3 of *Law, Legislation and Liberty*. In past times, he writes, the values that sustain a market order,

> were inevitably learned by all the members of a population con-
> sisting chiefly of independent farmers, artisans and apprentices
> who shared the daily experiences of their masters. They held
> an ethos that esteemed the prudent man, the good husbandman

and provider who looked after the future of his family and
business by building up capital, guided less by the desire to
consume much than by the wish to be regarded as successful
by his fellows. . .

At present, however, an ever-increasing part of the population
of the Western world grow up as members of large organisations
and thus as strangers to those rules of the market which have
made the great society possible. To them, the market economy
is largely incomprehensible; they have never practised the rules
on which it rests and its results seem to them irrational and
immoral (Hayek 1979: 111–27).

In short, a market order is possible only if the moral values
appropriate to it prevail. At present they do not. In a market
order, market outcomes and market power would, indeed, be ipso
facto legitimate. Unfortunately, we do not yet live in such an order.
Corrupted, late-twentieth-century men and women, products of
decades (perhaps even of a century) of creeping collectivism, do
not 'understand' the moral requirements of a market order and
are not ready for the dawn of market freedom. So before the
dawn breaks – indeed, before it *can* break – they must be remade.
And, for that, a cultural revolution is necessary. The enterprise
culture is, at one and the same time, the revolutionaries' instrument
and their destination. Just as the Bolsheviks discovered that the
corrupt and backward-looking human material bequeathed to them
by the Tsars was not ready for a stateless Leninist Utopia, and
concluded that the long-suffering Russian muzhik must be remade
into a new kind of Soviet Man before Utopia could arrive, so
the advocates of the enterprise culture have concluded that the
feckless, enterprise-eschewing, market-distorting human material
bequeathed to them by the postwar consensus and the long decades
of compromise and appeasement that led up to it must be remade
in the image of the entrepreneurial ideal before the market order
they seek can come into being.

This leads on to the 'external' answer; the answer that might be
expected to come from outside the enterprise-culture camp itself.
(It may perhaps be the same answer in different words.) This
is that the advocates of the enterprise culture are seeking, quite

deliberately, to change the parameters within which arguments about the morality of the market may take place; that they hope to change the moral environment within which market power and market outcomes are judged. They want to do this because they know – who better? – that in the postwar mixed economy the market has had to function within fairly narrow moral limits and because they wish to widen these limits. They wish to widen the limits for a number of reasons, of course, but it seems to me that one reason stands out above all the others. The nineteenth-century entrepreneurial ideal had to do with authority as well as with freedom. Central to it was the assumption that the owner-manager had an absolute right to do what he wished with his own: that any interference with his authority over the labour he hired was an attack on the rights of property. In much the same way, part of the point of the twentieth-century enterprise culture is to restore authority, in the state, in the firm and, for that matter, in public-sector organizations as well. To return to Hirschman's vocabulary for a moment, the object of the exercise is to create a state of affairs in which adjustment by Voice is unnecessary because everyone accepts the consequences of adjustment by Exit: in which the tedious, time-consuming and (for some) humiliating processes of consultation and negotiation that Voice entails can be short-circuited; and in which, in consequence, managers once again enjoy 'the right to manage', while governments have the right to govern. More simply, what is at stake is an attempt to legitimize a shift in the balance of social and economic power – a shift from the public sector to the private, as Harold Perkin (1989) has pointed out and, in my view, much more important, a shift in both public and private sectors from those at the bottom of hierarchies to those at the top.

At this point, however, enter a huge and embarrassing paradox. A crucial part of the object of the Thatcherite project is to limit the role of the state. There are two important reasons for this. One is ideological. Neo-liberals hold that the market is the realm of freedom, and the state the realm of coercion: that is one of the central premises of their whole creed. It follows that, as a matter of moral principle, that state's role should be limited. The second and more important reason is pragmatic. Neo-liberals also hold that the extension in the role of the state, which took place in the 1960s and 1970s, led to a vicious circle of overload and ungovernability. The state's reach came to exceed its grasp: the more it promised, the less it could perform; and the wider the gap between promise and performance, the more its authority declined. The obvious moral is that the state's role must be pruned back – not in order to weaken it, but, on the contrary, to strengthen it.

This is where statecraft – the 'old wine' of my title – comes into the story. As James Bulpitt (1985) has suggested, the Tory tradition is of a strong and authoritative state, which concentrates on what he calls 'high politics' while leaving 'low politics' to other agencies – to local government and to intermediate associations of all kinds. Macmillan in the early 1960s and still more Heath in the early 1970s departed from this tradition. Both embarked on interventionist economic policies, which dragged the state into the sphere of 'low politics' and which, at least potentially, also threatened its monopoly of 'high politics'. In both cases, the result was a demoralizing electoral defeat: in Heath's case, in circumstances that made the Conservative party's survival as a governing party appear problematical. Mrs Thatcher's real attraction did not lie in her new-fangled 'monetarist' economics: it was that economic liberalism provided a route by which her party could rescue the state from the toils of 'low politics' and, in doing so, return to the exceedingly old-fangled tradition of Tory statecraft.

Herein lies the paradox. The cultural revolution implied by the project of creating an enterprise culture can be carried out only by a strong and, above all, intrusive state, which intervenes incessantly in 'low politics'. Only the state can change the mix of incentives and disincentives that traps fallen late-twentieth-century men and women in the dependency culture of bloated public provision and attenuated private enterprise; only the state can humble or disarm the vast range of intermediate institutions that embody and transmit corrupting, anti-entrepreneurial values. If an enterprise culture is to come into existence, universities must be remodelled, the freedom of action of local authorities must be much more tightly curtailed, the self-governing professions must be 'marketized' and the trade unions must lose power. But all this runs counter both to traditional Tory statecraft and to neo-liberal ideology. The central theme of the politics of the 1980s was to be found in the working-out of that paradox – in the oscillation between the twin poles of the 'free economy' and the 'strong state': between the need to enhance the *power* of the state in order to create an enterprise culture and the need to diminish the *role* of the state in order to ensure that the enterprise culture is truly 'enterprising'.

At this point, some questions may be in order. How successful has the project been, and how successful is it likely to be? On one level, of course, it is bound to fail. It is plainly impossible, in the closing years of the twentieth century, to re-create the kind of enterprise culture that existed in the early nineteenth century. But failure will not necessarily undermine the legitimacy or the appeal of the project. The examples of the Church Militant and of the Communist Party of the Soviet Union show only too clearly that a millennarian ideal can often be rather like the carrot placed just in front of the proverbial donkey. The fact that the donkey never catches up with the carrot only leads him to redouble his efforts. The fact that the ideal is never realized only reinforces the faithful in their zeal, giving them an ever-growing list of obstacles to be overcome and of enemies to defeat. And, even if the enterprise culture is never attained, the attempt to attain it may have important consequences. In particular, it may block off other possible courses. One of Hirschman's most fruitful insights was that Voice – his alternative to Exit – depends upon Loyalty; that the processes of negotiation, discussion and mutual education upon which adjustment through Voice depends are likely to produce results only if those who engage in them are held together by ties of mutual obligation which endure through time. If, by strengthening Exit, Loyalty is eroded, if market forces attenuate the ties of community, the chances of returning to Voice at some time in the future are likely to diminish. Negotiated adjustment – the kind of adjustment implied by the European Commission's Social Charter – depends upon a communitarian ethic. Such an ethic may well be a casualty of current attempts to create an enterprise culture, even if they are not wholly successful. And in that case, there would be no other hole to go to.

References: Chapter 4

Beer, S. H. 1982. *Britain Against Itself: the Political Contradictions of Collectivism*. London: Faber and Faber.

Bulpitt, J. 1985. The discipline of the new democracy: Mrs Thatcher's domestic statecraft. *Political Studies*, 34, 1: 19–39.

Hayek, F. A. 1979. *Law, Legislation and Liberty, The Political Order of a Free People*. Volume 3. London: Routledge and Kegan Paul.

Hirschman, A. O. 1979. *Exit, Voice and Loyalty – Responses to Decline in Firms, Organizations and States*. Cambridge, Mass: Harvard University Press.

Hirst, P. and Zeitlin, J. 1989. *Reversing Industrial Decline?* Oxford: Berg.

Joseph, K. 1975. *Reversing the Trend – a Critical Reappraisal of Conservative Economic and Social Policies*. Chichester and London: Barry Rose.

Lash, S. and Urry, J. 1987. *The End of Organised Capitalism*. Cambridge: Polity Press.

Morgan, P. 1990. Address by Peter Morgan to the Annual Convention of the Institute of Directors. London: Institute of Directors.

Perkin, H. 1972. *The Origins of Modern English Society 1780–1880*. London: Routledge and Kegan Paul.

Perkin, H. 1989. *The Rise of Professional Society: England since 1880*. London: Routledge.

Zysman, J. 1983. *Governments, Markets and Growth: Financial Systems and the Politics of Industrial Change*. Ithaca and London: Cornell University Press.

5 Enterprise – towards the emancipation of a concept

TONY SKILLEN

I shall argue in this chapter that the notion of 'enterprise', when this is identified with the economic sphere, more specifically with capitalism, is conceptually limited when compared with broader European understandings. This identification, characteristic of the term's use in this country, also prevents the development of true enterprise.

Are capitalists entrepreneurs?

As a youth I studied economics in Australia. I was taught that the four factors of production were land, labour, capital – and enterprise. When I came to England, among many other corrections to my education was the information that the last was *not* to be included as one of the these factors. This is the British View.

I am not sure that my British instructors should be left with the last word. Indeed, I want to suggest that the 'British' refusal to separate out 'enterprise' as a factor of production is unsoundly based. The idea that 'enterprise' will come into animated existence just by virtue of the presence of the capitalist market, and hence needs no special attention, is probably a profound error in economic sociology. Thus, I intend to consider different views of the relation of capital to enterprise in economic thought. But I do not intend to leave it at that. It is a grotesque constriction to limit our notions of 'enterprise' and 'enterprise culture' to capitalist economics, indeed to the economic sphere generally. We need to remember the full scope of the virtue of enterprise. And we need to remember that enterprise is often, and sometimes necessarily so, sacrificed to economic concerns. First, though, a look at economics.

Adam Smith ([1776] 1937), like Adam Ferguson but more so, makes the spur to 'overcoming obstacles' and the 'exertion of vigilance and attention' a major virtue of the system of private ownership. Enterprise, for Smith, flows straightforwardly from the capitalist market system, and is not some additional component of it. By contrast, it seems that French political economists argued that 'enterprise' *was* a specific 'factor'.

This continental tradition, visible in Schumpeter's *Capitalism, Socialism and Democracy* (1943), depicts 'capital' as the merely monetary-mechanical wherewithal of production. In this sense the capitalist, as owner of this wherewithal, is possibly quite 'unenterprising'. He is but an accumulator, who needs to be persuaded by the entrepreneur's promise of success to part with his funds. It is the entrepreneur who animates and directs this resource, receiving 'profit' if his risk-taking generalship and energy are successful. In this tradition, then, the usurious capitalist – Mr Moneybags – merely gets 'interest' on what he advances to the entrepreneur.

Accordingly, Say, at the beginning of the last century, distinguishes the organizer and leader of production from the provider of capital (see Robbins 1968: 100).[1] Likewise, Pareto attacked, from a sociological as well as an economic standpoint, the 'confusion' of two different categories in the single term 'capitalists' (Pareto 1966: 263–5). The first category is property owners and owners of savings, while the second is true entrepreneurs. Whereas the entrepreneurs are marked by 'ingenuity', 'resourcefulness', and 'opportunism', the property owners and savers are 'conservative', 'timid', and 'rabbits' and include the salaried and clerical 'staffs' of public *and* private firms.

Returning to Schumpeter, his entrepreneurs, showing only intermittently in the epicyclings of economic systems, are essentially *innovators*, people who make market breakthroughs and achieve a period of advantage in disequilibrium. In a Weberian way, Schumpeter thinks of the normal tendency of business as one of routinization and self-protection, dominated not by enterprise but by system-maintenance. Schumpeter's work, therefore, fits in with Burnham (1945) and Galbraith's (1957) 'managerialism' doctrine, which stresses ownership and control as separate functions.

Ironically, this leads to a further distinction. For if 'enterprise' is essentially 'innovation', it is itself capable of 'professionalization' and 'routinization' in the form of research and development expertise. Writing before the advent of the joint-stock company, Say distinguishes between the 'organizer', who manages ('undertakes') the business, and the capitalist who lends him money. The organizer is also the one who stands to go bankrupt if the 'enterprise' fails.

It is thus apparent from this brief survey of the historical portrayals of 'enterprise' that there are three mutually detachable notions. First, there is the *'innovativeness'* notion, stressing vision, imagination and resourcefulness. Secondly, there is the *'managerial virtue'* notion, emphasizing 'effectiveness', leadership, 'superintendence', persistence and the ability to follow through an 'undertaking'. And finally, we have the *'liability to risk'* notion, characterized by vulnerability to failure, and prospect of profit.

It is the third component that differentiates the specifically capitalist entrepreneur, as it is the case that both innovativeness and managerial virtue are consistent with non-capitalist 'forms of enterprise'. Advocates of capitalism (such as certain proponents of Thatcherism) claim that only the third component, in its direct form – as distinct from professional 'managers' or 'innovators' who are subject to dismissal or sanctions from public or private owners if they are unsuccessful – is an adequate spur to generate the first two of the above notions of 'enterprise'. For there will be 'enterprise' only if there are also 'entrepreneurs'. Thus, Margaret Thatcher is concerned that the British people might not be spurred by the *'liability to risk'* aspect to exhibit *'innovativeness'* and *'managerial virtue'*. Her faith is that the revival of *'innovativeness'* and *'managerial virtue'* depends upon the *'liability to risk'*.

There is a significant slippage of meaning in Martin Wiener's provocative *English Culture and the Decline of the Industrial Spirit* (1981: 182–3). The book ends with praise for the Thatcher revolution and its revival of the missing 'industrial' spirit. But Wiener's praise depends on an identification of 'industrial' with 'capitalist'. After all, it is fairly well established that in many ways the Thatcher period has been bad for industry in this country. Certainly, finance capital has flourished under Thatcher. But Wiener himself, in a brief but telling discussion, has already shown himself a follower of Pareto and Say. He notes a damaging practical and cultural gulf between the elite financiers of the City of London – traditionalists, obsessed with safety and stability, and in a real sense conservative – and the provincial, patronized, under-capitalized captains of (northern) industry. Of course, not only do we now know more about the distinctive phenomenon of financial enterprise, but we are also familiar with the invasion of the City precisely by an enterprising cohort from less-cushioned backgrounds.

Wiener's historical account, then, mirrors Pareto's general one of a contrast and conflict between the entrepreneurial function and its concomitant ethos (that of the hands-on venturer), and the capitalist function and spirit (that of the investing accumulators). In this connection, it is essential to distinguish the *capitalist* from the *entrepreneurial* mentality.[2] If you are a pure, ideal-typical capitalist, your aim is accumulation – a quantitative goal, abstracted from any content – and, if you can get professional managers to assist in this aim, it is only to your advantage. As any copy of the *Financial Times* will tell you, however, there are ideal-typical entrepreneurs, who, having 'struggled' and built up their companies, sell them to start again on a new venture. Their activity is not 'abstracted' from content, but is nonetheless fickle in its attachment to content. But the distinction between these two kinds of entrepreneurs is false to the more 'neutral' Say notion of enterprise as 'undertaking', and so a second sense of 'enterprise' is worth distinguishing. In this sense, the 'entrepreneurial mentality' is shown, not only in building but also in maintaining the 'enterprise'. The ideal-typical entrepreneur of this type is wedded to his business and would regard the entrepreneur in the previous sense as promiscuously abandoning the ship in mid-ocean. Also important, from a sociological–cultural–political point of view, is that these latter entrepreneurs can be as conservative as the 'best' of the Pareto-like rentiers. After all, we are here in the world of the small businessman.

Although it is useful to think of these categories as picking out exclusive classes of individual, different, often competing, types of activity, the fact remains that such divergent types of outlook often cohabit in one individual's economic life. That we are dealing here in abstractions can be further emphasized by pointing out, contrary to tradition, that if *labour* is an economic category and not merely an empirical class ('I am a labourer') then it refers to what could be called 'sheer effort' in relative abstraction from 'enterprise' (for the 'abstractness' of economics, see Skillen, 1980). It is, as Marx observed, an empirical feature of capitalism both to de-skill and disenfranchise workers from their control over their productive life: that is, to render the labourer into the quintessence of 'labour' in this abstract sense. Yet every capitalist, every manager, needs a measure of enterprise in his workforce – of commitment, imagination and initiative. And a major tendency of modern, post-Fordist 'management science' consists largely in the serious appreciation of the measure of this need and the consequent importance of 'enriching' jobs to encourage and channel workers' enterprise.[3]

Lifting the economy's scales: enterprise as a virtue

'Enterprise', it is clear, is not a concept that by definition is tied to Smithian–Friedmanite–Thatcherite economics. It is an empirical question whether and to what extent laissez-faire, protected by the law-and-order state, generates and promotes economic enterprise. It is wrong for people to the left of advocates of 'private enterprise' to concede the notion and value of 'enterprise' to the right, leaving themselves raking in the muck for bad things to say about it. I have even heard one solemn left-winger say, on the basis of Macbeth's description of his grisly mission as an 'enterprise', that the term had a negative connotation before the advent of capitalism! Right-wing philosophy's attempts to appropriate concepts of justice, of freedom, or of citizenship have regularly been opposed. The other approach is to abandon such values to the right, to devalue them and then counterpose other values. Some feminist writing, for example, depicts 'justice' as an essentially masculine virtue, an abstract, detached, cold-blooded thing beside the care and compassion, upheld 'with a different voice' as superior. But to identify enterprise with market huckstering, with slapping a price on everything or with hawking your sister in the street, exhibits just such an approach. It augurs ill for a culture of the left if all *active* notions ('citizenship', 'freedom', 'enterprise'), with the exception of 'administration', are conceded to the right.

So far I have tried to open up conceptual space for a debate within the context of economics. But this context itself needs not only to be questioned but to be challenged. For the very priority of economics reflects a threat to 'enterprise', if that term is understood in its wider and original sense. This is something that teachers are aware of, in so far as 'market' and 'consumer' pressures lead administrators along unenterprising and conventional channels when it comes to allocating institutional resources. Academic researchers, long disciplined by the 'research grant' incentive to the extent that, for many, a question only arises if funds are available to address it, have long had their inquiring enterprise nobbled by their own careerist 'entrepreneurship' (see Skillen 1980). Overall, the utilization of a narrowly based economically defined notion of 'enterprise' results in actions that serve only to limit enterprise in its broader, more humanistic, sense.

Let us reflect on the ways in which enterprise, as I have more broadly defined it, has to struggle against 'enterprise' more narrowly envisaged, in order to flourish.

In Herne Bay, Kent, there is a charitably funded residential home for adults who are seriously handicapped and who have hitherto been in large traditional institutions. The aim of the place, since long before the Government's 'dumpist' policy of returning patients to 'the community', is to develop the independent capacities of the residents. 'Helping them to help themselves' is a difficult project since they have long been accustomed to being recipients of food and of being directed. Enterprise-acculturation requires a dedicated staff, approximately one for every two residents. It also needs permanent financial and technological backing, including protected employment. Here we see enterprise culture having to combat economies generated by market forces.

Secondly, residents of old people's homes are generally 'looked after' – fed, cleaned, placed in front of the television, and so forth. 'Physiotherapy' tries to attach an active dimension to this passive regime. If you visit one of these places you will see rows of women sitting by their beds. At certain times, tea is brought in. It is my impression that women seem even more depressed in these places than the men. Their self-respect had previously been formed on the subtle adjustments entailed by managing their households and looking after their families on a daily basis. Now they cannot get near a kettle. Safer, less disruptive, ultimately cheaper to do it all for them and dole out the anti-depressants! This provides a forceful illustration of enterprise culture struggling with welfare bureaucracy.

Next, consider the fact that drug agencies in Liverpool have been experimenting by offering heroin 'on demand' to addicts, with supervised injections and so on. Conservatives in this city have been up in arms mobilizing resistance. But there has also been resistance by drug consumers. The handout has widely been perceived as a 'square bore'. The drug culture, it seems, is not just the epitome of passive consumerism but is itself an enterprise culture. 'Scoring' entails an adventurous, risky and rebellious identity and way of life, for some a full-time occupation that supplied a high that the handout could not offer. So this example is of enterprise culture lined up against consumerism.

Threatened with shutdowns and redundancies, the Combined Shop Stewards' Committee at Lucas Aerospace in the 1970s collaborated to develop a Corporate Plan for new uses of existing technologies and plant (see Skillen 1978: 79–80). Independent auditors certified that there was a potential for profit in adopting this plan. The company turned it down, principally because its source as well as its content threatened 'managerial prerogative'. In this case, we find competition between enterprise culture and hierarchical authority.

To give a final illustration: many people, especially boy scouts, girl guides and woodcraft folk, organize paper drives, bottle collections, can-recycling schemes and similar activities. Officials receive the offerings in the name of environmental protection, and then, given that it is still cheaper to use new trees, new silicon and newly mixed ore, quietly hand the stuff over to the waste disposal contractors for dumping with the rest of the garbage. If it is rare for the dead to be raised, it is unheard of for the yet unborn to be actualized, let alone to be equipped with market power to express their interests. This can be seen as an example of enterprise culture versus capitalist imperatives.

Ordinary thought and ordinary language refuse to locate the value of enterprise solely within the boardrooms of capitalist firms. 'Initiative', 'risk' and 'imagination' are values as wide and as deep as human experience. The concept of enterprise indeed is a bit like 'courage' or 'integrity'. It is a *formal* virtue. By that I mean that, unlike, say, 'compassion', which specifies certain goals or concerns, true enterprise values are more or less neutral with respect to goals, to the *content* of activities. It is thus a mistake to identify enterprise with acting in a self-seeking fashion. We can be as enterprising in pursuit of altruistic or disinterested goals, as we can be of those of an egoistic variety. Indeed, we can be as enterprising as a group as singly.

Enterprise is a quality appropriate to the human condition. Humans need imagination, the capacity to struggle to surmount obstacles, to take responsibility and risks. They also need to be able to cope with and learn from failure as well as its 'twin imposter', success. Older cultures, most of which are remote from our bourgeois individualism, produce these virtues in their members, tempering them and channelling them with other values such as loyalty, compassion and respect. Not only do humans need enterprise, they exult in it, organize games that display and test it, and value it for itself as an attribute of the individual and the group.

Now of course, like courage, enterprise can be exhibited in reprehensible as well as good activity. In cultural terms this means that the 'arenas' of enterprise are characteristically circumscribed. It is, however, a feature of capitalist society to delimit that arena, to turn taboo zones into enterprise zones, where everything is up for grabs, and new 'territory' is forever being opened up. It is interesting also that the capitalist entrepreneur, unlike many of his predecessors, requires lack of enterprise on others' part to generate his competitive advantage.

Attention to these truisms, I would argue, should help us not only to be critical of the paternalistic dependency cultures associated with the postwar 'welfare state'. It should also open our eyes to the pinched duplicity of the New Right's conception of enterprise culture. Thus, unblinkered, the apostle of enterprise might see:

● the authoritarianism and rigidity of schooling in our society and the general passivity and irresponsibility of young people's lives.
● the confinement of labour in jobs increasingly de-skilled and regimented.

- the confinement of women to the status of unrecognized domestic slaves and pets. The idea of the world of enterprise as essentially masculine blocks awareness of the need to unite entrepreneurial and caring values and roles.
- the cruel reduction of the elderly to the sphere of the post-active, destroying both dignity AND ability and contribution.
- the erosion of democratic powers, local or functional, so that 'active citizenship', alleged to be part of the new enterprise culture, is reduced to Rotary Clubs' organizing clean-up campaigns in streets left in a mess by shrinking public services and expanding private despair.

In conclusion, there is a tendency to overemphasize the economic, thus identifying enterprise with capital and hence with capitalism. But thinking about enterprise differently – in the way inherited from the continental tradition – helps us to detach the notion from this usual identification, and to be reminded, for example, of the socialistically inspired Greater London Enterprise Board, with its partnerships and seed-funding of local, sometimes cooperative, businesses. It reminds us too of what as keen observers of life we know already, that enterprise is not necessarily a prominent feature of capitalist management. Hence, as monopolies continue to swallow up the high streets of human existence, it becomes an open question as to what specific forms of ownership and control are most conducive to the enterprise necessary in particular fields.

The government, instead, presents us with share ownership – with the passive, secure nest-egg as the enterprise culture spreads to the people. We are presented with the image of people detached from workers' organizations, desperate enough to hustle for any job as entrepreneurs-at-large on their bikes – offering themselves as that most 'entrepreneurial' of all objects, the individualized commodity.

Adventure is, to turn the verbal tables, a scarce commodity in the modern capitalist world. Developments in productive technology, so often running counter to the interests of producers and consumers, make possible less work, more enterprise in work, and better choice for consumers. But an enterprise culture worth both names – 'culture' as well as 'enterprise' – is going to have more scope and more need for enterprise than is dreamt of in today's dominant philosophy.

Notes: Chapter 5

1   Fifty years earlier, Richard Cantillon (Robbins 1968: 108; cf. Samuelson
    1981: 581, 726) had written that, distinct from those who received fixed
    wages, whether they be generals or footmen, are the 'entrepreneurs',
    defined as those whose income depends on their own skill, luck
    and negotiating capacities. Be they merchants or tinkers they 'live
    on uncertainty'. Cantillon's concept is important in the Thatcherite
    idea of a trans-class 'enterprise culture', in which it is accepted that
    one must be prepared to mount either one's bike or one's Boeing
    in pursuit of a living. Now, whereas Cantillon's translator writes
    'undertaker' for 'entrepreneur' (and likewise 'undertaking' – this bleak
    translating habit must partly explain as well as reflect the dismal lack
    of British economists' interest in 'enterprise'), Say's translation goes
    to the opposite extreme with 'adventurer'.
2   I have borrowed the term 'capitalist mentality' from Cohen (1978:
    300 ff), offering 'entrepreneurial mentality' as part payment.
3   See Skillen (1978) for a critical description of developments in man-
    agement 'science'. In Skillen (1981) I develop the contrast in Marxism
    between a 'romantic' view of the proletariat as potential collective
    entrepreneurs and a narrower view of class as a protective interest
    group whose 'enterprise' is restricted to waging anti-productive war
    against capital.

References: Chapter 5

Burnham, J. 1945. *The Managerial Revolution.* Harmondsworth: Penguin.
Cohen, G. A. 1978. *Karl Marx's Theory of History.* Oxford: Clarendon
    Press.
Galbraith, J. K. 1957. *American Capitalism.* Harmondsworth: Penguin.
Pareto, V. 1966. *Sociological Writings* (ed. S. E. Finer). London: Pall
    Mall.
Robbins, L. 1968. *The Theory of Economic Development.* London: Macmillan.
Samuelson, P. 1981. *Economics.* New York: McGraw-Hill.
Schumpeter, J. 1943. *Capitalism, Socialism and Democracy.* London: Unwin.
Skillen, T. 1978. *Ruling Illusions.* Hemel Hempstead: Harvester.
Skillen, T. 1980. The ethical neutrality of science and the method of
    abstraction; the case of political economy. *The Philosophical Forum,* xi,
    3 (Spring): 215–33.
Skillen, T. 1981. Working class interests and the proletarian ethic. *Canadian
    Journal of Philosophy.* Supplementary vol. vii: 155–70.
Smith, A. [1776] 1937. *The Wealth of Nations.* New York: Modern
    Library.
Wiener, M. J. 1982. *English Culture and the Decline of the Industrial Spirit.*
    Cambridge: Cambridge University Press.

PART 2

The morality of
enterprise values

6 Enterprise in its place: the moral limits of markets

RAYMOND PLANT

In this essay I shall consider what might be regarded as the moral limits of markets. As with most institutions, the very legitimacy of the market may well depend on recognizing that markets have to operate within certain boundaries and that they will lose their legitimacy if they operate beyond those limits.

In the 1970s the theory of government overload was popular. The claim was made that the British government had lost some of its authority because, since the Second World War, its role and functions had been extended into areas that were not of central concern to government and in which its competence was limited. Part of the programme of Mrs Thatcher was to increase the legitimacy of government by narrowing its scope and increasing its authority in a narrower area. Whether this project has been successful is not a matter for discussion here. What I am suggesting, however, is that something similar could happen in the case of markets. If markets and the motivations which markets rely on are extended in an uncritical way, then it is possible that they too could come to lose legitimacy, even in areas where they are appropriate. This essay should not, therefore, be construed as an anti-market one. Rather, I am concerned with making sure that the market, which has an absolutely necessary function in a free and pluralistic society, does not jeopardize people's loyalty by being continually extended into areas in which its legitimacy might be questionable.

My title is 'Enterprise in its place' though, rather than 'Markets in their place'. I have no general theory to offer about the psychological or cultural underpinnings of the market and the role of enterprise in this. However, it does seem that individuals have to have enterprising attitudes if markets are to work, and there has to be a cultural climate that favours enterprise for them to work effectively. In this sense, what might be called the enterprise culture appears to be a necessary, although not a sufficient, condition for the success of markets. This is why the development of the market economy in Eastern Europe is fraught with some dangers. People may see their economic salvation as lying in the extension of markets, but may have lost the cultural attitudes of enterprise and entrepreneurship that make the market work. Accordingly, they may well be disappointed in the results that markets without enterprise culture will bring. However, the main point for this essay is that, if enterprise is a necessary condition for a successful market order, then plotting some of the boundaries of markets will also involve putting enterprise in its legitimate place.

I believe that it is possible to identify three sorts of moral boundaries to markets. There may, of course, be more, but quite a lot is caught by the following: the moral underpinnings of markets, which should not be subject to market activity; what I shall call – following Michael Walzer (1983) – the moral boundaries to the sphere of markets; and the moral consequences of markets.

Moral underpinnings

In talking of the moral underpinnings of markets, I have in mind the idea that in order to work effectively the market requires certain moral attitudes on the part of those involved, and that there is some danger of these moral underpinnings being disturbed by markets themselves, thereby striking at the roots of their own effectiveness and efficiency. I shall discuss two examples of this, although no doubt there are others.

The first is that, although market relations undoubtedly rest upon self-interest, they equally rest upon contract; and contractual relations in turn depend upon a set of indispensable moral attitudes of trust, promise-keeping, truth-telling and taking-one's-word-as-one's-bond. As Emile Durkheim once pointed out, all that is in the contract is not contractual. That is to say, for contractual relations to work effectively, there has to be in place a set of moral attitudes and relationships that underpin contract. These, as much as self-interest and enterprise, are necessary conditions of the market order. If morality comes to be seen as a form of self-interest, then it is possible that these moral factors may come to be put into the pot of self-interested calculation; and this would be disastrous for the market itself. If the culture of society comes to be dominated by self-interested conceptions of morality, and business relationships turn into a wholly buccaneering, enterprising sort, then there is at least some danger – if there is no other countervailing set of moral values not based upon self-interest – that the moral assumptions on which the market exchange rests could, in fact, be eroded by a culture of self-interest.

This is an issue which goes back a long way in western history. Some sophists in ancient Greece argued that morality is a matter of self-interest, and that it would be foolish to attempt to act justly if one could get away with acting unjustly when it was in one's interests to do so. Many thinkers on both the left and the right of the political spectrum have argued that the capitalist system emerged from within western European Christianity, which protected moral values from the adverse effects of self-interest. However, with the growth of secularization, which is closely related to the growth of the capitalist economy, these Christian values of trust, truth-telling and promise-keeping have been eroded, turning our understanding of morality into one of self-interest. In these circumstances, the moral framework of values – on which capitalism has historically drawn to preserve the values that are essential to its own effective conduct – has become eroded by the very development of capitalism itself.

No doubt the maintenance of these values could be turned into a formal legal matter, so that there could be legal sanctions against a failure to keep to these moral assumptions. However, there are a couple of difficulties with this assumption that the moral prerequisites of markets could be turned into matters of the rule of law. The first is that the rule of law itself cannot operate very effectively where there is a collapse of the moral assumptions that the law is there to protect. The law does not exist in a moral vacuum. It has to be underpinned by widely accepted and diffused moral values. However, if these are turned into matters of self-interest, then the authority of law that seeks to preserve values that have a different basis might be undermined. This has become clear recently in the context of the regulation of financial markets. Some defenders of the market have been uneasy about some of these forms of regulation, because they see them as embodying the idea of victimless crime, in which someone can be guilty of an offence caused by the unrestrained pursuit of self-interest without there being an identifiable victim of this self-interested activity.

What seems to be lacking in such complaints is that the integrity of the market can itself be a victim of self-interest if it is not constrained by regulation of this sort. However, if the idea of these being victimless crimes were taken as a reason for easing such regulation, then the point I made earlier would become salient: that is, that the law in this area falls victim to the power of a self-interested view of the nature of morality, in which the maintenance of the integrity of the market itself, as opposed to protecting identifiable victims, is not seen as an important issue. The law can maintain this kind of function only if it is assumed that there is a general morality relating to the market, which has to be preserved. If, however, there is a sufficient change of attitude, so that all that counts is whether someone else's self-interest – the identifiable victim's – has been harmed, then it is difficult to obtain much social consent for having laws that protect some idea of the general moral integrity of the market.

In order to secure such consent, there has to be some wider appreciation of the moral integrity of the market. Of course, it might be argued that this could still make sense in terms of the long-term interest of those involved in market transactions or, alternatively, appealing to some kind of idea of 'universalizability': what would be the consequences for the market if everyone behaved like that? However, both of these strategies based upon self-interest still presuppose that there is some constraint on self-interest in market transactions, either of a long-term sort, or of a 'universalizable' sort. The potential problem is, though, that the prospects of short-term gains might well override such constraints unless there is some deeper-seated morality in society: what Hegel called *Sittlichkeit*, or 'ethical life' or 'civic virtue', which acts as a countervailing power to self-interest.

The second problem involved in turning these ethical matters into formal ones of legal sanction is that it is more costly and inefficient. If there are internalized values of a non-self-interested kind, which constrain behaviour in the market, then it is at least arguable that this is a less costly form of regulation than what would otherwise be a growing problem, requiring more and more regulation.

The second aspect of the moral underpinning of the market is in many ways parallel to the first, and was well-recognized by Adam Smith: that is, the maintenance of some sense of civic virtue and social obligation in relation to the market. On a purely self-interested view of the morality of the market, attitudes could arise in relation to economic behaviour that actually damage the market.

This could occur in two ways. First, on a self-interest view there would be every incentive for a trader to seek to secure a monopoly in the goods and services that he or she has to sell. Monopolies, again, are harmful to the free market, and also in some cases (such as newspapers and the media) harmful to society as a whole. But what argument could be put to a trader that he or she should not try to secure a monopoly if it is in his or her interests to do so? Again, the only appeal would be to some sense of the integrity of the market as a whole, or to a principle of universalizability, or to Adam Smith's own 'impartial spectator' theory: 'What if everyone behaved in that way?'

Again, however, this means that there has to be some constraint on self-interest, and this sense of constraint has to be there to support legal sanctions against monopoly. Without some sense of civic virtue, or orientation to values that are not of a self-regarding kind, market behaviour will require growing regulation in the interests of the market itself. Such regulation, in turn, may become increasingly problematic if there is not some more general concern to cultivate a sense of social and civic responsibility, which, as I have suggested, may become more and more difficult with the erosion of social values in favour of private and self-interested ones.

The second way in which this occurs is similar to the first: that is, from the point of view of self-interest, the individual trader may, in a wholly rational way, be a rent-seeker from government – seeking, that is, to secure privileges from government in terms of subsidies, tariffs or legal privileges. On a free market view these are, again, harmful to the market, and the government has to resist them. However, the same problem occurs again. The state has to act to resist this in terms of the integrity of the market, and in terms of a sense of fairness and justice in the society as a whole. In order to do so, it has to be able to appeal to a sense of civic virtue and consciousness, which goes beyond self-interest. Yet the growing role of market relations in society may erode society's capacity to take the steps necessary to protect the forms of virtue on which the market rests.

In this sense, therefore, I want to argue that the market certainly requires a sense of enterprise and self-interest, but it equally requires a sense of civic virtue without which the market itself cannot function effectively. The difficulty is that the growth of market relationships may gradually displace those forms of civic virtue and responsibility which, if they were internalized, could constrain individual behaviour in the interest of the market in an informal way; and may, in the longer term, erode the social basis of consent necessary for formal legal regulation when informal mechanisms have failed.

The sphere of the market

I now want to turn to a different set of moral boundaries, which might be encapsulated in the idea that the market does have a clear sphere, but that equally there are spheres in which market relationships are inappropriate; and that the market may damage its legitimacy in its own sphere if it transgresses those boundaries.

The idea behind this is drawn from Michael Walzer's *Spheres of Justice* (1983), in which he argues that goods and services in society have a social meaning and identity that are closely related to the culture of the society, and that must play a central part in deciding how these goods are to be distributed in that society: for example, whether they are to be distributed by markets, the state, or various kinds of voluntary associations.

I shall take two examples, which clearly imply some kind of dispute about the moral boundaries of the market. These boundaries are not fixed in some kind of theoretical or *a priori* way, but have to be seen to be closely woven into the culture of a particular society – in this case, the United Kingdom. The first example is whether the sale of human organs should be permitted: that is, whether there should be a market in bodily parts. On a strictly capitalist view of market principles, it is very difficult to see why there should not be such a market. The scope for a market is clearly quite wide. There could be a market in blood and blood-products; in kidneys; in sperm; in renting out a uterus for surrogate pregnancy; and so forth.

On a market view, at least three principles would favour a market in these areas. The first is that there is a clear demand for these organs among people who might be in quite desperate need of them. Secondly, the donor system that currently operates may lead to a shortfall in supply, as has certainly happened in the case of kidneys. Finally, if markets are usually construed as exchanges in property rights, then if a person owns anything, he or she owns the parts of his or her body. Indeed, most capitalist theories of property rights – from John Locke to Robert Nozick (1974) – follow from the idea of self-ownership.

The case for a market in organs and tissues has been put forcefully by advocates of the free market. The Institute of Economic Affairs has long argued for a free market in blood products, to run alongside the donor system; Woodrow Wyatt argued the case in *The Times* September 1989, when the issue of the sale of kidneys for the transplant operation in the London Humana hospital was in the news; and Simon Rottenberg (1982), the free market economist, published a chapter called 'The production and exchange of used body parts' in the Festschrift for Ludwig von Mises. All of these would see a clear role for markets, and for enterprise and entrepreneurship, in these fields. However, within our society, such advocacy has fallen on stony ground, and I think that most people would feel that some kind of moral boundary had been crossed by the market and the enterprise culture if they could be extended into such fields.

In his well-known book on the blood donor system in Britain, *The Gift Relationship* (1970), Richard Titmuss argued that if blood could be bought and sold, then anything could be. If human tissue is a marketable commodity, then there are really no social limits to 'commodification' and the scope for the enterprise culture. To its credit the government, despite its free market predilections, has set its face against a market in such contexts. This seems to be a clear case, to use Walzer's terminology, in which the market would be crossing into an inappropriate sphere. This is not, as I have said, based on *a priori* reasoning, but rather on the social understanding that we, as a society, have of such goods. It might, therefore, be crucial to the idea of legitimacy of the market itself that it does not try to cross such boundaries.

We might, of course, want to see whether this social understanding is based upon some clear principle, and this might be important in trying to determine a general limit to the kinds of goods that are subject to commodification. One possibility for a general principle might be an underlying attachment to the idea of respect for persons: that people should not treat themselves as commodities, or as means to the ends of others. This was certainly the basis of Kant's objection, when he discussed this issue in the eighteenth century in relation to the sale of teeth, hair and sexuality through the recruitment of castrati for Vatican choirs – although the point could be extended to prostitution as well. There are complex issues here which would also have a bearing on matters such as pornography and the general 'commodification' of the body; and also on the general issue of a market in health care, which makes money-plus-need the criterion of receiving care, rather than just need alone.

It may be that we do not have a consistent view of the moral boundary here. However, for present purposes, all that needs to be said is that the rejection of the sale of tissues and organs implies that there is a deep-seated moral boundary to at least some forms of bodily 'commodification' in Britain, and that this sets a clear boundary both to markets and to the enterprise culture. It may well be in the interests of the market that this boundary be maintained, for, as I have argued earlier, the market itself has to operate within a framework of moral principle if it is to be legitimate.

The second example of a similar sort is a complex one with many ramifications, which I cannot discuss in detail, but it is concerned with the way in which the extension of the market can displace the service ethic in society. In the view of many free-marketeers, the service ethic in the public sector in spheres such as health care, social work and education is something of a myth. The 'public choice' school of economists argues that those who work in welfare and educational bureaucracies in the public sector are, in fact, motivated in the same way as people in markets. The fact that someone earns his or her living as a doctor, nurse, social worker or teacher does not mean that they have stepped into some new moral realm in which they are motivated by the ethical demands of caring, service and vocation, unlike people in markets who seek to maximize their utilities. They do, in fact, seek to maximize their utilities by using their role in the public sector to increase their responsibilities, the scope of their bureaucracy, their status and their income; and they do this free from the threat of bankruptcy, and in ways that make it difficult for elected representatives to constrain their behaviour because of their professional knowledge and expertise.

Given this diagnosis, there is a case for either privatizing public services and subjecting them to market constraints, or invoking market principles within the public sector by mechanisms such as internal markets – or, if these solutions are not available, for tying providers down by performance indicators and greater specification through contracts and the like, to more definite and less discretionary forms of delivery. If people are motivated by utility maximization rather than the service ethic, then, the argument runs, they have to be constrained by market or quasi-market mechanisms. The caring professions should be demythologized into producer interest-groups, and their behaviour constrained in the same way as behaviour in the market is constrained by the customer.

This argument has many important aspects that cannot be discussed here. However, I do want to question one basic assumption, which seems to be involved in this analysis, which implies that the service ethic can be a feature only of voluntary organizations, in which people are not paid and therefore have no incentive to turn themselves into producer interest-groups as maintained by the 'public choice' model. This analysis assumption turns on accepting the argument that utility maximization is the basic form of human behaviour, or at least of behaviour for which one is paid. This assumption is, in itself, highly disputable; and I have suggested earlier that if it is accepted then some assumptions about civic virtue, which may be absolutely necessary to the market itself, are put into jeopardy.

It can also lead to some changes in behaviour among those in the public sector, which might, paradoxically, harm the service offered to the client, patient or customer, for if the service ethic is displaced by a contractual or a market one, there is a danger that people whose self-understanding is that they are offering a service, but are being constrained to behave as if they were in a market or a quasi-market. might then act only within the terms of the contract. This has, I think, already happened in schools. In my experience, there is a strong feeling among teachers that, if they are being put into this kind of position, then they will do what their contract specifies but nothing else. It would not then be open to government to appeal to an ethic of service to provide more than is specified in the contract, since the whole point has been to displace the ethic of service and replace it by contract or quasi-market relations.

Again, a market-oriented approach may lead to effects that are unintended. Can we in fact manage a society in which the ethic of service is displaced to the voluntary sector? Just as in the market, where appeal is made to virtues which may not be subsumable under those of private utility and private interests, so, too, in the state sector the introduction of markets, quasi-markets and the dominance of contract might well deprive us of ethical principles such as service and vocation, which are essential to the efficient delivery of services. We have to be very careful about the market again crossing an important moral barrier and replacing one ethic by another.

There is another deep issue here. In the public sector, which is part of government and should therefore be subject to the rule of law, we are concerned with things such as equity and treating like cases in like manner. These are not values served by markets, and there is no particular reason why they should be. However, they are central to government and to the rule of law. There is a clear danger that the introduction of market principles into the public sector might undermine these basic principles of public provision and, again, this provides some basic idea of moral restraint on what the role of the market might be in this context.

Moral consequences

The final sort of limit to markets that I want to discuss is in terms of outcomes. To what extent are the outcomes of economic exchange to be accepted as morally legitimate as they stand, whatever the degree of inequality to which they give rise? Here, the free market position has three main arguments at its disposal to support the claim that the outcomes of markets are not subject to a moral critique that could entail redistribution in the interests of social justice. The first is that market outcomes are the consequence of individual acts of free exchange. If each individual transaction is uncoerced, then the outcome is procedurally just, being the aggregate result of individual acts of free exchange. Given that its consequences are arrived at freely, there is no case for criticizing the market. Adherence to a just procedure, the market, cannot yield unjust results.

The second argument is that injustice can only be caused by intentional action. We do not attribute injustice to the results of unintended processes. However, a market is an unintended process in the appropriate sense. In a market, millions of people buy and sell whatever they have to exchange, and no doubt this individual buying and selling is undertaken intentionally. The 'distribution' of income and wealth arising from all these individual intentional acts is not itself intended by anyone. Since the distribution of income is not intended, it is by the same token not unjust, whatever its degree of inequality.

The third argument is that, even if there were a moral case for criticizing the market in the interests of distributive justice, we have no agreed criteria of distributive justice. We live in such a morally diverse and fragmented society that there is not the degree of social consensus to call upon to ground a set of principles of distribution. There are many possible distributive criteria: need, desert, entitlement, the contribution of labour, and so forth. All of these are, to some degree or another, principles of distribution; they are mutually incompatible and we have no resources in terms of social morality to underpin one set of principles compared with another.

Overall, taking these arguments together, market outcomes have to be accepted as being, in principle, unprincipled. In this situation, in which the privatization of morality has gone so far, all we can do is trust the outcome of the market. The market, in effect, embodies subjective wants and preferences, and one's value is not to be fixed by political means according to disputed principles of justice but rather by the subjective preferences and valuations of one's goods and services in the market.

This is a formidable and comprehensive critique of end state principles, such as social justice, which have usually been seen by social democrats, social liberals and democratic socialists as central to restraints on the capitalist market. The critique is so wide-ranging that I cannot deal with it fully here. However, I will make some skeletal points about each of the three arguments, which might then leave a foothold to develop a critique of market outcomes in these terms.

The argument that market outcomes are the result of individual acts of free exchange depends upon a number of rather large assumptions. The first is to do with property rights. Essentially, a market is about the exchange of property rights: the good that I own I sell in the market for the good that you own. If this exchange is to be legitimate, then property titles must be held to be legitimate. To impose a regime of market exchange on wider and wider areas of society on the basis of radical inequality of ownership takes it for granted that the property titles that have led through time to existing inequalities are, in fact, just.

It has often been noted that, although private property ownership lies at the basis of capitalist theories of market exchange, there has really been no widely accepted theory of private ownership, and certainly some of those that have been presented, such as Locke's, Nozick's and Hegel's, have very grave difficulties. Often, as in the work of Hayek (1960), the assumption is made that markets can be legitimately imposed on wide inequalities in property because: (a) we have no agreed criteria of distributive justice in terms of which property could be redistributed, and (b) property is probably in the hands of those where it can do the most productive good. The worst-off members of society will be helped by the trickle-down effect of the market more than they will be by redistribution, and if those who hold property hang onto it, then it is likely that this will create more economic dynamism to trickle down to the rest of society.

However, each of these arguments is highly contestable. The first argument assumes the truth of what I have been questioning. We cannot really argue that there cannot be a moral case for looking at property ownership, because any moral case will be so contested. This is the issue to which an answer is needed, not a reassertion of the argument. The second argument assumes the validity of the trickle-down effect. This is a matter shrouded in empirical controversy and depends a good deal on our understanding of poverty. However, there is a moral and conceptual argument raised by the assertion that the poor will be made better off by the market operating against a background of existing inequality, rather than any other alternative. Often this point is put in terms of a claim that the market empowers the poor more than political allocations of resources based upon an appeal to social justice. However, this is at the best dubious if we take the idea of power seriously.

Certainly, in the sense of 'power over', power is a positional good. That is to say, it is a good the value of which depends on some people not consuming it. The clear characteristic of a positional good is that, if it is equally distributed, its value disappears altogether. This seems to be the case with power in the sense I have defined it. If that is so, then power and empowerment cannot be subject to the trickle-down effect, just because positional goods cannot trickle down without disappearing. In order to empower the powerless, it is necessary to remove some of the power from the powerful. This cannot be done by creating more power to trickle down to the rest of society. The point at stake here is that inequality matters in terms of empowerment and it is far too bland an assumption to make that, if markets are imposed against radical social inequality, somehow the poor will be empowered. This cannot be the case if power is a positional good.

The second set of arguments dealt with the unintended nature of market outcomes and, therefore, the irrelevance of social justice. Let us accept for the sake of argument that market outcomes are unintended. We can then ask the question whether the unintended nature of an outcome makes any difference to whether that outcome can be the subject of a critique in terms of social justice. If outcomes are foreseeable for groups of people, then I believe social justice still has a place: at the level of personal morality it is possible to argue that we bear responsibility for the unintended but foreseeable nature of our actions. If market outcomes are foreseeable for groups of people, such as that those who enter the market with least are likely to leave it with least, then by parity of reasoning we could argue that we bear responsibility for the outcomes of processes that, although they may be unintended, are at least foreseeable. This responsibility is then in terms of social justice for the distributive consequences of foreseeable processes.

The free market theorist can hardly deny that market outcomes are foreseeable, because if it were not so there would be no basis to argue for the extension of markets. For example, the argument in favour of the deregulation of rent rests upon the assumption that it can be foreseen that this will increase the supply of private accommodation available for rent. The foreseeable consequences of markets lie at the heart of the case for markets and also lie at the heart of the possibility of a critique of their outcomes and of asserting our collective moral responsibility for them.

The final argument, that we do not have a public morality to underpin distributive justice, is a powerful one and takes us back really to the points I made in the section about the moral underpinning of markets. The assumption in that context was that the privatization of morality has gone so far, and the reduction of morality to self-interest has become so entrenched, that it is impossible for us to have a public or civic culture that would allow distributive justice to work in that context. I have already suggested that civic virtue is actually central to markets and their legitimacy, and I believe that moral pluralism can be overdone and in ways that would not only make social justice problematic, but also the moral assumptions on which markets rest.

All I can say here on this very big topic is that I believe that there are basic needs or, following Rawls (1973), primary goods that we have in common as members of a society such as ours, in the sense that these are goods that we need to achieve other sorts of goods. Among these are income, food, shelter, education, health care, and health education, together with the capacity to live a relatively free and autonomous life. These goods cannot be secured to individuals as of right, never mind with some degree of fairness or equality, by the market; and there is a role for an appeal to distributive justice in terms of these necessary conditions of human fulfilment. This is quite different from the assumption that all human goods should be distributed according to fixed criteria of social justice, a point that I made when discussing Walzer.

Overall, then, however important enterprise and the market are, there is still a good case for keeping them in their place. The 1970s saw nemesis succeed hubris in the context of the power of the state. If we are not sufficiently pluralistic in our thinking and if we mindlessly extend markets into inappropriate spheres, it may be that the 1990s might see market overload in the way we experienced government overload twenty years ago. The authority of government can be increased by limiting its scope; the legitimacy of markets may yet depend on keeping them in their proper place.

References: Chapter 6

Hayek, F. 1960. *The Constitution of Liberty*. London: Routledge & Kegan Paul.

Nozick, R. 1974. *Anarchy, State and Utopia*. Oxford: Blackwell.

Rawls, J. 1973. *A Theory of Justice*. Oxford: Oxford University Press.

Rottenberg, S. 1982. Production and exchange of used body parts, in I. M. Kirzner (ed.), *Method, Process and Austrian Economics. Essay 5 in Honour of Ludvig von Mises*. Lexington: D. C. Heath.

Titmuss, R. 1970. *The Gift Relationship: from Human Blood to Social Policy*. London: Allen & Unwin.

Walzer, M. 1983. *Spheres of Justice*. Oxford: Martin Robertson.

7 Adam Ferguson's critique of the 'enterprise' culture

TED BENTON

Adam Ferguson, one of the leading moral philosophers of the eighteenth-century Scottish Enlightenment, offers a sustained critique of the 'selfish system of philosophy', itself expressing the values and aspirations of the growing commercialism of his time. There are several most significant parallels between this earlier development and the recent changes in Britain. Ferguson's penetrating moral critique of what amounts to an earlier version of the 'enterprise culture' has considerable pertinence to the contemporary situation.

A certain view of human well-being and its institutional preconditions is currently in vogue. According to this view, the liberty and security of the individual are the principal – or exclusive – constituents of the good life. The purpose of government is to preserve this liberty and security, and whatever it attempts to do beyond this purpose is a despotic offence against the liberty of its subjects. Liberty consists in freedom of choice, and this, in turn, is taken to be equivalent to, or strongly dependent upon, the institutionalized market exchanges of private property owners. The defence of property ownership, and the promulgation of the market, is, it follows, the principal purpose of government.

One of the most appealing features of this view is that, unlike so many other utopian visions, it appears to harbour no unrealistic or elevated requirements of its constituent citizens. The effective participant in market exchanges needs to possess only a desire that requires satisfaction, and sufficient rationality to choose from among the goods on offer that which will satisfy the desire at least cost.

Given this view – that humans are motivated by self-interest, capable of cognizing their interests, and rationally calculating the most efficient means for their pursuit – all that is required is that their activities should be brought into interconnection by the institution of market exchanges. Provided that no external force intervenes to disrupt the spontaneous flow of self-interested action in the market, the consequence, intended or not, will be a harmonious coincidence of the satisfaction of the self-interest of each, and the aggregate interest of all. The happy consequence of a pessimistic realism about human nature is that, allowed to follow its course in an appropriate institutional context, it issues in a mutually supportive harmony of the security, satisfaction and liberty of each individual with the greatest good of all.

Easily the most frequently, if erroneously, invoked authority for this 'enlightened' synthesis of the self-interest view of human nature with advocacy of the market as the embodiment and presupposition of the liberty of the individual is Adam Smith ([1759] 1976). How paradoxical it must seem, then, that one of the most powerful and sustained critiques of these ideas should have been authored by Adam Ferguson, one of Smith's contemporaries and friends, and a fellow luminary of the Scottish Enlightenment.

Ferguson and Smith, with David Hume, William Robertson, John Millar and other lesser-known figures centred on Glasgow and Edinburgh, established a distinctive tradition of social philosophy during the eighteenth century. Central to this philosophy was a pervasive antagonism to what was called the 'selfish philosophy' or 'selfish system'. Perhaps the most provocative target of the Scottish philosophers' scorn was Bernard Mandeville, whose *Fable of the Bees* had won considerable notoriety through its espousal of the view that 'The Moral Virtues are the Political offspring which Flattery begot upon Pride', and that private vice was the source of public benefit ([1714] 1924: 51). Mandeville's view of human nature as essentially self-interested, and of morality as a matter of the appetites and aversions of the individual was derived from Thomas Hobbes, who was likewise the object of frequent critical references by Ferguson, Smith, Hume and their associates.

Although Hume was undoubtedly the greatest philosopher of the group, and Smith retains his celebrated status as one of the great founders of modern economics, it is Ferguson who provides the most telling sociological insights into the contradictory tendencies and dangers of the newly forming commercial society. Easily Ferguson's most important and original work was his *Essay on the History of Civil Society*, first published in 1766, and the main purpose of what follows is to offer an exposition and qualified defence of Ferguson's sceptical view of the relationship between market society and the liberty of the individual. Necessarily, this will also involve us in an exploration of his rival vision of human nature, happiness and virtue.

Civil society and civic virtue

Ferguson's *Essay* is ostensibly an account of the progress of human society from the 'rude' to the 'polished' state, a secularized theodicy of a genre already well established in the mid-eighteenth century. But if we understand by 'progress' not merely cumulative and directional change, but also a coincidence of that change with the realization of human well-being, 'perfection' or virtue, then we will miss Ferguson's central preoccupation. For him there is, indeed, cumulative and directional change in human history, but this brings in its wake the threat of corruption, misery and despotism, no less than the possibility of virtue, happiness and liberty. Indeed, it is hard to escape the conclusion that, for Ferguson, this trinity of values is more deeply threatened in the 'polished' commercial state than in earlier conditions of society.

With many of his contemporaries in the Scottish Enlightenment, Ferguson rejected the concept of 'state of nature' as a foundation for political philosophy. His objections to the idea, were, like Hume's, partly epistemological: *ex hypothesi*, the state of nature was not accessible to observation, and so could not be a proper object of positive knowledge. The only methodologically sound way of arriving at general principles in science is to ground them on 'just observation'. Applied to the human case, this method can yield but one conclusion: 'both the earliest and the latest accounts collected from every quarter of the earth, represent mankind as assembled in troops and companies' (Ferguson [1766] 1966: 3). Consequently:

> His mixed disposition to friendship or enmity, his reason, his use of language and articulate sounds, like the shape and the erect position of his body, are to be considered as so many attributes of his nature: they are to be retained in his description, as the wing and the paw are in that of the eagle and the lion. . . (Ferguson [1766] 1966: 3).

Humans are social by nature. It follows that the view of society as an 'artificial' creation, devised by individuals in order to realize purposes conceived independently of and prior to it, is incoherent. All that we do follows from our nature and the conditions in which that nature is exercised; there can be no opposition in human affairs between what is 'natural' and what is 'artificial'. It also follows that moral judgements may not be grounded on an appeal to the difference between the natural and the unnatural.

Ferguson follows Montesquieu in acknowledging the great diversity in human modes of social life and forms of government. The character of individuals, too, is shaped by habituation through 'forbearance or exercise' of their various faculties and dispositions. But this acknowledgement of diversity does not deter Ferguson from seeking the 'general characteristics' that constitute human nature. Indeed, following the Newtonian example, it is necessary first to establish these general characteristics if we are eventually to explain the diversity.

Some of our general characteristics we have in common with animals. Like them, we have 'instinctive propensities', or dispositions. These in the human case are of two kinds. One set is directed to the preservation of self and the race, while the other leads to society. Where we differ from animals is in the extent to which these initial dispositions are moulded or directed by our mental capacity for reflection and foresight, which are themselves exercised under varied external conditions of life. Among these conditions of life, Ferguson, unlike Montesquieu, assigns priority to the requirements and impositions of a definite mode of *social* life, and the values and purposes that prevail within it. Depending upon the condition of the social milieu and the relation of the individual to it, he may aspire to a happy and virtuous life, or fall into a state of extreme corruption. The transition from a 'rude' to a 'polished' state of society entails a clear danger of the second outcome. It is Ferguson's purpose in the *Essay* to warn of this danger, to examine its historical causes and to consider if and how it might be averted.

But, because social outcomes are products of a common human nature whose faculties and dispositions are exercised under diverse conditions of life, we are returned, once again, to the question of this common human nature. In addition to our self-preservative and social instincts, we possess capacities to recollect, and to reflect upon our actions, and a further disposition to evaluate, to judge good or bad, which we exercise primarily in relation to ourselves and other persons. Taken together, this ensemble of natural capacities and dispositions implies a further universal characteristic of humankind: one upon which Ferguson places great emphasis. This is their perpetual restlessness and dissatisfaction with their current state: their desire for improvement. Mankind is an 'active being' forever 'in train of employing his talents' (Ferguson [1766] 1966: 8).

This restlessness and desire of improvement, a universal character of *individual* humans, produces as its largely unintended and unforeseen consequence a distinguishing feature of the species: that is, its historical progress from a 'rude' to a 'polished' condition. Whereas the individuals of other species exhibit growth and development, in the human case these processes are continued at the level of the whole species. As we shall see, Ferguson recognizes that this phenomenon of historical development is more manifest in relation to the employment of some faculties than others, and herein lies one source of corruption and loss of liberty. But, in any event, whatever the moral character of the *outcome* of human restlessness, its status as a key fact of human nature is unmistakable.

But we do not understand the true nature of this human disposition restlessly to employ talents in projects of improvement if we think of it as a disposition that will be exhibited by individuals independently of their external conditions. This, with the other general characteristics of human nature, is fully expressed only in the appropriate milieu, and this milieu is society. To say that humans are by nature social is, for Ferguson, to say that society is the condition or context for which they are formed, and, therefore, the context in which alone their general and distinctive faculties are acquired and exercised. Individuals are most fully themselves, most fully human, the more they are bound together in society and the more they find within society the medium and the object of their activity. To imagine, or to observe (as in the case of 'wild-men'), human individuals independently of their involvement in social life as a source of illumination on human nature is a profound mistake.

We are not attached to society as a means of improving our material standard of life. Observation shows, on the contrary, that increase of luxury and 'external conveniences' is often accompanied by a loosening of the ties that bind individuals to society. Nor is it a matter of mere security: in times of national crisis and danger, we are frequently willing to sacrifice our lives in the service of society. Nor can the desire for mere honour and esteem explain the passions unleashed by the attachment to society. We are not, in fact, attached to society for any purpose extrinsic to it. We simply desire the society of others for its own sake, as an end in itself. But the passions that bind us to social life are not to be reduced to mere 'benevolence' or 'sympathy'. The intensity of our social loyalties also begets and feeds from equally intense hostility and enmity. The willingness to defend by force of arms one's society against its enemies is for Ferguson not only evidence of the power of our social bonds, but also one of the highest expressions of public virtue.

The corruption of commercial society

Implicit in this general view of human nature is a distinctive philosophical critique of the 'selfish system'. Hobbes, Mandeville and their ilk, in representing manifestly benevolent actions as in reality self-interested, are attempting to pass off as a discovery of science what is in fact a mere proposal to revise the use of language. In reducing a proper regard for the self to a matter of mere concern for 'interests', as distinct from the higher qualities and virtues of the person, the 'selfish philosophers' set up a mistaken opposition between the good of the individual and that of the public. Ferguson shared with Hume, Smith and the others, as we have seen, a view of human nature as intrinsically social, with benevolence and a desire for association with others among our innate dispositions. But where Ferguson differed, especially from Smith, was about Smith's attempt to ground morality in the very existence of such natural sentiments. Ferguson's critique of the 'selfish system' went further than that of his associates (at least in his own reading of them) in his insistence upon the irreducibility of moral virtue to any other kind of psychological attribute or disposition – whether pleasure, happiness, utility, or, as in Smith's case, sympathy.

But distinctive though it was, Ferguson's philosophical critique of the 'selfish system' is less notable than his historical and sociological analysis of the conditions in modern society which render it not *true* but *plausible*. The perspectives against which Ferguson's arguments are pitted are not *merely* the conceptual and empirical errors of speculative intellects. Their persistence and at least superficial plausibility also call for explanation. If human purposes are reduced to the satisfaction of bodily appetites and the preservation of property, if human happiness is confused with the pursuit of pleasure and avoidance of pain, and if morality is equated with utility, then what can have engendered such confusions but a society that comes close to making them true?

Ferguson's choice of empirical illustrations is an exemplary use of the comparative method to expose the insularity of his opponents' perceptions. Ferguson, in common with Smith and other Scottish moral philosophers of the period, not only drew upon the Stoic philosophy (especially for a conception of civic virtue), but also took a deep interest in classical history and civilization. Later in his career, Ferguson wrote a widely regarded history of the Roman Republic, and the *Essay* itself is replete with illustrations drawn from histories of classical Greece and Rome. He was clearly a keen reader of traveller's tales, and of the histories of non-European peoples. His own Highland background, too, no doubt endowed him with a certain sympathy for the positive qualities of social life in its 'rude' state, before the changes wrought by commercial society and constitutional government.

In the face of this weight of historical and anthropological evidence, the condition of commercial societies is represented as exceptional. In these societies, the instinctual disposition to sociability is least augmented by habituation, and social bonds are consequently at their most attenuated. In these societies, too, the instinct for self-preservation is most likely to take the form of an exclusive concern with possessions and mere bodily security – with 'interests' in Ferguson's disapprobatory use of the term. In the commercial nations, we have a form of society in which the paradigmatic personality-type, the predominant purpose of action, and the prevailing scale of values most closely approximate to those represented in the philosophies to which Ferguson takes greatest exception. There is a clear affinity or complicity between these philosophies and the commercial societies that spawn them. Ferguson's critique of these philosophies, as misrepresenting human nature, happiness and virtue, is then, at the same time, a critique of those forces at work in the society of his time that distorted or corrupted human nature, withdrawing from it the conditions of its fulfilment in a happy and virtuous life.

Ferguson tends to treat the commercial nations as a kind of experimental test situation, or 'worst-case' scenario for his theory of human nature. Exceptional though they are, these nations must continue to be viewed, in common with all other forms of society, as genuine expressions of human nature. Social bonds might be attenuated in such societies, but benevolent sentiments are still present – albeit less widely or keenly felt. Parental care is an example frequently cited by Ferguson, and we are reminded on the 'tolerable footing of amity' and restraint observed even in business transactions.

Wherever there exist societies that are 'polished' or civilized, and that also have attained a high development of the mechanical and commercial arts, then there are attendant dangers of corruption, national ruin, and despotism, or political slavery. But there is no necessity about the 'progress' from civilization to corruption, or, indeed, from corruption to despotism. Both civilization itself and the advance of material wealth and technique bear within them the seeds of corruption, but only under definite circumstances do these seeds germinate and grow. Moreover, different forms of government – democratic, aristocratic, monarchical and various admixtures – are consistent with the civilized state. A degree of ordered society, liberty and even virtue may be preserved even in the face of widespread corruption, depending on the form of government and the kind of requirement it makes upon its subjects for virtue and public spiritedness.

For Ferguson, the designation 'polished' or 'civilized' refers primarily to the achievement of an ordered, law-abiding society, in which internal conflicts are settled peacefully and in which there is security from external invasion. But these conditions of peace and security in the enjoyment of the fruits of labour also foster the development of the mechanical and commercial arts. The discovery is soon made that a division of labour that allows each individual to specialize in a single task makes possible a greater perfection in the goods produced as well as an increase in the efficiency and quantity in which they are produced: there is a steady accumulation of technical powers and of material wealth. In turn, the division of labour and specialization, in severing the immediacy of the connection between production and consumption, requires and stimulates the development of market relations and what Ferguson calls the 'commercial arts'. Finally, the development of the mechanical and commercial arts rests upon 'accidental' inequalities in property, faculties and dispositions, which it further progressively augments.

The societies with which Ferguson is concerned, then, share four intimately connected features. They may be characterized by any one of several possible forms of government, but all possess *some* form of constitutional government which, at the minimum, legally regulates transactions between individual subjects, provides security from external invasion, and includes a system of checks and balances by means of which the liberties of subjects are protected from possible excesses of the executive power itself. Secondly, there is a high level of development of technique and material production, manifested in a developed pattern of occupational specialization and differentiation. Thirdly, consumer goods are primarily produced for, and obtained by, market exchange. Fourthly, there are marked and entrenched inequalities in the ownership of property.

Ferguson thought that, notwithstanding the admitted benefits that flow from each of these features, their combination also renders a nation peculiarly liable to specific forms of corruption and to a consequent risk of decline, ruin and despotic rule. In particular,

Ferguson is concerned to demonstrate the actual incompatibility between such societies and a substantively democratic political order, as well as to identify a series of threats to the liberty of their citizens.

The two features most sharply incompatible with substantive democracy are the advanced division of labour and marked inequalities of property. Some specialized occupations elevate the mind and engage the heart, but many have the opposite effect on those whose life is spent in pursuit of them. Indeed, the increase in efficiency and perfection of production resulting from the division of labour is most marked precisely when the labourers are *least* required to think or to be creatively involved in their task:

> Many mechanical arts, indeed, require no capacity; they succeed best under a total suppression of sentiment and reason: and ignorance is the mother of industry as well as of superstition. Reflection and fancy are subject to err; but a habit of moving the hand, or the foot, is independent of either. Manufacturers, accordingly, prosper most, where the mind is least consulted, and where the workshop may, without any great effort of imagination, be considered as an engine, the parts of which are men (Ferguson [1766] 1966: 183).

This spine-chilling observation is the start of a long line of sociological concern with the social and human implications of modern manufacturing and industrial systems, and Ferguson has with some justification been accorded the status of one of the founding figures of modern sociology (see, for example, MacRae 1969, Meek 1954 and Swingewood 1970). Ferguson's own principal concern was with the degeneracy and narrowness of vision on the part of the labouring classes, which must follow from their place in the division of labour.

But if the division of labour alone has these baleful effects on those whose dispositions and faculties are moulded by it, then how much more serious the situation is when the effects of inequality of property are combined with them. Such classes as mechanics, labourers and beggars are constrained to devote their lives to procuring the means to a mere livelihood. They are necessarily occupied with menial tasks, and preoccupied with the degrading object of material security. Depending upon their diverse characters and situations, members of these classes are liable to become envious, avaricious, criminal, servile, and/or mercenary:

> we think that the extreme meanness of some classes must arise chiefly from the defect of knowledge. . . and we refer to such classes, as to an image of what our species must have been in its rude and uncultivated state. But we forget how many circumstances, especially in populous cities, tend to corrupt the lowest orders of men. . . An admiration of wealth unpossessed, becoming a principle of envy, or of servility; a habit of acting perpetually with a view to profit, and under a sense of subjection; the crimes to which they are allured, in order to feed their debauch, or to gratify their avarice, are examples, not of ignorance, but of corruption and baseness (Ferguson [1766] 1966: 186).

Now, for Ferguson, democracy is a form of government in which sovereignty rests with the collective body of the whole people, and in which all citizens are eligible for public office. For a democracy to thrive, its citizens must love equality, and must be willing to work for the public good without hope of personal profit. In short, the virtue of the citizens is a necessary condition for democratic government. This condition cannot be satisfied by modern commercial societies. Given the necessary preoccupation of the lower classes with mere survival, demeaning tasks, or with material interests, substantive democracy cannot be sustained in them. All that may remain are mere 'pretensions to equal rights'. Ferguson clearly regards the entrusting of major public office to the corrupted and degenerate lower classes of these societies as the height of folly – at most 'they may be entrusted with the choice of their masters and leaders' (Ferguson [1766] 1966: 187).

But the choice between democracy and the market society presented no great dilemma for Ferguson. Although democracy had a certain romantic attraction for him (he regarded the move away from democracy as inevitably involving a degree of corruption), he tended to regard it as an extreme and unsustainable form, as a 'paroxysm' of the political order. In enjoying the benefits of both material advancement and the security that comes from regular government, we must reluctantly accept political forms that fall short of substantive democracy. In practice, Ferguson always kept aloof from the Reform movement, consistently putting his loyalty to the established constitution and the system of class subordination it sustained before any appeal that an extension of the franchise might have had for him. In this respect, Ferguson's views were superseded by later socialist writers, who were able to make an analytical distinction between the increasingly capitalist commercial ordering of economic life, with its associated de-skilling and impoverishment of the working classes, on the one hand, and the increase in material wellbeing that could come from the cooperative organization of production and the rational application of knowledge in technique, on the other.

But even on his own premises, Ferguson's bleak conclusion does not follow. Economic insecurity and poverty could, and did, just as easily lead to an elevating and invigorating combination among the dispossessed as to their corruption through envy and servility. In the early trade union and socialist movements could be found a social milieu in which the exercise of the highest human capacities and dispositions, such as benevolence, honour, loyalty and courage was both required and made possible (see, for example, Thompson 1968, and Taylor 1983). That these virtues could be acquired and enhanced in a spirit of antagonism and competitive struggle is only to be expected in Ferguson's own view of human nature. If this modest revision of Ferguson's analysis is correct, it suggests that a healthy and vital labour movement is a necessary condition for substantive democracy in the advanced commercial states.

For Ferguson himself, however, a degree of liberty, order and virtue can be sustained in the face of the corrupting effects of the division of labour and economic inequality only if other forms of government (aristocratic, monarchical, or 'mixed') are allowed to prevail. Here, what is necessary is that the worst corruption of human nature should be confined to those classes least relied upon for public office. Even this, unfortunately, cannot be guaranteed and, in so far as the division of labour and specialization of function become an all-pervasive principle of social organization, it poses a threat not just to democracy, but to liberty itself.

Implicit in Ferguson's comments are three features of occupational specialization that are potentially undermining of civil liberties. First, occupational categories are identity-forming in ways that compete with identification with and loyalty to nation. Each occupational group has its own 'carriage', 'point of honour', system of manners and ceremonial, through which the character of the individual is formed. The resulting diversity of individuals and ranks 'suppresses' the bonds of similitude that make up the 'national character'. Secondly, as we have seen, lifelong preoccupation with a single activity must narrow the vision. Not participating in the wide diversity of social practices, the individual plays a necessary part in the whole without any comprehension of what that part is, or how it relates to the others: 'society is made to consist of parts, of which none is animated with the spirit of society itself' (Ferguson [1766] 1966: 218). This loss of overall vision renders the individual unfit to play a full role in public life. Thirdly, occupation specialization, concentrating the activity and attention of individuals on the sphere of private interest, withdraws them from the public domain:

> the separation of professions. . .seems, in some measure, to break the bands of society, to substitute form in place of ingenuity, and to withdraw individuals from the common scene of occupation, on which the sentiments of the heart, and the mind, are most happily employed (Ferguson [1766] 1966: 218).

These three pervasive consequences of the division of labour and occupational specialization – individualism, narrowness of vision, and 'privatism' – were, of course, important topics of interest in subsequent sociological analyses of industrial capitalism, most famously, perhaps, in the great French sociologist Emile Durkheim's *Division of Labour in Society* ([1912] 1964). The Hegelian–Marxist concept of 'alienation', too, includes as a significant element the effects of the division of labour in detaching and isolating individuals from one another and from the life of society. Ferguson's own concern is with the loss on the part of individual citizens of the motivation and capacities to play a full, active and disinterested part in public life. The consequence of this is a reduction in the public sphere itself, and a usurpation of power on the part of the executive. Incapable and unwilling to make sacrifices in defence of their liberties, a self-interested and preoccupied citizenry is liable to lose them.

When the exercise of public office itself becomes subject to occupational specialization, then the threat to liberty is yet more dire. The functions of warrior and statesman, the paramount public offices, are the ones most decisive for national wellbeing, as well as for preserving the conditions for the highest development of individual happiness and virtue. Accordingly, for these activities to fall prey to self-interested functionaries and men of narrow vision spells disaster for both national stability and the liberty of the individual. Ferguson lays greatest emphasis here on the threat to liberty posed by occupational specialization in the military sphere. By employing a professional army, the citizenry is apt to take its security for granted, and to lose the capacity for self-defence. The way is then open for the military machine they have created to be turned against their own liberties.

Values

Despite the seriousness of all these dangers to national wellbeing, virtue and liberty, Ferguson is clearly most exercised by a further threat to which the commercial nations are exposed. This threat is, perhaps, a culmination or synthesis of each of the others. Secure, regular government, the advancement of the mechanical and commercial arts, and unequal property, are, severally, conditions that pose specific threats of individual corruption and national decline. But none produces such effects of necessity, or in abstraction from the influence of the others. These conditions affecting economic and political life, to produce their most ruinous effects, must further give rise to a wholesale and pervasive shift in values:

> A change of national manners for the worse, may arise from. . .a change in the prevailing opinions relating to the constituents of honours or of happiness. When mere riches or court-favour, are supposed to constitute rank; the mind is misled from the consideration of qualities on which it ought to rely (Ferguson [1766] 1966: 238).

Under the influence of these 'prevailing opinions' social honour is assigned on the basis of wealth, or flattery of the powerful, independently of the intrinsic merit or virtue of its recipients. Happiness is confused with mere pleasure, and private interest is treated as the principal purpose of life. Public life, no longer the domain in which the highest purposes of the citizens are concentrated, becomes a mere means for the more successful pursuit of private interest.

It is the pervasiveness of this cultural complex, rather than the mere existence of political security, material luxury, the market and economic inequality, that is the 'Achilles' heel' of the modern commercial nations. The political and economic features of these societies *predispose* them towards the value-system and the personality-type, which we may without too much difficulty recognize in the 'enterprise culture' of our own time and place.

Under certain conditions (such as prolonged peace and security from external danger, disproportionate development of the 'mechanical arts' and accumulation of wealth, the use of consumer-goods as marks of rank or distinction, and narrow concern on the part of governments with mere security and property) a definite personality-type comes to pervade all classes in a commercial society with a prevailing set of values and opinions, of preoccupations and 'objects of care.'

What is it precisely about these values and preoccupations that makes them 'corrupting', and how do they lead to a loss of liberty and to national ruin? First, the valuation of property above personal qualities such as merit and virtue, and the adoption of wealth as the foundation of the system of class 'subordination' involve a devaluation of the person, and a corresponding transfer of human value to mere material or 'animal' objects and beings:

> He finds in a provision of wealth, which he is probably never to employ, an object of his greatest solicitude, and the principal idol of his mind. He apprehends a relation between his person and his property, which renders what he calls his own in a manner a part of himself, a constituent of his rank, his condition, and his character, in which, independent of any real enjoyment, he may be fortunate or unhappy; and, independent of any personal merit, be may be an object of consideration or neglect; and in which he may be wounded and injured, while his person is safe, and every want of his nature completely supplied (Ferguson [1766] 1966: 12).

The 'enterprise culture', then, involves a kind of self-alienation in which regard for 'self' is displaced by regard for property and/or mere material wellbeing, by a preoccupation with 'interest', while concerns properly addressed to the self take as their object mere material possessions. A house, ornaments, clothes, furniture, and so on, are substituted for merit and virtue as objects of esteem and social honour. But this alienation from self and its associated fetishism of commodities also implies an alienation between individuals and the social world, and consequently among individuals themselves. Where self-interest reigns supreme, the community, ceasing to be the object that directly engages the most powerful sentiments, becomes a mere instrument for individual advantage:

> The individual considers the community so far only as it can be rendered subservient to his personal advancement or profit: he states himself in competition with his fellow creatures; and, urged by the passions of emulation, of fear and jealousy, of envy and malice, he follows the maxims of an animal destined to preserve his separate existence, and to indulge his caprice or his appetite, at the expense of his species (Ferguson [1766] 1966: 238-9).

In establishing a merely utilitarian relation between the individual and the community, the preoccupation with 'interest' that characterizes the enterprise culture also reduces the relations between individuals themselves to matters of instrumental calculation, on a level with their relations to their non-human property:

> he has found an object which sets him in competition with his fellow creatures, and he deals with them as he does with his cattle and his soil, for the sake of the profits they bring (Ferguson [1766] 1966: 19).

Under the combined influence of these material and political conditions, and the shifts in the dominant value-system and practical orientations that they facilitate, human nature itself is corrupted and debased. Two basic character-types become pervasive: those who without moral restraint seek power and wealth on their own account, and those who equally without moral restraint make themselves the willing tools of the wealthy and powerful in order to acquire some share of their masters' acquisitions:

> On this corrupt foundation, men become either rapacious, deceitful, and violent, ready to trespass on the rights of others; or servile, mercenary and base, prepared to relinquish their own. Talents, capacity and force of mind, possessed by a person of the first description, serve to plunge him the deeper in misery, and to sharpen the agony of cruel passions; which lead him to wreak on his fellow creatures the torments that prey on himself. To a person of the second, imagination, and reason itself, only serve to point out false objects of fear, or desire, and to multiply the subjects of disappointment, and of momentary joy (Ferguson [1766] 1966: 239).

Crucially, these corrupting influences affect all classes and conditions of persons, including those classes upon which devolve the duties of public life.

Ferguson at one point even warns of the possibility of the Hobbesian war of each against each in the absence of the restraint of law. But such a war is not, for Ferguson, the consequence of unaided and unconstrained human nature. Rather it is a measure of the corruption and degeneracy of human nature under the combined influence of luxury, economic inequality, the division of labour and the consequential changes in values and practices:

> Under this influence, they would enter, if not restrained by the laws of civil society, on a scene of violence or meanness, which would exhibit our species, by turns, under an aspect more terrible and odious, or more vile and contemptible, than that of any animal which inherits the earth (Ferguson [1766] 1966: 12).

However, once this degree and spread of corruption are approached, even the restraint of law undergoes a transformation in its bearing on the liberties of subjects. The law serves only as a defence of liberty when it continues to be applied in that spirit, and with constant vigilance against abuse and usurpation. When these conditions are absent, 'they serve only to cover, not to restrain, the iniquities of power'. The influence of laws in preserving liberty, Ferguson contends, 'is not any magic power descending from shelves that are loaded with books, but is, in reality, the influence of men resolved to be free' (Ferguson [1766] 1966: 263–4).

So, with pervasive corruption and debasement of human nature, those who hold executive power seek to extend it by overcoming all obstacles to their designs, while those subject to executive power actively connive in the destruction of their own freedoms. Not merely unfit either to exercise or to defend their liberty, they actively seek its annulment. Once the citizenry has connived in the usurpation of the executive power, a process is set in motion in which all remaining centres of resistance are identified and eliminated:

> When he has fixed a resolution, whoever reasons or demonstrates against it is an enemy; when his mind is elated, whoever pretends to eminence, and is disposed to act for himself, is a rival. He would leave no dignity in the state, but what is dependent upon himself; no active power, but what carries the expression of his momentary pleasure. . . The tendency of his administration is to quiet every restless spirit, and to assume every function of government to himself (Ferguson [1766] 1966: 274).

The progression is complete: a privatized, self-interested and materialistic citizenry collaborates with a rapacious executive power, saturated by the same corruptive values and purposes, to yield despotic rule, political slavery, and national ruin.

Conclusion

Ferguson's critique of the 'selfish system' and his analysis of it as a philosophical expression of that form of corruption of human nature to which modern capitalist societies are peculiarly liable is a powerful, and, to my mind, largely convincing one. Nevertheless, in important respects it is limited or defective. I have already noted Ferguson's (understandable, in context) failure to distinguish analytically between progress in human technical powers, on the one hand, and the institutional forms and inequalities of a market society, on the other. Lacking this distinction, Ferguson was unable to separate the benefits that might come from a more equally shared material wellbeing from the corrupting combination of wealth and material insecurity in a class–divided market society. It was this analytical failing that also sustained Ferguson's apparent contempt for material wellbeing itself, as though this were properly the concern only of 'mere animals'. As Marx was to argue almost a century later (and, indeed, as the Stoics had argued centuries before) desires for food, shelter, clothing and so on are not *in themselves* demeaning or corrupt, but they become so only in a form of life which abstracts them from their rightful place in a wider context of human and communal purposes, and turns them, in this abstract form, into the sole or primary end of life itself. Finally, there is an unmistakable masculine – even militarist – cast to Ferguson's concept of the virtuous life. He explicitly distances himself from values sometimes associated with civilization, such as gentleness, generosity, and leniency towards one's enemies. He contrasts such values with the bold and warlike virtues of the classical civilizations, and attributes the change to the spread of 'antiquated' notions of chivalry in relation to women into our public life, and even into the conduct of war. He frequently uses the word 'effeminate' to characterize a life-style corrupted by luxury and withdrawal from the exertion of public life.

Notwithstanding these reservations, Ferguson's work contains the broad outlines of a quite startlingly prophetic sociological analysis of commercial civilization and the corruptions to which it is susceptible. Ferguson tends to think of advancement in the 'material arts', specialization and the division of labour, and the growth of commercial society as indissolubly intertwined processes. Although they lead to greater comfort, security and luxury, they nevertheless lead to a new system of domination and subordination, a lopsided development of the individual, a corrupting preoccupation among the lower classes with mere subsistence, and, above all, a dissolution of social bonds.

In so far as commercial society assigns status on the basis of material success, and allows its citizens to take their peace, security and luxury for granted (through, for example, allocating the function of national defence to a specialist standing army) then to this extent self-interested motivations are favoured, and the vigour of civic virtue declines. The highest and most worthy exertions of humanity can flourish only where the intensity of social bonds and civic virtue also flourish. The contrary tendency toward self-interested individual competition can lead only to a debasement of the aims and contents of individual action, and prepare the way for tyranny and despotism.

References: Chapter 7

Durkheim, E. [1912] 1964. *The Division of Labour in Society*. New York: Free Press.

Ferguson, A. [1766] 1966. *An Essay on the History of Civil Society*. Edinburgh: The University Press.

McRae, D. 1969. Adam Ferguson 1723–1816. In T. Raisin (ed.), *The Founding Fathers of Social Science*. Harmondsworth: Penguin.

Mandeville, B. [1714] 1924. *Fable of the Bees*, Vol. 1. Oxford: Clarendon Press.

Meek, R. 1954. The Scottish contribution to Marxist sociology. In J. Saville (ed.), *Democracy and the Labour Movement*, pp. 84–102. London: Lawrence & Wishart.

Smith, A. [1759] 1976. *The Theory of Moral Sentiments* (D. Raphael and A. MacFie (eds)). Oxford: Clarendon Press.

Swingewood, A. 1970. Origins of sociology: the case of the Scottish Enlightenment. *British Journal of Sociology*, 21, 2: 164–80.

Taylor, B. 1983. *Eve and the New Jerusalem*. London: Virago.

Thompson, E. P. 1968. *The Making of the English Working Class*. Harmondsworth: Penguin.

8 *The human impact of the market*

SEAN SAYERS

For the past decade, the British government has been ruthlessly pursuing free market policies. It has introduced market forces into many walks of life previously protected from them; and it has vigorously promoted the values of the 'enterprise culture'. The economic and social consequences of these policies have been dramatic and profound. On the one hand, there has been a radical economic 'restructuring': a ruthless sweeping away of much that was old and inefficient, and a considerable streamlining and modernizing of the economy. In the process, however, the lives of countless individuals have been disrupted. Communities, and even whole regions, have been devastated. Millions have been thrown out of work, or forced into new and often uncongenial occupations.

Reactions to these developments have tended to polarize into two opposite extremes. Much of the argument has been about economic issues. For the view that the free market approach has been effective in its intended aim of combating economic stagnation and stimulating new growth is widely questioned. However, there is also a moral dimension to the controversy, and this is what I shall be focusing on in this paper.

Thus the competitive market is recommended by its defenders, not only as the answer to economic problems, but also in moral terms: as an arena of freedom, where initiative and enterprise are given scope to flourish. These views have until recently been enjoying an unprecedented influence. Indeed, when Mrs Thatcher was being welcomed as an economic guru even in Moscow, some were proclaiming the universal triumph of free market capitalism and the final demise of socialism – the 'end of history' no less (Fukuyama 1989).

Many, however, remain profoundly sceptical. They see the market as an evil and alienating phenomenon. They emphasize the ways in which it has a harmful and destructive impact on individuals and communities. In short, they see nothing to celebrate in the free market, and they look upon the economic direction being taken in Eastern Europe and the Soviet Union with dismay and foreboding.

Neither of these responses is new; both echo earlier ideas that can be traced back to the beginnings of the capitalist era. And neither is satisfactory. A quite different approach is needed if we are to form a realistic picture of the impact of the market. This is what I shall argue.

The free market philosophy and its critics

To its defenders, the market is the very system of liberty in economic life; and one that leads to freedom in the wider social and political sphere as well. The market, according to this view, is made up of a mass of separate and independent individuals, all pursuing their own interests in their own ways, voluntarily competing and contracting with each other. In such conditions of free competition, it is argued, enterprise and initiative will develop and flourish quite spontaneously. For underlying this outlook is the theory of *homo economicus*, the philosophy of rational self interest: the view that human beings are by nature free and independent individuals, each acting in such a way as to maximize his or her own self-interest.

According to this view, enterprise – in the sense of the com-petitive pursuit of economic goals in the market – is a natural human inclination. An explicit 'enterprise culture' – a culture that values and encourages enterprise as such – is not needed to create enterprising individuals, but only to counteract the harmful and stultifying influences of a previous 'dependency'. Such individ-uals will emerge spontaneously in the liberating conditions of the competitive market. In these conditions, moreover, through the 'hidden hand' of the market, the interests of both buyers and sellers, consumers and producers, workers and employers, will all be met in the best possible way, leading to an efficient, dynamic and productive economy – the 'greatest happiness of the greatest number'.

This is the faith of the laissez-faire, free market philosophy. It has been put forward by apostles of free market capitalism, from the early political economists (Smith [1776] 1974) to the present day believers in the panacea of 'market forces' (Friedman and Friedman, 1962). It is a crude and simple philosophy, which can easily degenerate into dogma; and one that is so evidently inadequate and unrealistic as an account of human nature and social economic life that it is tempting to regard it as a mere rationalization of free market capitalism, as a piece of ideology pure and simple with no claim to serious philosophical attention.

No doubt it often takes that form. Nevertheless, there is an element of truth in it which should be recognized. Historically, the initial growth of the capitalist 'free market' necessitated the removal of the many impediments and restraints on its operation that characterized earlier feudal conditions: the bonds of serfdom, guild restrictions and monopolies, local tariffs and other barriers to trade and commerce, and so on. Likewise, in recent years, to create free market conditions, the government has systematically been removing trade union rights and immunities, minimum wage agreements, and much of the protective legislation governing health, safety and other conditions of work.

Seen in this light, the introduction of market conditions does indeed seem to involve the removal of restraints and restrictions, a liberation from them, and the creation of an economic situation of laissez-faire. At times, moreover, this has undoubtedly occurred under the pressure of already existing economic forces seeking greater scope in which to operate – forces that spontaneously develop when restraints are removed. A recent example is the introduction of new technology in printing and the subsequent expansion of the newspaper industry. The existence of an extensive black market in the Soviet Union suggests the presence there, too, of economic forces waiting to expand when they are permitted to do so.

However, the laissez-faire philosophy gives only one side of the picture; and there is another which must also be seen. For, on the whole, people do not voluntarily enter into competition in the market. The self-sufficient peasants and householders of pre-capitalist society did not generally put themselves onto the market and become employed wage labourers of their own free will. Through enclosure and clearance, they were deprived of their traditional means of livelihood. They were forced off the land and, by the threat of destitution, driven into overcrowded and unhealthy industrial towns, where they were subjected to relentless hours of soul-destroying factory work for near-starvation wages.

Similarly, in recent years, the introduction of market forces has not generally been welcome by those most directly affected by them. Steel workers, printers, miners – even doctors, lawyers and teachers – have all fiercely resisted the government's attempts to impose market competition in their areas of work. None of these groups has willingly embraced the enterprise culture, and 'got on their bikes' to go out in search of the opportunities supposedly offered by the competitive market; all have had to be forced to do so. So although there is some truth in the idea that the market is a system of freedom, of laissez faire, it is also and at the same time the case that the market has a coercive aspect, and the idea of the spontaneous growth of enterprise is at best only a part of the picture.

There is some truth in *both* sides here, I want to suggest. However, while the laissez-faire philosophy sees only the positive side, it is the negative side that is stressed by most critics. The market undermines and sweeps away established patterns of work and life. It destroys the self-sufficient pre-capitalist household and converts its members into wage labourers. It dissolves pre-capitalist communities into a welter of opposed individuals and competing self-interests. In place of the personal ties and communal bonds that characterize pre-capitalist societies, it puts purely commercial relations, an alienating 'cash nexus'. In places of the natural fors and rhythms of rural life, it subjects people to a fragmenting division of labour and degrading conditions of work. Moreover, these destructive effects are not a once-and-for-all phenomenon. As the experience of recent years has shown, the market continues to have a disruptive impact: dissolving even communities that it itself has created, like those in the older industrial regions.[1]

In absolute antithesis to the laissez-faire approach, these critics thus tend to portray the market in purely negative terms, as a coercive system that destroys individual and communal autonomy and self-sufficiency, and forces people into a regime of universal and all-round dependency. As a result of the market, according to Robertson (1985: 38), for example, 'individual people in their own households have lost the freedom, and the capacity, and the habit, to meet their own needs directly by their own work, and have become more and more dependent on paid employment outside their own control to provide them with money to buy goods and services'.

Moreover, such critics of the market also reject the values of the 'enterprise culture''' and the account of human nature, the theory of *homo economicus*, upon which they are based. People are not naturally competitive and self-interested. If, as a matter of fact, people become like that in modern society, it is because the social pressures of the competitive market system make them so. Capitalist 'enterprise' and the entrepreneurial spirit are the products of society, not nature. Naturally, people are cooperative, not competitive; their needs are few, simple and easily satisfied.

These ideas provide the basis for a radical critique of the free market philosophy. Its narrowly economic perspective is rejected in favour of an outlook that values personal relations, cooperation and community. The stress is on the human and moral dimension rather than the economic aspects of life; on the quality of life, rather than on the quantity of goods available; on personal, coopera-tive, communal, even spiritual, values, rather than material ones. From this perspective, the market and commerce are portrayed as destructive and negative phenomena. Even if they have led to a development of production, this has been to the detriment of individuals. Such critics thus tend to be, at the very least, sceptical of the values of economic development and material progress that are involved in the free market outlook. Often, indeed, they reject these values altogether, and instead look back to times when, as Gorz (1985: 48–9) puts it, 'social and personal relations were not dominated by market relations. They were governed by non-economic, non-monetary exchange . . . by solidarity and mutual aid.'

These ideas will surely be familiar. For commentators have been expressing misgivings such as these about the moral impact of capitalist commerce and industry since the time of Rousseau at least; and subsequent writers in this line include such important nineteenth-century social critics as Carlyle (1895), Ruskin ([1860] 1985) and Morris (1973)[2] These ideas are particularly influential at present. They have dominated a great deal of the recent criticism of free market policies and the 'enterprise culture' which has not been purely economic in character.

Towards an alternative perspective

These views are the diametric opposite of the free market philosophy: indeed, they constitute the romantic reaction against it. There is some truth in both of these philosophies, I have been suggesting; but ultimately, I now want to argue, both are one-sided and unsatisfactory.

Thus the free market philosophy sees the non-commercial relations of pre-capitalist societies as mere fetters and restraints on natural and spontaneous capitalist enterprise. This is an untenable and absurdly one-sided view. For such relations constitute the economic system of pre-capitalist societies; and, in their time, they provided a framework in which their economic and social life could grow and develop.[3] On the other side, however, it is just as absurd to imagine that non-market societies are purely voluntary and natural, as Gorz appears to do when he characterizes them in terms of 'solidarity and mutual aid'. This presents a grossly idealized and romanticized picture, which ignores the limitations and narrowness, the stifling closeness, of small rural communities and the self-sufficient family household, not to mention the squalor, brutality and other primitive features of pre-capitalist societies.[4]

In short, neither the laissez-faire philosophy nor its romantic opposite gives a satisfactory account of such societies. They are neither purely oppressive nor purely cooperative and voluntary; neither purely hostile to human nature, nor completely in accord with it. They cannot be understood in such absolute and either/or terms. They have an altogether more complex and contradictory human impact. They both provide the essential framework within which human beings grow and develop, produce and reproduce; and, at the same time, as specific and determinate structures, they limit those activities and confine them within certain bounds.

The same is true of market societies. These cannot be understood on the laissez–faire view that the market is a system of pure freedom, of voluntary individual contracts. For there can be no doubt about the coercive impact of the forces that the market unleashes. On the other hand, it is equally untenable to regard the market as a *purely* negative and destructive phenomenon, which merely divides and fragments communities into a mass of isolated and opposed individuals.

What is missing from both pictures is any appreciation of the fact that the market not only dissolves social relations, it also creates them. At the same time as it destroys existing social forms, it produces new ones: it establishes new relations, new connections, new bonds between people. The pre-capitalist peasant household is virtually a self-sufficient unit. Through its own work, it produces almost everything that it requires. Its relations with the outside world, its horizons, barely stretch beyond the boundaries of its own patch of land and immediate locality. The market breaks down this isolation and self-sufficiency. With its advent, the household no longer works only to satisfy its own immediate needs. It produces commodities for exchange. The products of its work are now destined for the market; they are destined to meet the needs of other consumers. Likewise, the needs of the household are no longer all provided for directly by its own labour – the household becomes more and more dependent on goods produced by others and obtained through the market.

The market thus destroys the isolation and self-sufficiency of the pre-capitalist household. But the result is not a mere collection of separate individuals. Rather, it is a new and wider network of relations.[5] For through the mechanism of the market, the work and needs of many people are brought together. Producers and consumers are brought within a common system, linked together and made interdependent. Increasingly, the members of the household find that their interests are bound up with those of other producers and consumers, often in far distant places. One of the first writers to understand this clearly was Hegel. The market constitutes what he calls a 'system of needs', through which 'the *labour* of the individual for his own needs is just as much a satisfaction of the needs of others as of his own, and the satisfaction of his own needs he obtains only through the labour of others' (Hegel [1807] 1977: 213).

Certainly, such market relations are, initially at least, purely economic ones. They may not even appear to be relations between *people* – social relations – at all. For they take the apparent form of relations between commodities, relations between *things* (Marx [1867] 1961: Ch. 1, sec. 4). This alien appearance notwithstanding, however, they *are* social relationships, and their impact gradually impinges on every aspect of the household: extending its horizons, changing its pattern of life, and drawing its members out beyond its confines into the wider world.

Furthermore, the development of the market goes together with a radical extension of the division of labour beyond the household. The household no longer produces everything that it needs, but depends upon the work of others for many of its requirements. Just as with the market, so too the division of labour is often portrayed as a purely negative phenomenon, the only result of which is to fragment and divide people. This is an equally one-sided view. For the tasks that a household or person needs to perform can be divided among different households or individuals only when they *cooperate* in such a way that each can depend on others to supply some of their needs. In short, the division of labour is only another expression for the *social organization* of labour, and its development means the expansion of social forms and social relations.

In short, there are positive as well as negative aspects to the human impact of the market. Despite all the destruction and misery that have accompanied – and still accompany – its imposition, there is also a constructive and progressive aspect to it. To be sure, the market destroys the basis for rural self-sufficiency, it shatters traditional communities and households, it severs established bonds and relations. In so doing, however, it breaks the ties that bind people to the land and the feudal lord. It drives them off the land; but in the process they are forced out of the isolation and seclusion, the fixed patterns and rhythms of rural life. Nor does the process stop here. As a result of the growth of the market, people are brought into a far wider network of relationships. They are taken out of the village and household, they are concentrated in towns and cities, factories and offices. Through the operation of the market their work is related to that of everyone else in a universal division of labour; it is given a value – an economic value – that is objective and universal. People are thus put into contact and communication; they are brought into the social world and into public life. Their horizons are extended, their consciousness widened, their energies increased.[6]

This is not to deny the misery and suffering that the market has caused and continues to cause. On the contrary, the point, rather, is that the market's human impact is *contradictory*; there is *both* a positive *and* a negative side to it. No doubt it is the negative aspects that are most immediately evident; the positive effects become apparent only later and in the longer term. In the longer term, however, they are unmistakable. Working people have not simply been degraded and alienated, oppressed and dehumanized by the inexorable advance of commercial capitalism during the last two hundred years or so, as the critics suggest should be the case. Rather, they have steadily developed and progressed, both physically and morally. They have achieved far higher levels not only of material welfare, but also of education, culture, and general awareness of the world; they have won for themselves a far greater sphere of social activity and participation in public and political life.[7]

The idea of progress

These claims will, I know, provoke a sceptical response in many readers. For it seems strange and paradoxical to describe a phenomenon as destructive in its impact as the market as being at the same time humanly positive and progressive. This is particularly puzzling if, as is often the case, progress is equated with increasing human happiness. The sense of progress intended here cannot be understood in these terms. However, it is this idea of progress which lies behind both of the positions that I have been criticizing.

Thus, the free market philosophy tends to identify progress with economic development pure and simple. This view is characteristic of the utilitarian assumptions and the account of human nature, the theory of *homo economicus*, which underlie the laissez-faire approach. Happiness is equated with material wellbeing; and the market is portrayed as a liberating environment that leads to economic growth and increasing prosperity.

Although critics of the market seldom dispute that its introduction has led to economic development, they reject these ideas in almost every other respect. In particular, they reject the equation of economic development with human progress. The market, they argue, is not just a means to economic development; neither does it 'liberate' natural enterprise. It is coercive system. As a result of its impact, human nature itself is changed; our needs and desires grow and develop. Moreover, as writers such as Rousseau ([1755] 1984) maintain, human needs and desires may expand more rapidly than our powers to satisfy them, with the result that economic development brings no improvement in the quality of life, no real increase in satisfaction or happiness.

There is some truth in both sides of this argument, I believe. For, on the one hand, it seems clear that there must be some connection between economic development and happiness; and yet, when we look at life in modern capitalist society, with its poverty and misery, its insecurity and alienation, it seems very doubtful that such conditions of life represent any real improvement over the way of life in earlier and simpler sorts of society.

Both of these approaches gauge progress in terms of happiness; although, of course, they have quite different conceptions of what happiness involves. This makes the issue between them particularly difficult to resolve, for happiness is a notoriously elusive concept. However, the idea of progress can be specified in terms that do not refer to happiness at all. Thus, in describing the progressive aspects of the market, above, I focused on the broadening range of activities and social relations, on the development of abilities and consciousness, to which it has given rise. The concept of progress involved can thus be specified in terms of self-development and self-realization – it is a non-utilitarian concept.

A number of writers spell out such a concept of progress, but none more clearly than Durkheim. Social development, he argues, makes possible a greater range of activity and awareness. That means that the individual can experience a wider variety of satisfactions, of which perhaps the intensity may be heightened. Equally, however, the range and intensity of the pains and discomforts experienced are also increased.[8] 'Happiness', says Durkheim ([1893] 1984: 188–9), 'does not increase because activity becomes richer, but is the same wherever it is healthy. The most simple creature and the most complex one experience the same happiness if they both equally realize their own nature. The average savage can be just as happy as the normal civilized person.'

In the historical process there has been a development of human activities and relations, of needs, powers and capacities, hence also of freedom; but whether this has resulted in any increase in happiness is doubtful. Nevertheless, to look upon these changes as beneficial and progressive is to imply that, even with all the suffering they have involved, they are desirable and humanly valuable. There is no question of harking back to an earlier stage. The present form of civilization, even with all its discontents, is preferable to what went before.

Marx and the market

Similar ideas are also involved in Marx's philosophy. Although, of course, Marx criticizes capitalism, and describes the destructive and alienating impact of the market with unequalled lucidity and force, he does not *merely* condemn these phenomena, or regard them as mere evils. Rather, he emphasizes their *contradictory* character. For at the same time, he insists, they also have a positive, progressive and even 'revolutionary' side.

This consists partly in the economic development to which capitalism gives rise and which, Marx believed, was creating the necessary material conditions for a higher historical stage of socialism. He even talks of this as 'one of the civilizing aspects of capital' (Marx [1894] 1971: 819). On this basis, Marx is often regarded as a narrowly economic thinker who, like the classical economists, sees progress in purely material terms. But this thought cannot be understood in this manner. For Marx is equally concerned to describe and analyse the wider human impact of these developments. This is perhaps most evident in his early writings on alienation, but the same themes recur throughout his work. This gives rise to the opposite, 'humanist' view, that Marxism is primarily a moral critique of the dehumanizing effects of capitalism along the lines I have been describing. Such an account is equally untenable. Despite the alienating and humanly destructive effects of the market, there is a revolutionary side here too. For it leads ultimately to the creation and growth of the proletariat, the industrial working class, as a social and political force.

Often, Marx's descriptions of the destructive and dehumanizing effects of capitalism appear to conflict with this line of thought, and deny its positive side altogether. In a characteristic passage, for example, he writes ([1867] 1961: 645), 'all the methods for raising the social productiveness of labour are brought about at the cost of the individual labourer. . .accumulation of wealth at one pole is. . .at the same time accumulation of misery, agony of toil, slavery, ignorance, brutality, mental degradation, at the opposite pole'. And there is much else like this throughout his work.

There are real problems of interpretation here, for there is lack of clarity and confusion in what Marx wrote on this topic, but it is beyond my scope to try to tackle those issues here. However, it is clear, at least, that *one* of the main strands of Marx's account of historical development and the role of the proletariat in it, makes sense only if the contradictory character of the impact of capitalism – its positive as well negative aspects – is recognized. For it is an essential element of his account of capitalism that, despite all the misery it causes, it also creates, not only the material conditions for socialism, but also the agents which will bring it about.

Indeed, Marx criticizes the utopian socialists of his time for their failure to appreciate just this point. 'They see in poverty nothing but poverty, without seeing in it the revolutionary, subversive side, which will overthrow the old society' (Marx [1847] 1955: 109). Like the romantic critics I have been describing, who are in many ways their contemporary descendants, the utopian socialists tend to portray capitalism as an entirely destructive and inhuman phenomenon, reducing the working class to a degraded, passive and impotent mass, 'without any historical initiative or any independent political movement' (Marx and Engels [1848] 1966: 88). But in reality, Marx argues, the result is quite different. In the end, what capitalism produces is 'its own grave-diggers' (Marx and Engels [1848] 1966: 59).

Quite clearly, there is a strong streak of idealization in Marx's picture of the working class. In modern industrial societies its revolutionary character is in doubt; indeed, with the recent rise of other radical movements, many now question whether it still constitutes the primary force for change and progress. This certainly raises fundamental problems for Marxism as a historical and political theory. However, the issue here is more basic. Even if Marx's expectations for the working class have not been fulfilled, there is still an important element of truth in his account. For it involves the view, which I have also been stressing, that the impact of the market on working people has not been entirely negative. Even if not as the agent of revolution, it has, as Engels says ([1845] 1969: 37), drawn 'into the whirl of history the last classes which had remained sunk in apathetic indifference to the universal interests of mankind'. It has meant an expansion of their horizons and consciousness, of their real relations and sphere of activity. In short, it has ultimately been a progressive phenomenon.

These ideas provide the framework for Marx's assessment of the impact of the market: an assessment in terms quite different from those I have been criticizing. For Marx rejects both the laissez-faire view that the market is the natural and final form of human economic life and, at the same time, the purely negative judgement of capitalism that is involved in the romantic approach. The free market is not his idea of human liberation; and yet his picture of socialism is the very opposite of the romantic vision of a rural idyll where small self-sufficient households and communities prevail, and where people lead 'simpler' and more 'natural' lives. 'Universally developed individuals', he insists (Marx [1857] 1973: 162), 'are no product of nature, but of history.'

In place of the absolute approaches of these other outlooks, Marx portrays capitalism as a specific and finite stage of economic and social development; and he assesses its impact in historical and relative terms. *Relative* to what went before it constitutes progress. However, there is nothing final or ultimate about it. On the contrary, it is a limited and inherently contradictory social form. Through the working out of its own processes of development, the conditions are ultimately created for a new – higher and more developed – form of social and economic life.

These new conditions and possibilities, which are generated within and by capitalism, provide the basis for a new assessment of the market. For relative *to them*, the market comes to be a fetter and a restraint on human development; it constitutes a conservative and backward force, and can be criticized on that basis.[9] In this way, Marx criticizes the market in a manner that is forward rather than backward looking. His critique is based not on absolute ideas of human nature, nor on the standards of earlier and less developed social conditions, but on possibilities that arise out of the social and economic forces that capitalism has itself created, but which it proves increasingly unable to employ and control in a beneficial and rational way.

In this way, Marx's assessment of the market is based on the view that capitalism will ultimately be superseded by a higher stage. Marx often appears to regard this process, in a quasi-Hegelian fashion, as inevitable (Elster 1985: 107–18). Such a view of progress is indefensible, if for no other reason than that humanity has now developed the power to destroy itself, and there seems no guarantee that it will not one day do so. However, the idea of progress can be developed in ways that do not involve the idea of inevitability. Thus, it can be conceived as a trend or tendency (Flew 1967); and the market can be criticized along the lines I have been outlining, as a fetter to progress so understood. What must be retained, however, are the beliefs that past development can be characterized in terms of progress, and that there are progressive tendencies discernible in present conditions.

Even these views are now widely questioned, and not just for philosophical reasons. For the very possibility of progress beyond capitalism and the free market seems to have been put in question by the actual course of history. On the one hand, capitalism has proved far more resilient and durable than Marx and many others in the nineteenth century ever imagined possible; while, on the other, it appears that history can go into reverse: gains can be lost. In the last decade in Britain, for example, many of the apparent advances won in the long struggle for socialism – in welfare provision, in trade union rights, in public ownership and control, etc. – have been reversed; and in the 'socialist world'[10] there appears to be a headlong rush to dismantle social and economic arrangements previously regarded as definitive of socialism, and to introduce private enterprise and the free market in their place.

These developments necessitate the most fundamental rethinking of the nature of Marxism and of socialism more generally; it is an illusion to believe otherwise. However, there is no basis in recent events, dramatic as they have been, for the conclusion that capitalism constitutes the final stage of human development and the 'end of history'. The repeated lesson of the history of capitalism since its early phase is that the pure free market is incapable of meeting many basic needs, or ensuring a satisfactory level of social provision. For this reason, nowhere in the advanced industrial world is the free market any longer allowed to operate unplanned and unchecked. In many major areas of economic life – such as agriculture, health care, basic housing, education, public transport, protection of the environment, etc. – government intervention and control have been found necessary, not for political or ideological reasons, but because the free market has proved unable to provide the minimum necessities in these areas (Galbraith 1990).

It is these needs, and the inability of the free market to meet them, that historically have given rise to the aspirations and demands for socialism. They have not vanished, and show no signs of doing so. While they continue to exist, socialism will remain on the political agenda. For a more effective and rational way of organizing social and economic life, while not inevitable, is surely possible and increasingly necessary. This, at least, is the conviction that underlies socialism and that provides the basis for its criticisms of capitalism and the free market.

Contemporary responses

I have been discussing these issues in abstract and general terms. To conclude, let me briefly consider something of their contemporary political and social significance. Britain emerged from the Second World War, unified by the war effort, as a relatively peaceful and harmonious society. This is portrayed – no doubt in an exaggerated and idealized, but still quite recognizable, way – in such films as 'Dixon of Dock Green' and the early Ealing comedies (e.g. 'Passport to Pimlico').

The Tory government of the last decade or so has destroyed all that; it has shattered the postwar political consensus. Through its free market policies it has unleashed economic forces that have devastated many traditional and long-established industries and communities, thrown millions out of work, and laid waste to whole regions. As a result, Britain has become one of the most divided, decrepit, polluted, coercive and riot-torn societies in Europe.

Many people have suffered in the process. They have been forced onto the defensive, and tend to see only the negative side of what has been happening. They regard market forces, the 'enterprise culture', and even economic change and development in general, as purely destructive and inhuman phenomena; and they look back longingly to the postwar situation, to the 'Dixon of Dock Green' world.

Such responses are understandable and perhaps even inevitable; but nevertheless they are unrealistic and unsatisfactory. Of course, there is a negative and destructive aspect to the changes that have been occurring – that is clear enough. But what is harder to see, and what I have been trying to bring out, is that there may also ultimately be another side to them as well. For the market not only destroys social bonds and relations, it also eventually gives rise to new ones, as new economic activity develops.

The Soviet Union and Eastern Europe are now embarking on a similar free market course. From our vantage point here, we must regard this with mixed feelings and a degree for foreboding. We know from our own experience that the result will not simply be a liberation of 'enterprise' and 'initiative'; even the success of the free market in promoting economic development is in doubt. However, what is certain is that it will cause widespread dislocation and distress, it will exacerbate social inequalities and divisions, it will tear apart the very fabric of society. In the longer term, however, if the introduction of market forces succeeds in leading these societies out of their present stagnation and towards renewed growth and development, then the positive effects will become increasingly apparent. In some of these societies, despite all the problems facing them, there are grounds for hope on this score; and, if those hopes prove well founded, the introduction of the market will constitute not the 'end of history', but rather a new beginning.

There is no guarantee of this, however, as we know to our cost. For in Britain, the government has proved very good at destruction; it has wiped out large sections of manufacturing industry and, in so doing, the communities that depended on it. But it has proved much less successful at the positive task of revitalizing and reconstructing the economy and the society. It should be criticized in these terms: in a forward and not backward looking way; not so much for the way in which it has been uprooting the past, but rather for the way in which it has failed to bring forward the future.

Notes: Chapter 8

1　'Uninterrupted disturbance of all social conditions, everlasting uncertainty and agitation distinguish the bourgeois epoch from all earlier ones. All fixed, fast-frozen relations. . .are swept away, all new-formed ones become antiquated. . .all that is solid melts in air' (Marx and Engels [1848] 1966: 44–5).

2　See also Wiener (1985) for a broad historical survey of this tradition of thought.

3　As Marx ([1857] 1973: 650) writes, 'guild industry, in its heyday, found in the guild organization all the fullness of freedom it required, i.e. the relations of production corresponding to it. After all, it posited these out of itself, and developed them as *its* inherent conditions, and hence in no way as external and constricting barriers.'

4　Gorz (1989: Ch. 11) is now more fully aware of these aspects.

5　Lenin ([1897] 1967: 91), is particularly clear about this. Market exchange, he writes, 'expresses a special form of *social economy*. . . It. . .*not only disunites* (it does that only in respect of the medieval associations, which capitalism destroys), *but* also unites men, compelling them to enter into intercourse with each other through the medium of the market. . .substituting unity. . .of a whole country, and even of the whole world, for local and social-estate associations'.

6　Mrs Gaskell's novel, *North and South* ([1855] 1970), gives a graphic account of these developments as they were observable in the middle of the nineteenth century.

7　Similarly, as a result of the market, the social position of women has been transformed. Certainly, market forces often operate coercively and oppressively in the lives of women, just as of men; they are not an unmixed blessing. Many women are forced by economic necessity to seek employment in the market, and this offten comes on top of an undiminished share of housework, as many recent writers have pointed out. As a result, women and the family are put under great strain. At the same time, however, the employment of women has led to their emancipation from the confines of the home, and their entry into public life. For all the alienation and stultifying narrowness of so many jobs, employment has provided women with opportunities to develop and exercise their talents and abilities in much fuller and wider ways than are usually possible in the private, non-market sphere of the home. Indeed, the market has been perhaps the greatest single force in the modern world leading to the liberation of women.

8 Mill makes a similar point in the course of distinguishing between higher and lower pleasures in *Utilitarianism* ([1861] 1962), Chapter 2.
9 For a fuller account see Sayers (1989).
10 I use this phrase *faute de mieux*. A year ago I would have talked of 'actually existing socialism', but this is rapidly ceasing to exist.

References: Chapter 8

Carlyle, T. 1895. *Chartism* and *Past and Present* in *Sartor Resartus and Other Writings*. London: Chapman and Hall.
Durkheim, E. [1893] 1984. *The Division of Labour in Society*, tr. W. D. Halls. London: Macmillan.
Engels, F. [1845] 1969. *The Condition of the Working Class in England*. London: Panther.
Elster, J. 1985. *Making Sense of Marx*. Cambridge: Cambridge University Press.
Flew, A. G. N. 1967. *Evolutionary Ethics*. London: Macmillan.
Friedman, M. and Friedman, R. 1962. *Capitalism and Freedom*. Chicago: Chicago University Press.
Fukuyama, F. 1989. The end of history?. *The National Interest*. Excerpts reprinted in *The Independent*, 20–21 September 1989.
Galbraith, J. K. 1990. Why the Right is wrong, *The Guardian*, 26 January 1990.
Gaskell, E. [1855] 1970. *North and South*. Harmondsworth: Penguin.
Gorz, A. 1985. *Paths to Paradise*. London: Pluto.
Gorz, A. 1989. *Critique of Economic Reason*. London: Verso.
Hegel, G. W. F. [1807] 1977. *Phenomenology of Spirit*, tr. A. V. Miller. Oxford: Clarendon Press.
Lenin, V. I. [1897] 1967. *A Characterization of Economic Romanticism*. Moscow: Progress.
Marx, K. [1847] 1955. *The Poverty of Philosophy*. Moscow: Progress.
Marx, K. [1867] 1961. *Capital*, Vol. I. Moscow: Foreign Languages Publishing House.
Marx, K. [1894] 1971. *Capital*, Vol. III. Moscow: Progress.
Marx, K. [1857] 1973. *Grundrisse*. Harmondsworth: Penguin.
Marx, K. and Engels, F. [1848] 1966. *Manifesto of the Communist Party*. Moscow: Progress.
Mill, J. S. [1861] 1962. *Utilitarianism and Other Writings*. London: Fontana.
Morris, W. 1973. *Political Writings*, edited by A. L. Morton. London: Lawrence and Wishart.
Robertson, J. 1985. *Future Work*. Aldershot: Gower.
Rousseau, J.-J. [1755] 1984 *A Discourse on Inequality*, tr. M. Cranston. Harmondsworth: Penguin.
Ruskin, J. [1860] 1985. *Unto This Last and Other Writings*. Harmondsworth: Penguin.

Sayers, S. 1989. Analytical Marxism and morality. In R. Ware and K. Nielson (eds), *Analyzing Marxism* (*Canadian Journal of Philosophy*, Supplementary Vol. 15). Calgary, Alberta: University of Calgary Press, pp. 81–104.

Smith, A. [1776] 1974. *The Wealth of Nations*. Harmondsworth: Penguin.

Wiener, M. J. 1985. *English Culture and the Decline of the Industrial Spirit, 1850–1980*. Harmondsworth: Penguin.

PART 3

The ethics of the enterprising self

9 Governing the enterprising self

NIKOLAS ROSE

In the summer of 1989, an advertisement began to appear regularly on the front page of *The Guardian* newspaper. It was for a private organization called 'Self-Helpline' and offered a range of telephone numbers for people to ring for answers to some apparently troubling questions. There were 'Emotional problems', from 'Dealing with infidelity' to 'Overcoming shyness'. There were 'Parenthood problems', from 'My child won't sleep' to 'I feel like hitting my baby'. There were 'Work problems', such as 'Am I in the right job' or 'Becoming a supervisor'. And there were 'Sexual problems' from 'Impotence' to 'Better orgasms'. For the cost of a telephone call, callers could obtain 'self-help step by step answers to dealing with your problems and improving the quality of your life'. They were assured that 'all messages are provided by our professionals qualified in medicine, counselling and business'. And, of course, the calls could be made anonymously, without the fear of being traced: the problem, and its solution, was a matter entirely for oneself (Self-Helpline 1989).

This little advertisement may seem trivial, and its concerns hardly germane to something as weighty as 'enterprise culture'. But the forms of political reason that yearn for an enterprise culture accord a vital *political* value to a certain image of the self. And this image of an 'enterprising self' is so potent because it is not an idiosyncratic obsession of the right of the political spectrum. On the contrary, it resonates with basic presuppositions concerning the contemporary self that are widely distributed in our present, presuppositions that are embodied in the very language that we use to make persons thinkable, and in our ideal conceptions of what people should be. It is these presuppositions that this advertisement displays. The self is to be a subjective being, it is to aspire to autonomy, it is to strive for personal fulfilment in its earthly life, it is to interpret its reality and destiny as matters of individual responsibility, it is to find meaning in existence by shaping its life through acts of choice. These ways of *thinking* about selves, and these ways of *judging* them, are linked to certain ways of *acting* upon selves. The guidance of selves is no longer dependent upon the authority of religion or traditional morality; it has been allocated to 'experts of subjectivity' who transfigure existential questions about the purpose of life and the meaning of suffering into technical questions about the most effective ways of managing malfunction and improving 'quality of life'.

These new practices of thinking, judging and acting are not simply 'private' matters. They are linked to the ways in which persons figure in the political vocabulary of advanced liberal democracies – no longer as subjects with duties and obligations, but as individuals, with rights and freedoms. Specific styles of political discourse may be ephemeral, and the salvationist rhetoric of enterprise culture espoused by the British conservatism of the 1980s may fade away. But the presupposition of the autonomous, choosing, free self as the value, ideal and objective underpinning and legitimating political activity imbues the political mentalities of the modern West, as well as those now sweeping what used to be termed 'Eastern Europe'. How are we to evaluate it?

Notions of personhood vary greatly from culture to culture, and there are many ways of accounting for such variation, connecting personhood to religious, legal, penal and other practices bearing upon persons, and to wider social, political and economic arrangements. Recently, the French philosopher and historian Michel Foucault has suggested some productive ways of thinking about these issues, by linking practices bearing on the self to forms of power. Foucault's work is instructive partly because it rejects two ways in which we habitually think about power and subjectivity. We often think of power in terms of constraints that dominate, deny and repress subjectivity. Foucault, however, analyses power not as a negation of the vitality and capacities of individuals, but as the creation, shaping and utilization of human beings *as* subjects. Power, that is to say, works through, and not against, subjectivity (Foucault 1982; see Miller 1987). Further, we think about political power largely in terms of oppositions between 'the state' and 'private life', and locate subjectivity within the latter. But Foucault conceives of power as that which traverses *all* practices – from the 'macro' to the 'micro' – though which persons are ruled, mastered, held in check, administered, steered, guided, by means of which they are led by others or have come to direct or regulate their own actions (Foucault 1979a; Miller and Rose 1988, 1990). To analyse the relations between 'the self' and power, then, is not a matter of lamenting the ways in which our autonomy is suppressed by the state, but of investigating the ways in which subjectivity has become an essential object and target for certain strategies, tactics and procedures of regulation.

To consider the terms that are accorded so high a political value today – autonomy, fulfilment, responsibility, choice – from this perspective is certainly to question whether they mark a kind of culmination of ethical evolution. But this does not imply that we should subject these terms to a critique: for example, by claiming that the rhetoric of freedom is an ideological mask for the workings of a political system that secretly denies it. We should, rather, examine the ways in which these ideals of the self are bound up with a profoundly ambiguous set of relations between human subjects and political power. Following Foucault, we could use the term 'government' as a portmanteau notion to encompass the multiple ways in which the self has become related to power (Rabinow 1984; Gordon 1986, 1987). Government embraces all those concerns with managing and administering social and personal existence in the attempt to introduce economy, order and virtue.

We can explore these relations along three interlinked dimensions. The first dimension, roughly 'political', Foucault termed 'governmentality', or 'mentalities of government': the complex of notions, calculations, strategies and tactics through which diverse authorities – political, military, economic, theological, medical, etc. – have sought to act upon the lives and conducts of each and all in order to avert evils and achieve such desirable states as health, happiness, wealth and tranquillity (Foucault 1979b). From at least the eighteenth century, the capacities of individuals, as subjects, as citizens, as selves, have emerged as a central target and resource for authorities. Attempts to invent and exercise different types of political rule have been intimately linked to conceptions of the nature of those who are to be ruled. The autonomous subjectivity of the modern self may seem the antithesis of political power. But Foucault's argument suggests an exploration of the ways in which this autonomization of the self is itself a central feature of contemporary governmentality.

The second dimension suggested by Foucault's writings is roughly 'institutional'. However, it entails construing institutions in a particular 'technological' way, that is, as '*human* technologies'. Institutions from the prison, through the asylum to the workplace, the school and the home can be seen as practices that put in play certain assumptions and objectives concerning the selves that inhabit them (Foucault 1977). These are embodied in the design of institutional space, the arrangements of institutional time and activity, procedures of reward and punishment, and the operation of systems of norms and judgements. They can be thought of as 'technological' in that they seek the calculated orchestration of the activities of selves. They attempt simultaneously to maximize certain capacities of individuals and constrain others in accordance with particular knowledges – medical, psychological, pedagogic – and towards particular ends – responsibility, discipline, diligence, and so forth. In what ways and with what consequences are our contemporary notions of subjective autonomy and enterprise embodied within the regulatory practices of distinctively 'modern' forms of life?

The third dimension for investigation of the modern self corresponds to a roughly 'ethical' field, in so far as ethics are understood in a 'practical' way as modes of evaluating and acting upon one's self that have obtained in different historical periods (Foucault 1988; see Rabinow 1984). Foucault examined these in terms of what he called 'technologies of the self', techniques 'which permit individuals to effect by their own means or with the help of others a certain number of operations on their own bodies and souls, thoughts, conduct and way of being, so as to transform themselves in order to attain a certain state of happiness, purity, wisdom, perfection, or immortality' (Foucault 1988: 18). Ethics are thus understood as means by which individuals come to construe, decipher, act upon themselves in relation to the true and the false, the permitted and the forbidden, the desirable and the undesirable. Hence, we might consider the ways in which the contemporary culture of autonomous subjectivity is embodied in our techniques for understanding and improving ourselves in relation to that which is true, permitted and desirable.

'Enterprise culture' can be understood in terms of the particular connections that it establishes between these three dimensions. For enterprise links up a seductive ethics of the self, a powerful critique of contemporary institutional and political reality, and an apparently coherent design for the radical transformation of contemporary social arrangements. In the writings of 'neo-liberals' such as Hayek and Friedman, the wellbeing of both political and social existence is to be ensured not by centralized planning and bureaucracy, but through the 'enterprising' activities and choices of autonomous entities – businesses, organizations, persons – each striving to maximize its own advantage by inventing and promoting new projects by means of individual and local calculations of strategies and tactics, costs and benefits (Hayek 1960; Friedman 1982). Neo-liberalism is thus more than a phenomenon at the level of political philosophy. It constitutes a mentality of government, a conception of how authorities should use their powers in order to improve national wellbeing, the ends they should seek, the evils they should avoid, the means they should use and, crucially, the nature of the persons upon whom they must act.

Enterprise is such a potent language for articulating a political rationality because it can connect up these general political deliberations with the formulation of specific programmes that simultaneously '*problematize*' organizational practices in many different social locales, and provide rationales and guidelines for transforming them. The vocabulary of enterprise thus enables a political rationality to be 'translated' into attempts to govern aspects of social, economic and personal existence that have come to appear problematic. Enterprise here not only designates a kind of organizational form – individual units competing with one another on the market – but more generally provides an image of a mode of activity to be encouraged in a multitude of arenas of life – the school, the university, the hospital, the GP's surgery, the factory and business organization, the family, and the apparatus of social welfare. Organizations are problematized in terms of their lack of enterprise: it is this that epitomizes their weaknesses and their failings. Correlatively, they are to be reconstructed by promoting and utilizing the enterprising capacities of each and all, encouraging them to conduct themselves with boldness and vigour, to calculate for their own advantage, to drive themselves hard and to accept risks in the pursuit of goals. Enterprise can thus be given a 'technological' form by experts of organizational life, engineering human relations through architecture, timetabling, supervisory systems, payment schemes, curricula and the like, to achieve economy, efficiency, excellence and competitiveness. Regulatory practices can be transformed to embody the presupposition of the enterprising self, striving for fulfilment, excellence and achievement.

Hence, the vocabulary of enterprise links political rhetoric and regulatory programmes to the 'self-steering' capacities of subjects themselves. Along this third dimension of political rule, enterprise forges a link between the ways we are governed by others and the ways we should govern ourselves. Enterprise here designates an array of rules for the conduct of one's everyday existence: energy, initiative, ambition, calculation and personal responsibility. The enterprising self will make a venture of its life, project itself a future and seek to shape itself in order to become that which it wishes to be. The enterprising self is thus a calculating self, a self that calculates *about* itself and that works *upon* itself in order to better itself. Enterprise, that is, designates a form of rule that is intrinsically 'ethical': good government is to be grounded in the ways in which persons govern themselves.

For many critics, this vocabulary of enterprise is obfuscating rhetoric: the apotheosis of the 'capitalist illusion' that persons are 'sovereign individuals'. Such an assessment is facile. The language of enterprise is only one way of articulating ethical presuppositions that are very widely shared; that have come to form a common ground for almost all rationalities, programmes and techniques of rule in advanced liberal democratic societies. Government in such societies is not characterized by the utopian dream of a regulative machinery that will penetrate all regions of the social body, and administer them for the common good. Rather, since at least the nineteenth century, liberal political thought has been structured by the opposition between the constitutional limits of government on the one hand, and the desire to arrange things so that social and economic processes turn out for the best without the need for direct political intervention. Thus, the formal limitations on the powers of 'the state' have entailed, as their corollary, the proliferation of a dispersed array of programmes and mechanisms, decoupled from the direct activities of the 'public' powers, that nonetheless promise to shape events in the domains of work, the market and the family to produce such 'public' values as wealth, efficiency, health and wellbeing.

The autonomy of the self is thus not the timeless antithesis of political power, but one of the objectives and instruments of modern mentalities of government. Liberal democracy, if understood as an art of government and a technology of rule, has long been bound up with the invention of techniques to *constitute* the citizens of a democratic polity with the 'personal' capacities and aspirations necessary to bear the political weight that rests on them. Governing in a liberal-democratic way means governing *through* the freedom and aspirations of subjects rather than in spite of them. It has been made possible by a proliferation of discourses, practices and techniques, through which the self-governing capabilities of individuals can be brought into alignment with political objectives.

The problem of the regulation of 'private' spheres, produced by liberal–democratic forms of government has been solved, in large part, by means of the specific powers of 'expert' knowledge: the 'rationalizable' techniques deployed by medics, social workers, psychiatrists, psychologists, counsellors and advisers. Governing in a liberal-democratic way depends upon the availability of such techniques that will shape, channel, organize and direct the personal capacities and selves of individuals under the aegis of a claim to objectivity, neutrality and technical efficacy rather than one of political partiality. Through the indirect alliances established by the apparatus of expertise, the objectives of 'liberal' government can be brought into alignment with the selves of 'democratic' citizens.

Technologies of the self

Many authors have commented upon the rise of a therapeutic culture of the self, and have sought to link this to more general political transformations. The most superficial analyses have consisted of a reprise on the familiar theme that capitalism breeds individualism, the obsession with therapy being the corollary of the illusion of atomistic self-sufficiency. More considered analyses have made similar melancholy assessments (Rieff 1966; Lasch 1980; MacIntyre 1981; Bourdieu 1984). But rather than disdaining these doomed attempts to fill the absence caused by the demise of religion, cultural solidarities or parental authority, Foucault's approach encourages us to view therapeutics as, in certain respects, continuous with these. Therapeutics, like religion, may be analysed as techniques of the self through which human beings are urged and incited to become ethical beings, to define and regulate themselves according to a moral code, to establish precepts for conducting or judging their lives, to reject or accept moral goals.

This is not the place to trace the relations between contemporary therapeutics and earlier technologies of the self (Rose 1990; cf. Foucault 1985, 1986a). Let me continue to explore just one significant theme: the allocation of authority over 'the conduct of conduct' to expertise. Expertise is important in at least three respects, each distinguishing the present regime of the self from those embodied in theological injunction, moral exhortation, hygienic instruction or appeals to utilitarian calculation. First, the grounding of authority in a claim to 'scientificity' and objectivity establishes in a unique way the distance between systems of self-regulation and the formal organs of political power that is necessary within liberal democratic rationalities of government. Secondly, expertise can mobilize and be mobilized within political argument in distinctive ways, producing a new relationship between knowledge and government. Expertise comes to be accorded a particular role in the formulation of programmes of government and in the technologies that seek to give them effect. Thirdly, expertise operates through the particular relation that it has with the self-regulating capacities of subjects. For the plausibility inherent in a claim to 'scientificity' and rationalized efficacy binds subjectivity to truth, and subjects to experts, in new and potent ways.

The advertisement with which I began this chapter operated under a significant title: 'Self-Help'. Although this notion has a long history, today it signifies that the regulation of personal existence is not a question of authorities seeking to impose norms of conduct through an intrusive state bureaucracy backed with legal powers. Nor is it a matter of the imposition of moral standards under a religious mandate. Self-help, today, entails an alliance between professionals claiming to provide an objective, rational answer to the question of how one should conduct a life to ensure normality, contentment and success, and individuals seeking to shape a 'life style', not in order to conform to social conventions but in the hope of personal happiness and an 'improved quality of life'. And the mechanism of this alliance is the market, the 'free' exchange between those with a service to sell and those that have been brought to want to buy.

Contemporary individuals are incited to live as if making a *project* of themselves: they are to *work* on their emotional world, their domestic and conjugal arrangements, their relations with employment and their techniques of sexual pleasure, to develop a 'style' of living that will maximize the worth of their existence to themselves. Evidence from the United States, from Europe and the United Kingdom suggests that the implantation of such 'identity projects', characteristic of advanced liberal democracies, is constitutively linked to the rise of a new breed of spiritual directors, 'engineers of the human soul' (Rose 1990). Although our subjectivity might appear to be our most intimate sphere of experience, its contemporary intensification as a political and ethical value is intrinsically correlated with the growth of expert languages that enable us to render our relations with our selves and others into words and into thought, and with expert techniques that promise to allow us to transform ourselves in the direction of happiness and fulfilment.

The ethics of enterprise – competitiveness, strength, vigour, boldness, outwardness and the urge to succeed – may seem to be quite opposed to the domain of the therapeutic, which is associated with hedonism and self-centredness. And indeed, contemporary culture is ethically pluralist: the differences that Max Weber examined between the 'styles of conduct' appropriate to different 'spheres of existence' – spiritual, economic, political, aesthetic, erotic – have not been abolished (Weber [1915] 1948). But despite such ethical pluralism, these diverse ethical regimes are governed by a single *a priori*: the 'autonomization' and 'responsibilization' of the self, the instilling of a reflexive hermeneutics that will afford self-knowledge and self-mastery, and the operation of all of this under the authority of experts who claim that the self can achieve a better and happier life through the application of scientific knowledge and professional skill. And the triumph of expertise lies in its promise to reconcile the tensions formed across the soul of the individual who is forced concurrently to inhabit different spheres. For the new experts of the psyche promise that modes of life that appear philosophically opposed – business success and personal growth, image management and authenticity – can be brought into alignment and achieve translatability.

Freud, it will be recalled, advertised psychoanalysis thus: 'You will be able to convince yourself,' he wrote to an imaginary patient, 'that much will be gained if we succeed in transforming hysterical misery into common unhappiness. With a mental life that has been restored to health you will be better armed against that unhappiness' (Breuer and Freud 1895, in Freud, 1953–7, Vol. 2, p. 305). His successors formulate their powers rather differently. The London Centre for Psychotherapy points out that psychotherapy takes time, yet it offers 'far more fulfilling relationships and greater self expression. Family and social life, sexual partnerships and work are all likely to benefit' (London Centre for Psychotherapy 1987). Advocates of behavioural psychotherapy hold only that 'the client's "symptoms" can be regarded as discrete psychological entities which can be removed or altered by direct means' (Mackay 1984: 276). But 'therapy' is generalized to include such 'symptoms' as sexual orientation, anxiety, lack of assertiveness and the wish to increase self-control. And 'therapy' is extended to such goals as 'greater self-awareness', which should not only 'facilitate the change process but should lead the client to reappraise his life style', 'the development of problem-solving skills', and increasing 'overall perceived self-efficacy'. In the more avowedly 'humanistic' and 'alternative' therapeutic systems, from Rogers's 'client-centred therapy' to Perls's 'Gestalt therapy', from Berne's 'transactional analysis' to Janov's 'primal therapy', versions of the same hope are held out: you can change, you can achieve self-mastery, you can control your own destiny, you can truly be autonomous (cf. Rose 1990).

Become whole, become what you want, become yourself: the individual is to become, as it were, an entrepreneur of itself, seeking to maximize its own powers, its own happiness, its own quality of life, through enhancing its autonomy and then instrumentalizing its autonomous choices in the service of its lifestyle. The self is to style its life through acts of choice and, when it cannot conduct its life according to this norm of choice, it is to seek expert assistance. On the territory of the therapeutic, the conduct of everyday existence is recast as a series of manageable problems to be understood and resolved by technical adjustment in relation to the norm of the autonomous self aspiring to self-possession and happiness.

Therapeutics has transformed work – mental and manual – into a matter of personal fulfilment and psychical identity. The employment relationship becomes significant less for the cash reward it offers than for the subjectivity it confers or denies. An entire discourse upon jobs, careers and unemployment has taken shape, conducted in therapeutic rather than economic terms (Miller 1986). The confident, thrusting self-images of the entrepreneur seem far from such therapeutic ethics. Yet this opposition is illusory. For therapeutics can forge alliances between the liberation of the self and the pathways to personal success, promising to break through the blockages that trap us into powerlessness and passivity, into undemanding jobs and underachievement. Hence, therapeutics can appeal to both sides of the employment contract: it will make us better workers at the same time as it makes us better selves. Therapy can thus offer to free each of us from our psychic chains. We can become enterprising, take control of our careers, transform ourselves into high fliers, achieve excellence and fulfil ourselves not *in spite of* work but *by means of* work.

Therapeutics has psychologized the mundane. Everyday life, from debt, through house purchase, childbirth, marriage and divorce is transformed into 'life events', remediable problems of coping and adjustment. Each is to be addressed by recognizing forces of a subjective order – fears, denials, repressions, lack of psycho-social skills – and similarly subjective consequences – neurosis, tension, stress, illness. The quotidian affairs of existence have become the occasion for introspection, confession and management by expertise. Although this may appear to entail precisely the forms of dependency to which the spirit of enterprise is opposed, this opposition is misleading. For therapeutics, here, impels the subject to 'work' on itself and to assume responsibility for its life. It seeks to equip the self with a set of tools for the management of its affairs, so that it can take control of its undertakings, define its goals, and plan to achieve its needs through its own powers.

Our contemporary regime of the self is not 'anti-social'. It construes the 'relationships' of the self with lovers, family, children, friends and colleagues as central both to personal happiness and social efficacy. All kinds of social ills, from damaged children to ill health to disruption at work and frustration at home have come to be understood as emanating from remediable incapacities in our 'interactions' with others. Thus, human interaction has been made amenable to therapeutic government, and therapists have sought to take charge of this domain of the interpersonal, knowing its laws, diagnosing its ills, prescribing the ways to conduct ourselves with others that are virtuous because they are both fulfilling and healthy. Yet, however 'social' this field may be, it can be turned to the account of the enterprising self: for, in recognizing the dynamic nexus of interpersonal relations that it inhabits, selves can place these relations under conscious control and the self can learn the skills to shape its relations with others so that it will best fulfil its own destiny.

Freud, it has been argued, built psychoanalysis upon a tragic vision. Humans were unable to escape suffering; the duty of the living to tolerate life was denied and hampered by those who promulgated illusions that the pains of existence could be transcended to ensure happiness (Rieff 1959; Richards 1989). But grief, frustration, disappointment and death pose dangers to the regime of the autonomous self, for they strike at the very images of sovereignty, self-possession, omnipotent powers, secular fulfil-ment and joy through lifestyle to which it is welded. Hence, for the new therapeutics of finitude, suffering is not to be endured but to be re-framed by expertise, to be managed as a challenge and a stimulus to the powers of the self. In transcending despair through counselling or therapy, the self can be restored to its conviction that it is master of its own existence.

Although they are heterogeneous and often originate in con-texts and moralities that seem quite discrepant from the world of enterprise, each of these therapeutic systems of spiritual direct-ions operates upon an ethical terrain that can be made entirely consonant with the imperatives of the enterprising self: work on yourself, improve the quality of your life, emancipate your true self, eliminate dependency, release your potential. The healthy self is to be 'free to choose'. But, in embracing such an ethic of psychological health construed in terms of autonomy, we are condemned to make a project out of our own identity and we have become bound to the powers of expertise.

The presuppositions of the self

A recent recruiting poster for the Royal Navy, on the side of a London bus, emphasized one key phrase: 'choose your way of life'. This is indicative of a transformation, probably most emphatic over the last couple of decades, in the types of self that are presupposed in practices for the institutional administration of individuals. For the power of the forms of knowledge and techniques that I have termed the 'expertise of subjectivity' lies in the new alliances that they make possible between the aspirations of selves and the direction of life in factory, office, airline, hospital, school and home. The self-steering capacities of individuals are now construed as vital resources for achieving private profit, public tranquility and social progress, and interventions in these areas have also come to be guided by the regulatory norm of the autonomous, responsible subject, obliged to make its life meaningful through acts of choice. Attempts to manage the enterprise to ensure productivity, competitiveness and innovation, to regulate child rearing to maximize emotional health and intellectual ability, to act upon dietary and other regimes in order to minimize disease and maximize health no longer seek to discipline, instruct, moralize or threaten subjects into compliance. Rather, they aspire to instil and use the self-directing propensities of subjects to bring them into alliance with the aspirations of authorities.

One key site has been the workplace (Rose 1990; Miller and Rose 1990). A new vocabulary of the employment relation has been articulated by organizational psychologists and management consultants, in which work has been re-construed, not as a constraint upon freedom and autonomy, but as a realm in which working subjects can express their autonomy. Workers are no longer imagined merely to endure the degradations and deprivations of labour in order to gain a wage. Nor are workers construed as social creatures seeking satisfaction of needs for solidarity and security in the group relations of the workplace. Rather, the prevailing image of the worker is of an individual in search of meaning and fulfilment, and work itself is interpreted as a site within which individuals represent, construct and confirm their identity, an intrinsic part of a style of life.

The world of work is re-conceptualized as a realm in which productivity is to be enhanced, quality assured and innovation fostered through the active engagement of the self-fulfilling impulses of the employee, through aligning the objectives of the organization with the desires of the self. Organizations are to get the most out of their employees, not by managing group relations to maximize contentment, or by rationalizing management to ensure efficiency, but by releasing the psychological striving of individuals for autonomy and creativity and channelling them into the search of the firm for excellence and success. It now appears that individuals will ally themselves with organizational objectives to the extent that they construe them as both dependent upon and enhancing their own skills of self-realization, self-presentation, self-direction and self-management. Expertise plays the role of relay between objectives that are economically desirable and those that are personally seductive, teaching the arts of self-realization that will enhance employees as individuals as well as workers. Economic success, career progress and personal development intersect in this new expertise of autonomous subjectivity: work has become an essential element in the path to self-realization, and the strivings of the autonomous self have become essential allies in the path to economic success.

A second key site is consumption. Again, expertise has forged alignments between broad socio-political objectives, the goals of producers and the self-regulating propensities of individuals. Politico-economic analyses and calculations have come to stress the need for a constant expansion of consumption if economic wellbeing is to be maintained in the interests of the national budget, the profitability of the firm and the maintenance of levels of employment. A complex economic terrain has taken shape, in which the success of an economy is seen as dependent upon the ability of politicians, planners and manufacturers and marketers to differentiate needs, to produce products aligned to them, and to ensure the purchasing capacity to enable acts of consumption to occur. Yet political authorities can act only indirectly upon the innumerable private acts that comprise consumption, through such measures as policies on advertising, interest, credit and the like. It is the expertise of market research, of promotion and communication, underpinned by the knowledges and techniques of subjectivity, that provides the relays through which the aspirations of ministers, the ambitions of business and the dreams of consumers achieve mutual translatability.

These objectives are to be achieved by instrumentalizing autonomy, and promising to promote it. Consumers are constituted as actors seeking to maximize their 'quality of life' by assembling a 'life-style' through acts of choice in a world of goods. Each commodity is imbued with a 'personal' meaning, a glow cast back upon those who purchase it, illuminating the kind of person they are, or want to come to be. Design, marketing and image construction play a vital role in the transfiguring of goods into desires, and vice versa, through the webs of meaning through which they are related, the fantasies of efficacy and the dreams of pleasure that guide both product innovation and consumer demand. Through this loose assemblage of agents, calculations, techniques, images and commodities, consumer choice can be aligned with macro-economic objectives and business advantage: economic life can be governed and entrepreneurial aspirations realized, through the choices consumers make in their quest to fulfil themselves.

The sphere of consumption, and the mechanisms of its promotion and moulding, can be extended to incorporate problems that were previously governed in other ways. Health stands as an exemplar of this transformation. Healthy bodies and hygienic homes may still be a public value and a political objective. But we no longer need state bureaucracies to enjoin healthy habits of eating, of personal hygiene, of tooth care and the like, with compulsory inspection, subsidized incentives to eat or drink correctly, and so forth. In the new domain of consumption, individuals will *want* to be healthy, experts will instruct them on how to be so, and entrepreneurs will exploit and enhance this market for health. Health will be ensured through a combination of the market, expertise and a regulated autonomy (Rose and Miller 1989).

Perhaps the most striking example of the complex processes through which these new networks have been constructed and operate is the regulation of 'the family'. For some two centuries, the family has been a central ideal and mechanism for the government of the social field (Donzelot 1979). 'Familialization' was crucial to the means whereby personal capacities and conducts could be socialized, shaped and maximized in a manner that accorded with the moral and political principles of liberal society. From at least the mid-nineteenth century, diverse projects sought to use the human technology of the family for social ends: for eliminating illegality, curbing inebriety and restricting promiscuity, imposing restrictions upon the unbridled sensualities of adults and inculcating morality in children. These had to resolve the paradox that liberalism construed the family as quintessentially private, yet simultaneously accorded it all sorts of social consequences and social duties: a concurrent 'privatization' and 'responsibilization' of the family.

Expertise resolved this basic problem at the junction of the family mechanism and the goals of liberal government. It enabled a harmonization between the promotion of the family as a locus of private aspirations and the necessity that it become a kind of 'social machine' for the production of adjusted and responsible citizens. Initially, it was the malfunctioning family that was the central concern. How could one minimize the social threat such families posed without destroying them by removing their endangered members? How could one act preventively upon those sectors of the population thought to harbour the seeds of social risk? Expertise was to ensure that the malfunctioning family would neither be lured into dependency by especially favourable treatment, nor forced into resistance by measures that were frankly repressive. Instead, it would be instructed in health, hygiene and normality, encouraged to see its social duties as its own concerns, and thus returned to its obligations without compromising its autonomy and its responsibility for its own members.

During our own century, attention has gradually but decisively shifted from the prevention of maladapttation to the production of normality itself (Rose 1985). The family now will meet its social obligations through promising to meet the personal aspirations of its members, as adults construe the maximization of the physical and mental welfare of their offspring as the privileged path to their own happiness. Once such an ethic comes to govern family life, individuals can themselves evaluate and normalize their parental and conjugal conduct in terms of the images of normality, of parental conduct and family life, generated by expertise. Bureaucratic regulation of family life is no longer needed to ensure a harmony between social objectives and personal desires. The ethics of enterprise can infuse the 'private' domain that for so long appeared essentially resistant to the rationale of calculation and self-promotion. Through this new mechanism, the social field can be governed through an alliance between the powers of expertise and the wishes, hopes and fears of the responsible, autonomous family, committed to maximizing its quality of life and to the success of family members.

The government of the self

In *The Cultural Contradictions of Capitalism*, Daniel Bell suggested that there was a fundamental opposition between the calculative relation to existence that was required within industrial capitalism and the 'cult of the self', the hedonistic culture that had apparently undercut the Protestant ethic that provided an integrative moral foundation for society at the same time as it chimed with economic needs (Bell 1979). The reflections in this chapter suggest that this analysis is misleading. In the heady days of the 1960s, cults of the self promised a liberation of the individual from all mundane social constraints. But today, the therapeutic culture of the self and its experts of subjectivity offer a different freedom, a freedom to realize our potential and our dreams through reshaping the style in which we conduct our secular existence. And, correlatively, mentalities of government and technologies of regulation operate in terms of an ethic of the self that stresses not stoicism or self-denial in the service of morality and society, but the maximization of choice and self-fulfilment as the touchstone of political legitimacy and the measure of the worth of nations. For both left and right, political culture is to be reshaped to secure ways of life that are fitting for free, sovereign individuals. Neo-liberalism has been a powerful contributor to this reorganization of the problematics of government, questioning, from a particular ethic of individual sovereignty, the legitimacy and the capacity of authorities to know and administer the lives of their subjects in the name of their wellbeing. But the vocabulary of the enterprise is only one way of articulating this more fundamental transformation in mentalities of government, in which the choices of the self have become central to the moral bases of political arguments from all parts of the political arena. Within this new political culture, the diverse and conflicting moral obligations of different spheres of life – at work, at play, in the public arena, in the family, and in sexuality – can achieve a mutual translatability, once each is articulated in terms of a self-striving to make its everyday existence meaningful through the choice of its way of life.

Mentalities of government in the first half of this century operated in terms of an image of the citizen as a social being. They sought to open a kind of contract between government and citizens, articulated in the language of social responsibilities and social welfare. In these forms of political thought, the individual was a locus of needs that were to be socially met if malign consequences were to be avoided, but was reciprocally to be a being to whom political, civil and social obligations and duties were to be attached. This political rationality was translated into programmes such as social insurance, child welfare, social and mental hygiene. Pedagogic technologies from universal education to the BBC were construed as devices for forming responsible citizens. Planned and socially organized mechanisms were to weave a complex web that would bind the inhabitants of a territory into a single polity, a space of regulated freedom.

During the past twenty-five years or so, this rationality of government has entered a chronic crisis, manifested in the appearance of counter-discourses from all parts of the political spectrum, left and centre as well as right. 'Welfare' is criticized as bureaucratic and inefficient, as patronizing and patriarchal, as doing nothing to tackle or redress fundamental inequalities, as a usurper of private choices and freedoms, as a violation of individual rights and much more. These counter-discourses are not only articulated in terms of a different vision of the respective roles of the state, the market, pluralism, civil society and the like. They are also predicated upon a different notion of the proper relations between the citizen and society. Across their manifold differences, these critiques of welfare are framed in a vocabulary of individual freedom, personal choice,

self-fulfilment and initiative. Citizenship is to be active and individualistic rather than passive and dependent. The political subject
is henceforth to be an individual whose citizenship is manifested
through the free exercise of personal choice among a variety of
options. The Home Secretary may argue that 'The idea of active
citizenship is a necessary complement to that of the enterprise
culture' (Hurd 1989, quoted in Barnett 1989: 9) while his left
wing critics argue that 'there can be no such thing as an active
citizen in the United Kingdom until there are *actual* citizens' (p.
11) and clamour for a written constitution and democratic rights.
But all shades of political opinion now agree that citizens *should* be
active and not passive, that democratic government must engage
the self-activating capacities of individuals in a new governmental
dispensation, that it is upon the political consciousness and commitments of individual subjects that a new politics will depend.

Such a notion of the active political subject should, I suggest, be
understood in terms of its consonance with the rise of regulatory
technologies that enable the subject at home and at work, in acts
of consumption and pleasure, to be governed 'at a distance'. We
should analyse notions like 'the active citizen', not merely as rhetoric
or ideology but in terms of the ways in which contemporary
political rationalities rely upon and utilize a range of technologies
that install and support the civilizing project by shaping and governing subjects and enhancing their social commitment, yet are
outside the formal control of the 'public powers'. To such basic
nation-forming devices as a common language, skills of literacy and
transportation networks, our century has added the mass media of
communication, with their pedagogies through documentary and
soap opera; opinion polls and other devices that provide reciprocal
links between authorities and subjects; the regulation of lifestyles
through advertising, marketing and the world of goods; *and* the
experts of subjectivity (Rose 1990). These technologies do not
have their origin or principle of intelligibility in 'the State', but
nonetheless have made it possible to govern in an 'advanced liberal'
way, providing a plethora of indirect mechanisms that can translate
the goals of political, social and economic authorities into the
choices and commitments of individuals.

Not all political subjects are embraced in the new regime of the
self. Those 'on the margins', literally 'outside society', are governed

in other, harsher ways when they threaten the values of the new liberal order, abandoned when they do not. Yet despite its 'dark secrets', neo-liberalism is significant, and not merely an ephemeral or corrupt phenomenon, because it was the right, rather than the left, that succeeded in formulating a political rationality consonant with the new regime of the self. Political authorities can now rely upon a range of technologies through which citizens themselves can act upon themselves in order to avoid what they have come to consider undesirable and achieve what they have come to think will make them happy. Citizens now no longer need to be instructed by their 'political' authorities in how to conduct themselves and regulate their everyday existence. We can now be governed by the choices that we ourselves will make, under the guidance of cultural and cognitive authorities, in the space of regulated freedom, in our individual search for happiness and the fulfilment of our autonomous selves.

A critical ontology of ourselves

This investigation of the forms of self that are presupposed within modern social, economic and political relations evokes a central question addressed by Max Weber. Wilhelm Hennis has suggested that Weber's work should be read as a sustained reflection on *Menschentum*, the history of what humans are in their nature and how human lives are conducted (Hennis 1987). Weber thus addresses a question of enduring importance: the forms of life entailed within certain economic relations, the modes in which different religious systems and forms of religious 'association' shape and direct the practical conduct of everyday economic and vocational existence, the ways in which these and other forces, such as the modern press, mould the subjective individuality of individuals and shape their *Lebenstil* or life styles at particular historical moments.

This interpretation of Weber has been linked, by Colin Gordon, to the concerns of Michel Foucault (Gordon 1986; 1987). In the last period of his work, Foucault returned on a number of occasions to Kant's essay of 1784 entitled *What is Enlightenment?* (Foucault 1986b). He argued that one of the central roles of philosophy since Kant's question was to describe the nature of our present and of ourselves in that present. To ask the question 'what is enlightenment?', for Foucault, is to recognize the importance of historical investigations into the events through which we have come to recognize ourselves and act upon ourselves as certain kinds of subject. It is to interrogate what we have become, as subjects, in our individuality, and the nature of that present in which we are.

Such an investigation would not attempt a psychological diagnosis of the modern soul. Rather, it would seek to document the categories and explanatory schemes according to which we think ourselves, the criteria and norms we use to judge ourselves, the practices through which we act upon ourselves and one another in order to make us particular kinds of being. We would, that is to say, endeavour to describe the historical *a priori* of our existence as subjects. And, perhaps, we should take as a starting point the notions of subjectivity, autonomy and freedom themselves.

In this chapter I have suggested that subjectivity is inherently linked to certain types of knowledge, that projects of autonomy are linked to the growth of expertise, and that freedom is inextricably bound up with certain ways of exercising power. But I have not intended to imply that such notions are false and should be subjected to a critique, or to recommend a nihilism that proclaims the corruption of all values. If the faithful incantation of weary political nostrums is inadequate to the task of serious analysis of the conditions and consequences of our 'age of freedom', so too is knowing sociological relativism or fashionable 'post-modern' irony. If this point requires reinforcement, it would be amply supplied by the part played by the language of freedom, individuality and choice in the recent revolutions in Eastern Europe. Hence, my aim has not been to expose or to denounce our current ethical vocabulary, but to open a space for critical reflection upon the complex practices of knowledge, power and authority that sustain the forms of life that we have come to value, and that underpin the norms of selfhood according to which we have come to regulate our existence. To claim that values are more technical than philosophical is not to denounce all values, but it is, perhaps, to suggest the limits of philosophy as the basis for a critical understanding of ethics.

From such a perspective I have tried to indicate a general change in categories of self-understanding and techniques of self-improvement, which goes beyond the political dichotomy of left and right, and which forms the ethico-political terrain upon which their programmes must be articulated and legitimated. I have argued that the rationalities of liberal government have always been concerned with internalizing their authority in citizens through inspiring, encouraging and inaugurating programmes and techniques that will simultaneously 'autonomize' and 'responsibilize' subjects. I have suggested that, during the present century, a complex network of experts and mechanisms has taken shape, outside 'the state', but fundamentally bound up with the government of health, wealth, tranquillity and virtue. A host of programmes and technologies has come to inculcate and sustain the ethic that individuals are free to the extent that they choose a life of responsible selfhood, and have promoted the dreams of self-fulfilment through the crafting of a lifestyle. And I have argued that the potency of a notion of an 'enterprise culture', however short-lived its particular vocabulary might prove to be, is that it embodies a political programme grounded in, and drawing upon, the new regime of the autonomous, choosing self.

Note: Chapter 9

The argument in this chapter draws upon evidence presented in more detail in my book *Governing the Soul: The Shaping of the Private Self* (1990), and on my work with Peter Miller presented in Rose and Miller (1989) and Miller and Rose (1990). My thanks to the editors of this volume for helpful comments on an earlier version.

References: Chapter 9

Barnett, A. 1989. 'Charlie's army', *New Statesman and Society*, 22.9.89, pp. 9–11.
Bell, D. 1979. *The Cultural Contradictions of Capitalism*, 2nd edn. New York: Basic Books.
Bourdieu, P. 1984. *Distinction: a Social Critique of the Judgment of Taste*. London: Routledge and Kegan Paul.
Donzelot, J. 1979. *Policing the Family*. London: Hutchinson.
Foucault, M. 1977. *Discipline and Punish: The Birth of the Prison*. London: Allen Lane.
Foucault, M. 1979a. *History of Sexuality*, Vol. 1: *An Introduction*. London: Allen Lane.

Foucault, M. 1979b. On governmentality. *Ideology and Consciousness*, 6: 5–21.

Foucault, M. 1982. The subject and power. In H. Dreyfus and P. Rabinow (eds), *Michel Foucault: Beyond Structuralism and Hermeneutics*. Chicago: University of Chicago Press.

Foucault, M. 1985. *The Use of Pleasure*. London: Penguin Viking.

Foucault, M. 1986a. *The Care of the Self*. New York: Pantheon.

Foucault, M. 1986b. Kant on Enlightenment and revolution. *Economy and Society*, 15, 1: 88–96.

Foucault, M. 1988. Technologies of the self. In L. H. Martin, H. Gutman and P. H. Hutton (eds), *Technologies of the Self*. London: Tavistock, pp. 16–49.

Freud, S. 1953–7. Studies in hysteria. In *Standard Edition of the Collected Works of Sigmund Freud*. London: Hogarth Press.

Friedman, M. 1982. *Capitalism and Freedom*. Chicago: Chicago University Press.

Gordon, C. 1986. Question, ethos, event: Foucault on Kant and enlightenment. *Economy and Society*, 15, 1: 71–87.

Gordon, C. 1987. The soul of the citizen: Max Weber and Michel Foucault on rationality and government. In S. Whimster and S. Lash (eds), *Max Weber, Rationality and Modernity*. London: Allen and Unwin, pp. 293–316.

Hayek, F. A. 1960. *The Constitution of Liberty*. London: Routledge and Kegan Paul.

Hennis, W. 1987. Max Weber's theme: personality and life orders. In S. Whimster and S. Lash (eds), *Max Weber, Rationality and Modernity*. London: Allen and Unwin, pp. 52–74.

Lasch, C. 1980. *The Culture of Narcissism*. London: Abacus.

London Centre for Psychotherapy. 1987. Untitled brochure. London: London Centre for Psychotherapy.

Mackay, D. 1984. Behaviourial psychotherapy. In W. Dryden (ed.), *Individual Therapy in Britain*. London: Harper and Row.

MacIntyre, A. 1981. *After Virtue*. London: Duckworth.

Miller, P. 1986. 'Psychotherapy of work and unemployment'. In P. Miller and N. Rose (eds), *The Power of Psychiatry*. Cambridge: Polity.

Miller, P. 1987. *Domination and Power*. London: Routledge and Kegan Paul.

Miller, P. and Rose, N. (1988). The Tavistock Programme: the government of subjectivity and social life. *Sociology*, 22, 2: 171–92.

Miller, P. and Rose, N. (1990). Governing economic life. *Economy and Society*, 19, 1: 1–31.

Rabinow, P. (ed.). 1984. *The Foucault Reader*. Harmondsworth: Penguin.

Richards, B. 1989. *Images of Freud*. London: Dent.

Rieff, P. 1959. *Freud: The Mind of the Moralist*. London: Gollancz.

Rieff, P. 1966. *The Triumph of the Therapeutic*. London: Chatto and Windus.

Rose, N. 1985. *The Psychological Complex: Psychology, Politics and Society in England, 1869–1939.* London: Routledge and Kegan Paul.

Rose, N. 1990. *Governing the Soul: The Shaping of the Private Self.* London: Routledge.

Rose, N. and Miller, P. 1989. Rethinking the state: governing economic, social and personal life. Unpublished manuscript.

Self-Helpline. 1989. Advertisement: 'Who else would you ask if you wanted an answer to these questions', *The Guardian*, 18 August 1989, p. 1.

Weber, M. [1915] 1948. Religious rejections of the world and their directions. In H. H. Gerth and C. Wright Mills (eds), *From Max Weber.* London: Routledge and Kegan Paul.

10 Enterprising kinship: consumer choice and the new reproductive technologies

MARILYN STRATHERN

There is, we are told, an argument 'for letting the future shape of the family evolve experimentally. No doubt people should be discouraged from taking high risks. . .And it goes without saying that new forms of family life must only be tried voluntarily. But subject to these qualifications, we *prefer a society* predisposed in favour of "experiments in living" to one in which they are stifled' (Glover *et al.* 1989: 63; my emphasis).

Thus the Glover Report on Reproductive Technologies to the European Commission. The committee was asked to consider ethical and other social issues raised by the techniques that (as they put it) 'extend our reproductive options' (Glover *et al.* 1989: 13). By reproductive option they mean primarily fertility, although their concern extends from artificial insemination, in vitro fertilization and 'maternal surrogacy' to future implications of gene therapy and embryo research. They suggest that these new techniques will enable us to influence the kinds of people who are born. Indeed, the techniques are bracketed together under the opening observation that perhaps our time will be seen as 'the era when we became able to take control of our own biology, and in particular to take control of our own reproductive process' (p. 13).

But what are we supposedly taking control of? What is being reproduced? In many cultures of the world, a child is thought to embody the relationship between its parents and the relationships its parents have with other kin. The child is thus regarded as a social being, and what is reproduced is a set of social relations. At the least, the child reproduces parents' relational capacities in its own future capacity to make relations itself, as often indicated for instance in marriage rules. Yet the future that the Glover Report holds out to us, with its benign language of voluntarism and preference, is rather different. What is apparently at stake is the fate of human tissue, and what these techniques will reproduce is parental *choice*. The child will embody the desire of its parents to have a child.

Consequently, conflict of interest is expressed as a matter of who wants what. Hence, the brief discussion of donor anonymity turns on what the donating man 'wants' and whether or not the social parents will 'want' their family complicated by a relationship with the biological father (p. 24). Again, the question of surrogacy contracts turns on the couple 'wanting' the child to be healthy, 'wanting' to end the relationship with the surrogate mother (p. 69), and so on. In the language of desire, the question of rights turns on the right to fulfil what one wants, and in a much larger way that is the justification for the enabling technologies. They help persons to fulfil themselves.

This has for long been a significant if unremarkable cultural motivation, in both Britain and Europe, for having families. The point is that the kind of people on whose opinions the Glover Report drew now see themselves in a world that is developing technologies specifically to enable this desire. That potency can eclipse or summate the diversity of factors that lead to children being born. Hence the equation between reproduction and fertility: what is 'extended' is the choice to have children.

Extending the choice

I put it thus to draw attention to certain elements contained in such ways of presenting ourselves to ourselves. And to get away from the idea that these ideas about having children affect only the having of children. For there is a kind of tunnel vision to much of the discussion that assumes that all that is at issue is childbearing, and that the only people concerned are those who have personal problems to solve. However, I am not addressing the capacity of any of us to have or not have children, and nothing of what I say either approves or denigrates those whom the technologies aid. My direction is elsewhere.

By 'ourselves' I do not claim to speak on behalf of contemporary British society, but simply to identify myself with those who are exposed – whether they wish for it or not – to a range of ideas and images now in cultural currency. We do not have to be governed or preoccupied by such ideas in order to be aware of their significance; it is sufficient that they have been conceived, expressed and thus made available as vehicles for further ideas. The issue, then, is not whether these technologies are good or bad, but with how we should think them and how they will think us. The issue is the forms of thought they present through which we shall look on other aspects of human affairs, such as kin obligation, nurture, friendship and so forth.

Glover and his associates make a gesture in that direction: they state that the problems raised by the new reproductive technologies 'require a response by society as a whole' (Glover *et al.* 1989: 15). By this, they mean what framework of law should exist: how far 'should these decisions affecting the future of the family and affecting which people are born, be left to emerge from the decisions of individuals or couples, and how far should there be a deliberately planned public policy?' Society's intervention is thus thought of as endorsing public opinion in the form of policy measures, and the policies will be about parents and children ('the family' in their account is simply a parent-and-child group). Yet it is a rather narrow view of everything we might wish to think of as pertaining to society to bundle it all up in policy measures, as it is an extraordinarily impoverished view of culture to imagine that how we conceive of parents and children affects only parents and children.

Culture consists in the way analogies are drawn between things, in the way certain thoughts are used to think others. Culture consists in the images that make imagination possible, in the media with which we mediate experience. All the artefacts we make and the relationships we enter into have in that sense 'cultural' consequences, for they give form and shape to the way we think about other artefacts, other relationships. A simple example: the Report draws on a contrast between rigidity and flexibility in order to contrast two sets of opinion. Although we can imagine contexts where either quality might be preferable, built into the contrast is a preference for flexibility – extension is good for its own sake. The metaphor imparts a concreteness to the contrast between opinions. We draw on such metaphors all the time.

It is because we do this all the time that the issues here are serious. The new reproductive technologies (hereafter NRT) are presented as opening up reproductive options, indicating a vision of a biology under control, of families free to find their own form. However fantasized these images of future choice are, it is also the case that in the name of enlarging the possibilities of human fulfilment, techniques are refined, medical advice is given and we hold on to the hope that human beings will find benefit only from genetic engineering (see, for example, Ferguson 1990): a fantasia of options on the one hand and actual decisions being implemented on the other. However we look at it, procreation can now be *thought about* as subject to personal preference and choice in a way that has never before been conceivable. The child is literally – and in many cases, of course, joyfully – the embodiment of the act of choice.

Yet not just the children born by such techniques: so also those not born by them, and so also those not born at all. Glover *et al.* (1989) notice in passing: 'Not to make these choices will itself be a choice' (p. 56). They do not refer simply to the decision to have a child; by this stage in the Report they are referring to the future possibility of determining sex and other genetic characteristics.

Perhaps there is nothing remarkable about all this, except for one thing. Until now, it has been part of most of the indigenous cultural repertoires in Europe to see the domain of kinship, and what is called its biological base in procreation, as an area of relationships that provided a given baseline to human existence. Kin relations, like genetic makeup, were something we could not do anything about. More powerfully, when these relations were thought of as belonging to the domain of 'nature', nature also came to stand for everything that was immutable, that was intrinsic to persons or things, and as those essential qualities without which they would not be what they were. It is not just that kin relations were regarded as constructed out of natural materials, but that the connection between kinship and the natural facts of life symbolized immutability in social relations.

By now my point must be obvious. What do we do with the idea that a child embodied its parents' wishes, that families will find whatever form its members desire, that kinship might no longer be something one cannot do anything about? How will this all work as an analogy for other relationships? If until now kinship has been a symbol for everything that cannot be changed about social affairs, if biology has been a symbol for the given parameters of human existence, what will it mean for the way we construe any of our relationships with one another to think of parenting as the implementing of an option and genetic makeup as an outcome of cultural preference? How shall we think about what is inevitable and not really open to change in relationships, a question that bears on the perception of people's obligations and responsibilities towards each other?

Parents as customers of parenting services? Biology under control? Customers respond to a market, not to 'society'; biology under control is no longer 'nature'. Shall we find ourselves bereft of analogies – shall we no longer be able to 'see' nature, or 'see' society for that matter? For if kinship and procreation have been understood as belonging to a domain of nature, if nature has in turn symbolized what we have taken as inevitable constraints on the conduct of social life, then society by contrast has been thought about as human enterprise working on these givens, and thus a realm of endeavour carved *out of* the natural world. If the givens of our existence vanish, by what shall we measure enterprise? – I go ahead of myself. Let me remain with the fact that we now live in a world where, alongside whatever other thoughts we had about parent-child relations, must come the thought that the child ought to exist by choice. In this world the idea of choice is already embedded in a matrix of other analogies.

This matrix is the Enterprise Culture. As the Glover report to the European Commission indicates, it is a culture more widespread than the particular manifestations in Britain with which this book is chiefly concerned. Nevertheless, it is useful to draw on Keat's (1991) account of the British version.

The value given to preference and choice in decision-making over the NRT already reveals the workings of analogy on analogy. Those who seek assistance, we are told, are better thought of not as the disabled seeking alleviation or the sick seeking remedy – analogies that also come to mind – but as customers seeking services. The new technology, meanwhile, enables persons to achieve desires that they could not achieve unaided. However, a further enablement is required to take advantage of the services (cf. Pfeffer 1987): money is literally enabling of the enabling devices. We can think of these services not just as human enterprise being exerted on behalf of those who wish to be enterprising, but as a business that caters for those who will make a business out of being a family.

Yet there is something about the market analogy that is less than benign. It tends to collapse all other analogies into itself, the effect being rather like that of money itself which, in differentiating everything, makes itself the only source of difference. For instance, Keat refers to the collapse of the distinction between production and consumption when production is consumer-led and when consumption becomes a business itself. This reverses the normal order we imagine that production takes, that you first find out what can be sold and then make it. Yet more than reversal is at issue. What worked about the dialectic between productive consumption and consumptive production was that each term was a reference point for the other, a given point of departure, whereas what seems to characterize the present dispensation is that we are unwilling to cede such stable reference points because of the particular one that we privilege. The producer manufactures according to the consumer's choices, and the consumer purchases according to the choices the manufacturer lays out. Choice has become the privileged vantage from which to measure all action. Yet choice is by definition destabilizing, for it operates as much on whim as on judgement. That at least is the cultural vision.

Consumers and producers live alike by one another's choices. In fact, we could say that producers turn out the embodied choices of their customers, and consumers choose among the embodied choices of those who provide the services. We glimpse a world full of persons embodying the choices of others. Perhaps one day we shall find some way of being able to reproduce the choices without the bother of putting them into bodies.

The absurdity offers the real glimpse of a situation where choice might cease to be enablement. In fact, we could have made that connection long ago. If we are to look for what is 'rigid' about the enterprise culture, for what stifles enterprise, for the new givens of our existence, it lies in the hidden prescription that we *ought* to act by choice. This is not sophistry; it is a point of political concern.

Prescribing the choice

Not everyone has been tunnel-visioned about the NRT. Notable exceptions are found in the works of feminist scholars, and many of my observations simply remake observations already made (for a recent review, see Franklin and McNeill 1988). There is the question of prescriptive fertility, for instance, that accompanies what we could call prescriptive consumerism: that is, the idea that if you have the opportunity to enhance yourself you should take it. Feminists are aware of pressures put on persons to appear to be fulfilled in certain ways. For, in the enterprise culture, one's choices must always be self-enhancing, the catch being that the self and its enhancement will be recognized only if it takes specific forms.

Thus Pfeffer (1987) asks why, in the late twentieth century, personhood has become equated with the capacity to reproduce, almost to the point of the difference between the fertile and infertile becoming analogous to that between the donors and recipients of charity. New techniques of 'fertilization' do not remedy fertility as such, but childlessness; they enable a potential parent to have access to the fertility of others. A new divide between have and have-not is implied, in so far as technology has already opened up to personal choice the 'decision' to have children. The enterprising self, as Keat says, is not just one who is able to choose between alternative ways, but one who implements that choice through consumption (self-enhancement) and for whom there is, in a sense, no choice *not* to consume. Satisfaction is not in this rhetoric the absence of desire, but the meeting of desire. To imagine an absence of desire would be an affront to the means that exist to satisfy it.

The sense that one has no choice not to consume is a version of the feeling that one has no choice not to make a choice. Choice is imagined as the only source of difference: this is the collapsing effect of the market analogy. Like the Warnock Report (1985) before it, the Glover Report goes out of its way to comment on commercialization in transactions involving gametes. We can think of reasons why commerce is discouraged. Yet the point is surely that the market analogy has already done its work: we think so freely of the providing and purchasing of goods and services that transactions in gametes are already a thought-of act of commerce. All that rearguard action to protect the idea of the family from the idea of financial exploitation, to re-conceive such transactions as altruistic or acts of love or as real gifts between persons, are after the event – these ideas have no other ideas to fall back on. If kinship is to be an enterprise like anything else, then where are the relationships that will enable us to think of gamete donation as a gift? Glover *et al.* (1989: 88) say that in 'families and between friends, gifts are more common than sales'. But gifts pass between friends and kin precisely to indicate the non-transactable part of their relationship. With whatever nuance of taste or sentiment, one gives to express a solidarity or celebrate a relationship that, once in place, has no choice about it. If the idea of a gift sounds hollow or off-key in reference to gamete transfer, it is because the enterprise culture provides many more and readier ways of thinking about a calculating self.

Enterprise culture

Prescriptive consumerism dictates that there is no choice but always to exercise choice; its other side is prescriptive marketing. Culture is being 'enterprised-up'.

I was once – naively – appalled on meeting a colleague (from another profession admittedly) who cheerfully admitted being on the way to the library in order to 'scholar up' a paper, to add the references that would make it look scholarly. Naively, because I had imagined scholarship was in the nature of the product. Now, in exercising their choices, consumers are concerned both with product identity and with product identification. The exercise of choice that defines the active citizen is market choice, not just because of the kinds of rules of the game associated with free bargaining or an equation between enterprising selves and business enterprises, but because the market deals in things that have been marketed. That is, they are designed for selling, made to specifications that anticipate consumer wants, presenting back to the consumer 'choice' in the form of a range of products out of which 'choice' can visibly be made. To choose responsibly, our active citizen must know what is being offered, much of this knowledge being filtered through appearance: things must look what they are supposed to be. Apples must look like apples.

We might say they have to be appled-up: varieties selected for marketing are those that have the most apple-like qualities. Qualities essential to the realization of choice become displaced, as it were, from the product onto what is presented for the consumer's discrimination.

Marketed products are quality-enhanced. Quality is not there to be discovered: those attributes that define things are made explicit, even superadded, in the course of the marketing process. Marketing does much of the selection for you, and consumer activism is generally in the area of greater determination over what the producer claims to present. So we select for quality where quality means both an innate characteristic – firmness, taste – and an enhanced version – unblemished flesh, shiny skin. The term 'quality' has always had this ambiguity. But the marketing of products forces an interesting collapse of its two senses. The natural, innate property and the artificial, cultural enhancement become one. To select an apple for its appleness is to discriminate between those that conform more and those that conform less to cultural expectations about what the natural apple should be. Glover *et al.* (1989) raise the question of whether handicapped people and those born with physical blemish can have a totally fulfilled life.

There is a little more at stake here than one might think. This is not a new essentialism but a collapse of the difference between the essential and the superadded. The market*ed* apple is 'the apple and a bit more', that is, a fruit that will attract the consumer for its appleness. What is collapsed is the difference between what is taken for granted in the nature of the product and what is perceived to be the result of extra human effort. Nature marketed is neither nature nor culture.

Although in referring to apples I have, so to speak, natured-up my example, the same point can be made with respect to manufactured articles, for whether utilitarian or luxury their qualities are enhanced by the efforts of advertiser and marketeer. Indeed, they are not 'marketable' without 'extra' attention being drawn to their 'inherent' characteristics. It is of some further significance that what we take as the domain that stands for what is natural, inherent and so forth in human affairs is not immune from an elision of a similar kind.

Among various models for human affairs that have held sway over the last two hundred years has been a distinction between the taken-for-granted in human relationships and the culturally constructed, between the natural individual and the society that socializes it into its own mould. This is one of many such binarisms that have moulded the development of social science and is arguably where our model of enterprise comes from – its natural parents, if you like. In this model, human beings are enterprising creatures who 'construct' and make what they will 'out of' the givens of existence and environmental constraints. We would thus contrast enterprise, that is, culture or society in the twentieth-century sense, endless variety testifying to an endless ingenuity, with other factors that appear given, immutable, universal, of which biological reproduction, like sexual difference, has until now been a prime example.

The contrast between human ingenuity (enterprise) and natural constraints is replicated in microcosm in European thinking about kinship. Anthropologists in the European tradition argue that there are many different ways in which cultures enterprisingly construct families and type of kin relations, but of course human beings everywhere are dealing with the same raw material, the facts of nature: of procreation, childbirth and a finite life span. This is roughly where Western social science theorizing is at. Every book with the sub-title 'the social or cultural construction of' teases away at the fundamental distinction between cultural enterprise and natural givens. The same model can be replicated within culture. Hence, one may analyse ideology as the cultural construction of other cultural values; or what one knows at one level to be an outcome of social arrangement, at another level one apprehends as a constraint. The English have always pitted against all the opportunities of an enterprising career or life-course the givens of class and childhood background, symbolized in the immutability of kin connections.

To enterprise (vb) kinship is to touch on an area of central significance to the English (and also no doubt British and European) idea of what enterprise is all about. It collapses the idea of culture as human enterprise working against or out of nature. One will no longer think one can do nothing about the sex of one's children, about birth abnormalities and about the characteristics they will inherit, any more than one will be able to regard one's own endowment as a matter of fate. One's fate will be to put up with the results of other persons' enterprises.

There is a footnote here about the fate of a subject such as anthropology, in so far as anthropology has prided itself on its own enterprise in uncovering other people's cultures as enterprises. It uncovers what people take for granted and shows them for the cultural artefacts they are, revealing other people's naturalisms as cultural constructs. Bit of a facer, then, to find oneself in a culture that is becoming cultured-up, that is, where it is not substantive products or values that are marketed but the activity of producing value itself – where what a culture values of itself is its own enterprise.

Disembodied choice

Let me end with an allegory for the reproduction of choice without body, of a culture that is all enterprise. It comes from a suggestion promoted by Howard (1988). His idea is that anthropologists, as the writers of ethnographies and the analysers of societies, should take advantage of new technology already available. The offspring of this new technology would be the hypertext.

Hypertext is produced by hypermedia – multimedia computer programming that 'allows a user to use a variety of pathways through nested information', so that a reader of hypertext 'is constantly presented with branches of information to explore and must make a series of choices while [so] exploring' (Howard 1988: 305). Hypertext is designed to be read on a screen interactively – a prospect that quite carries the author away. He imagines an ethnographic account of a wedding:

> Let me take a hypothetical example. A reader/viewer might be presented with a pictorial scene from a wedding. . . One button will play a movie of the scene so that the reader can watch the ceremony performed, complete with audio. Having watched the movie, one could then examine the event as a series of stills, and explore the information nested under [a bank of] buttons. Clicking on a button attached to a person would bring up to

the screen a set of new buttons, each labeled according to the kinds of information nested beneath it. One button might bring up the individual's genealogy, with information about how she is related to the bride and groom. . . Another button might bring up a short biography, sketching her personal history. Within this sketch might be additional buttons leading to more detailed information, about specific roles this person plays, her achievements, responses to psychological tests, etc. Still another button might bring up a written text of things the person said during the ceremony; by clicking on specific words in the text a dictionary entry might be activated, or another button might bring up an exegesis illuminating the significance of a phrase, or other aspects of word usage. Yet another button might present an inventory of the contributions in materials and labor the person made to the event, with each item connecting to information about the nature of the items (pp. 306–7).

The parallels with the social world of the enterprise culture are evident.

First, all the information is on a par. Although clumps of it are nested, one can apparently make pathways anywhere. Secondly, it makes evident that it is not relationships internal to the material that are being exposed, but the activity of the connecting mind that pushes the button that makes the pathways that makes the connections. Thirdly, the apparent choice is an illusion, for two reasons. (a) The reader *has* to push the button; he or she can only make a choice. You cannot spill coffee on this text, or glance back at an earlier chapter, or suspend judgement, or just let it wash over you: you have to interact with the thing. (b) The choices are someone else's, the author's prior pathways; because the author has selected and nested the information, the reader's choices are made against the background of the author's prior ones. Nonetheless, Howard (1988: 309) presents as a further 'choice' the ability of the reader to decide whether to explore information according to his/her own interests or to be guided through pre-structured pathways.

However, this last instruction throws up an assumption written into the vision of hypertext that makes it fall short of complete enterprise. It rather quaintly takes for granted that the information about the wedding exists as an extraneous datum: that is, as the body of data *about which* writer and reader are so enterprising. It is this given that allows the writer to have a creative time getting to work on the analysis of the wedding; while to the reader the nests and selections are a further given datum, and he or she has a creative time finding his or her own pathways through the information.

> The media would permit multiple relationships between textual materials and interpretation, and since so much more textual material could be included, there would be less reason to be selective. . . . A much wider range of materials could be accommodated, including those that did not particularly interest the ethnographer but might be of central concern to some readers (p. 307).

All the materials in the world!

One's mind reels at the possibilities. Until, of course, one realizes what enterprise really means. If there is nothing that is not created by choice, one has to take away the given status of the materials themselves. Take away the independence of the background against which the choices are made. Suppose the wedding were organized *for* the multimedia.

If the couple have any cultural finesse they will be making their own hypertext. Not an album of photographs, but a computer programme in which they will be able to relive various pathways through their wedding day, depending on the preference of the moment. In fact, they may well plan the occasion with multiple interpretations in mind, think about the alternatives they will be able to present later to themselves, in short, make choices on their wedding day that they can re-live as choices when they push the programme buttons. One's own pre-selected selections? Not much enterprise left for the future after all.

This chapter was intended as an exercise in cultural caricature – drawing attention to features through exaggeration. By the same token, the very idea of enterprise comes to seem a caricature of individual endeavour. The enterprise culture may well find it has not reproduced enterprise. The chances are that a culture that *thinks* itself enterprising will simply reproduce more and more technologies for its marketable reproduction.

Note: Chapter 10

Following the conference at Lancaster, a version of this chapter was published in *Cambridge Anthropology*, and I am grateful for permission to draw on it here. My thanks to the editors for their advice, and to Russell Keat and Nigel Rapport for clarifications. Some of the points are amplified by the author in a longer work: *After Nature: English Kinship in the Late Twentieth Century*, Cambridge University Press (forthcoming).

References: Chapter 10

Ferguson, M. W. J. 1990. Contemporary and future possibilities for human embryonic manipulation. In A. Dyson and J. Harris (eds), *Experiments on Embryos*. London: Routledge.

Franklin, S. and McNeill, M. 1988. Review essay: recent literature and current feminist debates on reproductive technologies. *Feminist Studies*, 14, 3: 545–60.

Glover, J. *et al.* 1989. *Fertility and the Family. The Glover Report on Reproductive Technologies to the European Commission*. London: Fourth Estate.

Howard, A. 1988. Hypermedia and the future of anthropology. *Cultural Anthropology*, 3, 3: 304–15.

Keat, R. 1991. Introduction: starship Britain or universal enterprise? In R. Keat and N. Abercrombie (eds), *Enterprise Culture*. London: Routledge.

Pfeffer, N. 1987. Artificial insemination, in-vitro fertilisation and the stigma of fertility. In M. Stanworth (ed.), *Reproduction Technologies*. Oxford: Polity Press.

Warnock, M. 1985. *A Question of Life: The Warnock Report on Human Fertilisation and Embryology*. Oxford: Blackwell.

11 The personal right to identity: a polemic on the self in the enterprise culture

ANTHONY P. COHEN

'Thatcherism' does not have a body of thought sufficiently coherent and consistent to justify its description as a 'philosophy'. The contributors to the Lancaster conference on 'The Values of the Enterprise Culture' showed that, on issues as disparate as those of economic theory and theological influence, Thatcherism is an eccentrically hybrid beast. Rather than a set of logically related propositions, there are rhetorical devices and slogans. The *Enterprise Culture* is one such; and, indeed, the existence of an 'enterprise culture' in contemporary Britain is evident only in its axiomatic assertion. Central to this rhetoric is that of 'the individual'. Thus, we find predicated upon this rhetoric such notions as individual responsibility, individual initiative, individual freedom, even a deconstructionist atomism that denies the very existence of 'society' in favour of its individual components. The individual is projected as the object of government action – to which is opposed the collectivist state.

This is a paradoxical opposition, since the state is the political and legal instrument of government policy. While Thatcherite rhetoric abhors the state, the Thatcher government has also vastly augmented its power. The state now routinely intervenes in areas of policy (curriculum and educational philosophy; broadcasting practice; moral conduct and religious life) in which it had previously appeared to tread lightly, except, perhaps, in times of exceptional national crisis.

The paradox is instructive because it appears to parallel another, which it also explains. The enterprising, personally responsible, free individual, vaunted by the government, stands on the wreckage of the *self*-conscious, self-directing idosyncratic individual who resists conformity, rejects the social categories that provide the basis of marketing and planning strategy, the individual who assimilates to herself/himself the classifying and homogenising devices of the mass society rather than the other way around. This autonomous individual is the victim of the privilege accorded in Thatcherite practice to economic power: sacrificed to economies of scale; made contemptible not only by economic weakness, but by a refusal to conform to a *regimented*, and therefore, bogus individualism. The integrity of this individual is dismissively impugned ('wet'), for she/he is 'not one of us'. The individual of Thatcherite rhetoric is the creature of an authoritarian view of the self. To it may be opposed the autonomous *self*-directing, 'authorial' self.

'Individualism' has long been the hackneyed and rather abused term employed by writers to characterize English society. Lukes (1973) showed cogently that the word has very discrepant meanings in different philosophical traditions. Applied to England, it may refer to liberation from ideological, dogmatic or other coercive orthodoxies (Morris 1987), or to the obligation on men to forge their own economic destinies without the support that elsewhere may be drawn from the practice of partible inheritance (MacFarlane 1978). It has been used metonymically to describe the value of domestic privacy (see Strathern, in press) and, jurisprudentially, to refer to a doctrine of legalistic egalitarianism.   It has been deployed to emphasize the ego-centred nature of bilateral kinship and cognatic descent systems, which are allegedly typical of Britain (see, for example, Fox 1965), as well as to refer to a spurious 'freedom of conscience', which has been simultaneously promulgated as a principle and denigrated as a practice by conservative opinion, without apparent embarrassment at the contradiction.

To these various constructions of individualism may be juxtaposed the idea of *individuality*. If this exists at all, it is either as a class-specific value, reserved to those who have the rights of birth or 'achievement' (however defined) to 'be themselves'. Opposed to this rather limited notion of meritocratic or eccentric individuality is the anonymous, individuality-denying working-class terrace or tower block, the union 'mass' meeting, the package tour, the queue for the stalls, the indiscriminate spaces of the 'public' bar and the football terrace. The tabloid compulsion to stereotyping in Britain clouds our perception of, and even impugns other people's claims to, individuality.

The confusion of 'individualism' (as a doctrine of economic activity) with 'individuality' (as a defence of autonomy and personal discretion) is related to a profound chauvinism in English discourse. Its origins can be only a matter of speculation, but it is apparent in the (imperial) *self* and (native) *other* discriminations of British colonialism and, later, of British social anthropology. But this discrimination may have itself been founded upon an earlier and deeply rooted class chauvinism that reserved intellect, sensitivity and self-awareness to the superior orders and denied them to the plebeian others. In literature, drama, historiography and political theory, individuals belong to the upper and middle classes; the rest form a virtually undifferentiated mass from which only the most exceptional may ever become singularly recognizable. It required the exceptional insight and skill of a Dickens or a Tressell to make working-class self-consciousness and personal distinctiveness intelligible and acceptable.

But the more recent history of the individual in popular discourse seems to have become even bleaker. To be elevated above the anonymous ranks of the tabloid society, one would seem to have to demonstrate exceptionality of a questionable kind: to have made or lost a fortune; to be peculiarly gifted at hitting balls with any of a variety of implements; to have had unusual sexual liaisons; perhaps to have an unconventional manner of speech or personal conduct. And even such exceptional people are liable to find themselves reduced, by ridicule or denigration, to the ranks at the earliest opportunity – as if they have somehow jeopardized a sacred equilibrium by being noticed or noticeable.

It is for historians and social philosophers to locate the origins of such anti-individuality, but the preponderance of such an ethos during the era of the putative 'enterprise culture' is self-evident. The 'freedom' of the individual now has about it the peculiar scent of nineteenth-century utilitarian liberalism, in which one was free to work or not to work – that is to say, free to eat or to starve. In Thatcherite Britain, one is now 'free' to choose between private and public health care, schooling and housing – a freedom that takes little account of the empirical circumstances of the individual who may be the beneficiary of such largesse. The reform of the social benefit system has left young people 'free' to choose between what may well be an inadequate or exploitative youth training placement, and a home in a cardboard box on London's South Bank.

The speciousness of this freedom is not wholly attributable to the politics of Thatcherism. Geoffrey Robertson shows, in his authoritative *Freedom, The Individual and the Law* (1989), that even the legalistic protection of individual rights in Britain hovers somewhere between the rudimentary and the non-existent. What should astonish us is not just the paucity of the freedoms enjoyed by the individual, but our banal complacency about it. More often than not, its assertion in political debate elicits the smug 'Any Questions' response: 'I suppose people are better off in the Soviet Union?' To be fair, this is a formula more frequently trotted out as an informed defence of apartheid in South Africa – but perhaps that is because we are so little aware of the tenuous nature of individual freedom in Great Britain – and this enhanced, perhaps wilful, unconsciousness is indeed one of Thatcherism's triumphs.

My concern here is not with freedoms under the law, or under the economic and political regimes, but with the most fundamental of *personal* freedoms, the right to selfhood or to the authorial identity. Of course, the possibility of an absolute freedom in these terms is spurious. We are named at birth, and are thereby entailed. We may subsequently be nicknamed and thereby have attributed to us a character that is none of our own doing and against which we may feel powerless to react (see, for example, Pitt-Rivers 1972; Cohen 1987). We are typed and labelled in a plethora of ways, all or most of which may be quite beyond our capacity to prevent. However, that is not to say that these imposed identities displace our own self-consciousness, for all that they may constrain it. My complaint is that in the social sciences, as in life, we have allowed ourselves to be dazzled by the labels and the processes of labelling, and have lost sight of our interest in the individual's *self*-perception. Whether or not the label sticks, the individual thus labelled may have a view of herself/himself that is not consonant with it. It is this *self*-perception that then motivates and informs her/his subsequent behaviour, *not* that of the labeller, from whose supposed vantage point it is usually described and explained.

The individual in the putative enterprise culture is thus an attenuated creature, limited both by the discourse of generalization and
by the matrix of economic individual*ism* on which this kind of
enterprise would appear to be predicated. It is difficult to see
how the doctrine of the profit-motive could be reconciled with
a view of the self-directing individual. Of course, an individual
may be both self-aware and driven by profit-seeking. But the
use of the profit-motive in Thatcherite economic policy (as, for
example, in privatization and contracting-out schemes) appears to
be a manifestation of a naive belief in stimulus–response theory, in
which the stimulus of profit and fear of failure induce the response
of competitiveness. In this view, the self adopts a maximizing
persona, which is imprinted on all entrepreneurs – from the oppor-
tunistic academic to the punter who cashes in his water shares
for a quick profit and a fortnight in the sun. In practice, the
entrepreneurial self and the authorial self are not mutually exclusive
– precisely because the motivations of the former are far more
complex than their representation in Thatcherite theory. People do
not respond simply and unambiguously to the tempting carrots of
base (or debased) self-interest: hence the widespread dissatisfaction
with the poll tax, even among many people who may benefit from
it financially. (It should be noted that the 1990 local election results,
which increased the Conservative vote in the London boroughs
of Ealing, Wandsworth and Westminster, were aberrant when
compared with those throughout the rest of the country, and
have been attributed to other local factors.) Thatcherite economy-
management operates on the assumption of a grotesquely simplistic
notion of causality: offer people high interest rates, and they will
stop spending their money; offer them lower taxes, and they will
spend the additional cash on home-produced goods; offer them
productivity deals, and they will work harder; offer them lower
local authority rates, and they will vote Conservative. It is a
depiction of the individual whose self-direction has been beaten
into dust by the reflex hammer of self-gratification.

Yet, the talk is of the individual and of personal freedom. If
they are not all the products of artifice and/or stupidity, how
can these contradictions be explained? The answer may lie in a
kind of credulousness that fails to distinguish between theoretical
construction and empirical pragmatics. The former is a view of

the individual as essentially simplistic and typical; the latter, one of profound complexity and disparity. There are at least three such theoretical constructions that surface repeatedly in the Thatcher canon. The first is one which varies between 'human nature', 'the British People', and Judaeo-Christians (see Raban 1989). It attributes self-seeking as a species-trait to individuals and justifies it so long as it is exercised within a particular cultural code. The second construes behaviour in terms of a stipulated conscious motive, thus defining as unnecessary the *investigation* of motivation. The rhetoric of the mandate thus attributes a certain kind of political intention to voting – in the absence of evidence for it. It is a very Hobbesian notion: that people *consciously* make a contract with each other to satisfy to the optimal extent their individual interests – although this consciousness may be a mere figment of the observer's imagination. With it goes an Oakeshottian suspicion of collectivity and organization. Individuals-as-atoms present much less of a problem to conservative doctrine than individuals-in-composite bodies. The third is the attitude that too much thinking is bad for people: they really want to be told what to do; or, at least, to be told what alternative courses of action they may choose. They may like the idea of a menu, but would like it all the more if the range of choice is not too great. They may like best of all when they are told, 'There is no alternative.'

But it would be absurd to lay all the blame for the subversion of self at the door of Thatcherism. It has been a long time with us, not least in our popular conceptualization of the person as the child of its parents and the 'representative' of its social groups and categories. There is nothing peculiarly British about a 'social' view of the person. It is to be found, in different forms and with differing emphases, throughout the world. These cultural doctrines of personhood have been constituted in social anthropology as theories of the self: of the self as 'licensed' by culture and as determined by the principles of the social structure, in any given society. The individual has thus been represented as a reflex of corporate group, of lineage, of kinship and descent ideology, and so forth. Sociology has dealt with the individual with even less subtlety by deploying the notion of 'role' to refer to the atomic unit of society. In most social science approaches to identity, the individual (or group) is depicted simply as a contingent *ego* to some *alter*: as if identity consisted in mutual contradefinition to the exclusion of a self-directedness (see Boon 1982). Indeed, the entire sociological school of 'symbolic interactionism' was founded on the premise of the individual symbolizing herself/himself *in interaction with others*, a view that has continued to inform the study of ethnicity for more than twenty years.

But, in contrast to these perceptions of the individual, both legal and lay discourse in Britain treats the individual in an apparently contradictory fashion, as 'personally responsible'. The paradox may be resolved by interpreting 'personal responsibility' in terms of obligations to one's putative group rather than to oneself. Breaking the law is an offence 'against' society which, as Hegel argued in *Philosophy of Right* ([1820] 1942), requires society itself to 'negate its negation'. 'Cowardice in the face of the enemy', or deserting the House team, are treated less as matters of failing just oneself than as 'letting the side down' – failing others. Marrying out of one's religion, or class, or ethnic group, may be depicted as an act of social betrayal rather than of the free, autonomous self. Indeed, pleading a personal right to self-direction may be dismissed as 'self-indulgence'. In every respect it would seem that the self is subordinated. The 'responsible individual' on whose shoulders rests the whole weight of enterprise ideology is required to exercise that responsibility in very particular ways; or, at least, is required to refrain from practising it in ways that do not conform to the principles of acquisitive conservatism. Scholarship and the arts have now, somehow, to be productive of some material benefit. Personal discretion – on, say, whether to support the poll tax or to buy private health insurance – can only be exercised in specified ways if it is not to reveal a deficiency of personal responsibility. The individual is thus strapped into an ideological straitjacket in which she/he is the replicate of an idealized player in the market game: everyone plays the *same* game, everyone wants the same things, everyone thus shares the same values, responds to the same stimuli, observes the rules of the game.

In his classic essay, 'Post-liberal democracy' (1964), C. B. Macpherson showed the difference between the nineteenth-century theory of laissez-faire capitalism, in which producers were disciplined and constrained by the market, and the modern economy, in which competition is largely a fiction, in which markets are managed either by international monopoly capital, by speculators, or by government intervention. In this form of enterprise, the consumer does *not* dictate what goods come on to the market and at what price. Rather, she/he consumes what is made available by producers at a price largely of their own choosing (cf. Speier, 1969). Conditions may have changed since Macpherson published his essay, but surely not in favour of the individual? The political market is similarly curtailed. We choose from a limited range of options, and are told that whatever emanates from government is the product of *our* will.

This pernicious combination of economic and political market management has left us in the invidious condition of being persuaded to experience and express *our* selves by wearing some designer's labels, by drinking *their* coffee, driving *their* cars. Manufacturing entrepreneurs were quick off the mark in associating mass production and mass marketing with the 'massification' of the individual. In order to entice me to consume *their* products as an expression of *my* identity, they create an entire persona for me: I am Sony-man, or Mitsubishi-man, perhaps both together. If I opt not to conform to their inventory, I am treated merely as having swopped one stereotype for another, labelled 'alternative', which will itself soon enough be colonized by the mainstream market. In this manipulative strategy, style replaces the self.

I have to confess that I am style-illiterate: I am aware only that I am seeing it if somebody tells me. Rather than seeing style, I see individuals. Would it be presuming too much to suggest that that is true of most people, and that therein lies the fallacy of the manipulative strategy? The people who are most persuaded by it are those who invent and practise it: marketers, planners, tabloid journalists and politicians. The assumptions they make that other people think with their categories may simply be naive, a naivety evident in the clumsy inaccuracies and inappropriateness of so much policy and planning. Who, besides them, can be satisfied with or have any interest in the reduction of complex, self-conscious individuals to mere categories? Anonymity and typicality is in the eye of the *beholder*. We have privileged that eye and neglected the *beholden*. In doing so, we risk committing their error in ignoring self-consciousness or defining it out of existence.

It has to be admitted that social anthropology, the most sensitive of the social sciences, has itself long succumbed to a similar fallacy: ethnographically manipulating individuals into analytic categories that are continually confounded by the complexities of reality. We may often be reluctant to concede that the error does lie with our categories, and instead tend to blame the (mis-)categorized for their aberrant behaviour. Social and management policy have been conducted in a similar manner. If employees behave too much like individuals and too little like company or organization members, management practice treats them like a pathology to be corrected. 'Step up the daily dose of corporate culture and stop the rot!' It is curious that we seem inclined to recognize the individual only in exceptional circumstances – those of obvious pathology or abnormal achievement – *as if we oppose 'normality' to individuality*. Perhaps that is an indication of the extent to which selfhood has been lost. But our growing awareness of the inadequacies of our customary practice, borne in on us in recent years by an efflorescence of critiques and experimental genres, may also serve to alert us to the self-denying tendencies of contemporary society and to the irony of their exaggeration in the so-called 'enterprise culture'.

I do not advocate here a view of the autonomous, free-floating individual. That would be absurd. My emphasis, rather, is on the individual who, despite all the subversion of individuality nevertheless retains the reflexes of self-awareness and self-consciousness; and who, despite the apparent uniformity of behaviour, cannot be reduced to type or category because that very uniformity may well mask vital differences of meaning. I do not underestimate the philosophical difficulties of rehabilitating the self in social (and especially in anthropological) analysis. I am also aware that I am conflating a number of concepts in this argument – self, individual and person – whose discriminations have been the object of much academic endeavour. These are matters both of semantics and substance, with which I have been trying to deal elsewhere, and I hope they may not divert us from my present central point, in relation to the enterprise culture, which is how we are to take account of the self-conscious individual or the 'authorial' self. How are we to demonstrate that there is, or that there may be, a clash between our constructions (anthropological and lay) of other people, and their own perceptions of themselves? How are we to incorporate our own experience of this contradiction into our understanding of other people? If *we* cannot progress on this, we cannot hope that anyone else will. I emphasize that this is not just an academic and methodological issue, because our own practice has mimicked that of people in far more powerful positions than we occupy, and therefore offers a heuristic for the analysis of the consequences of their operations. We have proceeded inexorably from the supposed invisibility or inaccessibility of self to its denial, by subordinating it to some 'social' construction. We have thereby denied the individual. In so far as our explanatory models have denied people their own selves, we have left ourselves free to supply their reasons for them: we have constructed them in the images of our own theoretical rationalizations. Of course, we may even have constructed their own putative self-consciousness in this way. We invent people, and are then stumped when our fictions turn out to be confounded in practice. Acknowledging self-consciousness or self-direction does not preclude the possibility of this kind of error, because we are still left with the difficulties of eliciting 'self', and we have also to recognize that looking for it may itself be tantamount to an invention. Nevertheless, we do require this discipline, not least in order that we become alert to the fictionalizing dangers of our over-generalized models, and those with which those other, more powerful people operate.

We can only speculate about the extent and nature of people's resistance to categorization. However, there is ample evidence that people are fighting back in a struggle for identities that are more sensitive to themselves. Anthropologists can hardly be surprised by the tenor of these campaigns. We know well that the higher the societal plane on which identity is based, the more generalized the identity, the flabbier, less eloquent, more contentious it is. Tribe is vacuous relative to clan, clan to lineage, lineage to segment and household, and so on. From this perspective we can see that statehood *and* nationality are insubstantial as premises of identity. Are we again going to misread people so badly as to treat the disintegration of the Soviet bloc as simply a matter of nationalisms, as if there were nothing more fundamental? How then would we explain the *intra*-national, intra-*sectarian* divisions within Israel, Sri Lanka, Peru, Armenia, Afghanistan, Northern Ireland, diasporic Islam, British Anglicanism, and so

on? Of course we could fall back on such old warhorses as ethnicity, religious and linguistic sectarianism, regionalism, doctrinal
factionalism, and so forth, but this would merely be to replicate the
same kind of self-denying or self-neglecting generalization, albeit at
an inferior level. People's attachment to collectivities is mediated
by their *personal* experience. *We* know that about ourselves; we
have to try to incorporate that knowledge into our understanding
of others.

Everywhere people are reappropriating their identities or are
creating them anew, whether as ethnicity, locality or whatever.
They may use shared *forms* in this process of reassertion, but we
should not mistake these for *uni*formities or orthodoxies of identity.
Like all symbols, these forms may be regarded as expedient means
of expression, not to be confused with the *substance* of expression.
These forms are motivated in their own, idiosyncratic ways by
individuals. It is, after all, a self-aware, self-conscious individual
who steps onto the commuter train. If the best we can do ethnographically for this person is to categorize him or her as 'a
commuter', we shall not be doing any better than Mrs Thatcher,
for whom 'free' individuals are cloned by the market, or else are
aberrant nuisances.

At the risk of exaggeration, I would suggest that the issue of
personal identity might be brought into appropriately prominent
focus by invoking the metaphor of 'personal rights'. Our attention
has customarily been concentrated on *rites* of identity, such as
initiation, through which individuals are regarded as being led
into approved social constructions of the person. But this focus
neglects the fraught and agonizing clash between a person's sense
of self and the identity imposed on him/her. The notion of identity
as a personal right may seem obscure, or stretch implausibly the
category of 'rights'. In anthropology, as in other pertinent disciplines, 'rights' appears to imply either an issue of legal concern,
or the integrity of the person or group in relation to the state
or to some other duly constituted authority. Identity does not fit
obviously into these boxes. A recent survey of anthropological
literature on human rights is divided into nearly seventy classes,
from 'The concept of the primitive' to 'Indigenous peoples' water
rights' and 'Bridewealth, dowry death and suttee' – but it does not
include 'identity' (Downing and Kushner 1988). We might conclude

that it is simply improper to speak of identity as a human right; or that identity is not seen as being a pressing matter of concern (perhaps because it is not regarded as subject to abuse); or, by contrast, that we have overly emphasized the legalistic criterion of the category 'rights'.

The last suggestion would seem to be most worth pursuing. There is little doubt that, if a state explicitly interfered in, curtailed, or in other ways threatened a person's identity – say, by interrogation, in a penal regime, even through the peculiar disciplines of the armed forces – this *would* be seen as a matter of the abuse of rights and liberties. Goffman's 'total institution' (cf. Goffman 1968), if one such existed, would surely command the attention of civil liberties groups. I am therefore led to the odd conclusion that it is only in the breach that identity is regarded as an issue of rights. This must be unsatisfactory. Further, there is no obvious reason why 'rights' should be reserved as a matter of legal definition. 'Right' is a common topic of popular discourse, argued out over the kitchen table (in relation to domestic and family obligations) at least as much as in court or legislature. It would be unacceptable to dismiss the first as semantically improper because of its verbal confusion with the second.

The 'right to identity' is a sensitive and subtle matter, and that is perhaps one reason why it has previously been dealt with more adequately by novelists than by social scientists. What has the academic literature to put against John Ellison's *The Man who Cried I Am*, or Paul Bailey's *Gabriel's Lament?* Anthropologists may well be inclined to argue that the subject is concerned with social relations rather than with the individual. But it is precisely in our rendering of social relationships that we underprivilege the sense and definitions of themselves that individuals take into their social relationships, and we therefore render them inadequately. In treating identity as simply contingent or relational, we privilege A's version of B over B's version of B, and very often disregard the latter altogether as being either irrelevant or methodologically inaccessible.

Further, identity is an expression of difference. By failing to accommodate it, we are complicit in that very denial of difference on which the enterprise culture's fraudulent notion of individualism is based. We ourselves become part of the processes of homogenization and 'creolisation' (Hannerz 1987) that we describe and document. If public discourse and policy planning are ever to be rescued from the grotesque simplifications (with their grotesque consequences) in which our masters and mistresses indulge and pleasure themselves, then the primacy of difference has to be placed very firmly on the agenda. They will continue, as always, to dismiss difference as eccentric, or to reduce it to such gross categories as ethnicity, class, or region. We have to insist that difference is a matter of consciousness, not of official recognition – indeed, of *self*-consciousness. The trampling of individual identity is replicated at more macrosocial levels in the trampling of ethnic, religious, tribal, linguistic, gender and other group identities. The dismissibility of identity is a basic enabler of so much that is destructive in social and economic process, from the felling of the rain forest to the 'touristification' of other cultures. Conservation itself has become one of those many things which *we* do to or for *others*. It is not self-indulgent to suggest that the assertion, protection, conservation of our *selves* is a prerequisite for our more 'selfless' activities. This may look dangerously like a Thatcherite prescription to 'look after Number One'. It is not. It is, rather, a plea to recognize the shallowness of the model of self on which Thatcherite enterprise is based, and to be alert to the dangers inherent in our own academic practice of validating it.

On the one (Thatcherite) hand, the individual is a performing self – a person recognizable from the dominant traditions of western social science. We cannot see the actor (since we say that she/he is methodologically out of reach), so we settle for the script, which we invent ourselves through our ingenious use of categories. In our fantasy 'enterprise culture', we have invented the selfish self and neglected the self-conscious self. On the other hand, there is the individual who is an authorial self, an almost silent voice whispering against the winds of political discourse (and socioanthropological analysis), '*I* am still here, but you can't hear me because you *won't* hear me. But you could – if you would!' It is my conviction in the dogged survival of this insistent voice that persuades me that Thatcherism is wrong about individualism; that social scientists have been wrong in treating personal and collective identity as simply the products of social relativities.

We have to make deliberate efforts to begin to understand the subtleties, inflections and varieties of individual thought that are concealed by the categorical masks we invent so adeptly. The denial of self to the people over whom power is exercised can render them defenceless. We may be attuned academically and politically to recognizing this among those selves whom we categorize as vulnerable. But will we recognize it when the Big Bang eventually fizzles out into the exhausted whimper, and shirt-sleeved market-makers swop their hot screens for the occupational therapist's raffia? Will we say, 'they were broken by the pressures of the international economy'? Or, that they were broken by the pressures we created for them, of having to be 'yuppies' with a recognizable life-style, from dockland flat to designer stubble, and within which they were finally unable to recognize themselves and found that they had lost their right to be themselves, had lost their right to identity?

References: Chapter 11

Boon, J. A. 1982. *Other Tribes, Other Scribes: Symbolic Anthropology in the Comparative Study of Cultures, Histories, Religions and Texts*. Cambridge: Cambridge University Press.

Cohen, A. P. 1987. *Whalsay: Symbol, Segment and Boundary in a Shetland Island Community*. Manchester: Manchester University Press.

Downing, T. E. and Kushner, G. 1988. *Human Rights and Anthropology*. Cambridge Mass.: Cultural Survival Inc.

Fox, R. 1965. Prolegomenon to the study of British kinship. In J. R. Gould (ed.), *Penguin Survey of the Social Sciences*. Harmondsworth: Penguin, pp. 128–43.

Goffman, E. 1968. *Asylums*. Harmondsworth: Penguin.

Hannerz, U. 1987. The world as creolisation. *Africa*, 57, 4: 546–59.

Hegel, G. W. F. [1820] 1942. *Philosophy of Right*, tr. T. M Knox. Oxford: Clarendon Press.

Lukes, S. 1973. *Individualism*. Oxford: Blackwell.

MacFarlane, A. 1978. *The Origins of English Individualism*. Oxford: Blackwell.

Macpherson, C. B. 1964. Post-liberal democracy. *Canadian Journal of Economics and Political Science*, 30, 4: 485–98.

Morris, C. 1987. *The Discovery of the Individual, 1050–1200*. Toronto: University of Toronto Press.

Pitt-Rivers, J. 1972. *People of the Sierra*. Chicago: Chicago University Press.

Raban, J. 1989. *God, Man and Mrs Thatcher*. London: Chatto & Windus.

Robertson, G. 1989. *Freedom, the Individual and the Law*. Harmondsworth: Penguin.

Speier, H. 1969. The worker turning bourgeois. In H. Speier (ed.) *Social Order and the Risks of War*. Cambridge, Mass.: MIT Press, pp. 53–67.

Strathern, M. (in press). *After Nature: English Kinship in the Late Twentieth Century*. Cambridge: Cambridge University Press.

12 *Enterprise, omnipotence and dependency: a psychoanalytic approach to political culture*

BARRY RICHARDS

This chapter will try to indicate something of what present-day psychoanalytic thinking may have to offer to the understanding of political culture. The use of psychoanalysis in the study of political society is now an area of growing and exciting scholarship, as evidenced in the work of diverse writers such as Janine Chasseguet-Smirgel (1986), Stephen Ducat (1988), Paul Hoggett (forthcoming), Joel Kovel (1988), Marie Langer (1989), Lloyd de Mause (1984), Paul Parin (1985), Michael Rustin (1989), Vamik Volkan (1988), Victor Wolfenstein (1981) and others.

In fact, notwithstanding the image of psychoanalysis as an individualistic and inward-looking discipline, an image which of course has had some basis in reality, there has always been within it a tradition of social and cultural criticism. Significantly for our purpose here, some of this work has focused on the psychological meaning of market relations and their impact on character development. The best known and most important work in this vein is that of Erich Fromm, the psychoanalyst who was closely associated with the Frankfurt School in the 1930s, and whose attempts then to synthesize psychoanalysis and Marxism were an important contribution to the development of critical theory. In one of his books, *Man for Himself*, first published in 1947, Fromm outlined a set of character types, or, as he also called them, orientations. All orientations are present to some degree in the individual, but the degrees of development and dominance of each depended on the prevailing social relations. In the twentieth century one particular orientation had become dominant, Fromm asserted; this he termed the marketing orientation, an organization of character 'rooted in the experience of oneself as a commodity' (Fromm [1947] 1986: 68). Self-esteem is dependent on one's market-value, and in one's relations with others the same pernicious calculative principle is dominant. 'The premise of the marketing orientation is emptiness, the lack of any specific quality which could not be subject to change' (p. 77) according to the demands of the market.

This work of Fromm's remains of value, both as a suggestive theoretical schema and as an example of the integration of a humanistic ethic into psychocultural analysis. However, Fromm did not provide much of an account of the bases of this character-type in early development, and moreover we must now take into account some important developments in post-Freudian psychoanalysis, which Fromm, though himself a leader in a certain kind of psychoanalytic revisionism, was unable to do. I am referring in particular to the postwar developments of psychoanalysis in Britain, to the elaboration of the Kleinian and so-called object-relations schools of psychoanalytic theory.

To some extent, steeped as they are in British and European traditions of humanism, these newer theories can be heard to confirm the kind of analysis offered by Fromm. They can be deployed to support the concern with authenticity that is evinced in Fromm's concept of the marketing orientation. The writings of the British psychoanalyst Donald Winnicott (see, for example, Winnicott 1960), are particularly amenable to this kind of theoretical manoeuvre, in that his concept of the False Self (which was also taken up in modified form by R. D. Laing) can be mapped onto a humanist–Marxist understanding of the cash nexus and its denial of human need. I attempted to do something of this sort in some earlier work (Richards 1984), where I argued that the psychoanalytic descriptions of the schizoid state of mind, in which False Self functioning has eclipsed inner truth, could complement the traditional analysis of alienation. Object-relations theory can on this view deepen that analysis, by opening it out to a set of hypotheses about the origins of schizoid traits in particular modes of parenting, themselves in turn the products of social change.

This sort of approach has some usefulness in the project of trying to understand what present-day cultures of enterprise might be about, psychologically speaking. However, it does not take us to the core of what I would now see as the potential contribution of present-day psychoanalysis, and into which some of this tradition of left-psychoanalytic cultural critique may be assimilated. But first there is a general point to make about the kind of exercise I am sketching.

It concerns the nature of disciplinary boundaries and objects within an interdisciplinary undertaking. Psychoanalysis is distinctively the discourse of inner worlds and their impact on outer ones. It has no special knowledge of the structure of the social world, and so its delineation of the public manifestations of the private unconscious is best done in conjunction with other disciplinary inputs from the social sciences. Moreover, the focus of convenience of psychoanalytic inquiry, when turned towards the public sphere, is the realm of *rhetoric* rather than that of more concrete forms of action. The unconscious impulse can find more complete expression in the play of words than in the building of social institutions. This is not to say that social institutions cannot and do not at times embody dramatizations of unconscious wishes, but it is to recognize that all sorts of compromises with reality and between contending social forces have to be made in the more material and institutional forms of social practice.

There is a methodological reason as well as a substantive reason for focusing on words and ideas. There *could* be a psychoanalytically based study of the enterprise culture, which concerned itself with the psychological correlates and consequences of specific new institutional and cultural features: that is, with the effects on individuals of the material and social realities of enterprise. However, that would require some substantial fieldwork of a kind that has not been undertaken. The approach I am suggesting, a psychoanalytic study of the rhetorics of enterprise, can proceed with less ambitious and expensive empirical data, by sampling specific discursive formations: government statements, media language, research reports and academic theories, polemical tracts and so on.

One of the main contributions of psychoanalysis in the present context can be to help us to look critically at the rhetorics of the enterprise culture and to explore their emotional meanings, their unconscious significance, in order to help us take the moral temperature of contemporary political culture. Further (though it is not possible to pursue it here), if the things people say, and the psychological meanings attached to what they say, are not entirely the same as the things they do, if the rhetorics of the enterprise culture are different in emphases or in overall direction from the realities, then in looking at the tensions between the two we may learn something of how stable the present realities are, and of what currents of moral feeling must be taken into account by any programmes of change.

Let me now say something about the new insights and for-mulations concerning individual development to be found in current psychoanalytic thinking. Any attempt to sum up what these developments might be encounters a problem, which is that psychoanalysis is not a monolithic body of knowledge; it encompasses a number of doctrinally different positions (and a number of different attempts to transcend those differences). It includes various programmes of rational, empirical enquiry – some clearly positivistic, others arguably realist – as well as strong hermeneutic traditions, and persistently influential strands of romanticism and mysticism. Its different variants espouse different degrees and kinds of environmentalism, and are differently disposed towards eclecticism and towards 'scientificity'. Some quite divergent conceptions of human nature and possibility can be found within its literature. So I can give you only my own rendering of what seem to me to be the most important and most general of later developments. I am drawing upon the work of Klein (cf. 1986) and some of her followers, of the British object-relations theorists and of a number of other recent psychoanalytic authors, among whom the French analyst Janine Chasseguet-Smirgel (1986) and the American Otto Kernberg (see, for example, 1980) are of particular significance, for me at least.

One set of these developments centres on a new statement of the Freudian theory of the reality principle. The fundamental task of development is seen as resignation to reality, but not in the classical Freudian language of the renunciation of pleasure, where pleasure may be conceived of in a fairly simple, bodily sense. In much present-day psychoanalytic theorizing the fundamental strug-gle is between the reality principle and omnipotence; the illusion of omnipotence is, throughout much of infancy and early childhood, the main psychic means we have for defending ourselves against the terrors that must attend any non-illusory experience of reality and our helplessness in it. ⟋ *having a lot of power* .

For in reality, especially as infants and children, we are of course anything but omnipotent. We depend utterly on others, whose inevitable inability to meet *all* our needs and desires signals to us the possibility, however unlikely in reality, of abandonment. The purpose of the illusion is to obliterate dependency needs. In the baby's mind, the rage it will also inevitably feel against those who must sometimes disappoint it compounds the fear of desertion: will they turn away from me because I have hated them? Within this structure of feeling, fantasies of self-sufficiency, complete control, immortality and other forms of omnipotence are the only resource we can reliably call upon to mitigate the anxieties that our actual insufficiency and vulnerability dispose us to. We protect ourselves against the terrors of dependency and guilt by imagining that they do not exist, by insulating ourselves inside the illusion of omnipotent invulnerability. If we are all-powerful, if other people do not really exist as independent agents and subjects, then we need not fear being abandoned by them, nor need we regret our rage at them.

Over time, if parents and others are experienced as sufficiently reliable and are thus able in their care and love of the infant to make the fear and guilt tolerable, then these feelings can be dealt with in other, better ways – they can be confronted instead of being banished by the omnipotent wish. Impressions of early caregivers are the elemental stuff of psychic development; whatever capacities the parents have to meet the baby's dependency needs and to tolerate its hatred will thus become part of the basic structure of the baby's developing psyche. Around these internalizations of others there may thus cohere a self that is able to endure the painfulness of life, the inner reality of anxiety and guilt, and the external reality of others. External reality cannot be fully experienced while inner realities are avoided, so while overcoming omnipotence is essentially an internal struggle, to replace impotence with potency and competence, it has profound implications for our relationship to the external world.

To the always incomplete degree that omnipotence has been overcome, we have psychologically grown up, and have at least the psychic potential for functioning as responsible citizens. To the

[margin handwriting: Inner struggle + External factors to Overcome Omnipotence]

extent that in all of us it does not happen, we remain wedded to illusion, to infantile and potentially destructive ways of experiencing the world, because we have not fully taken on board the intractable otherness of reality and its refusal to correspond to our wishes, in particular the otherness of other people. The omnipotent world-view is a narcissistic one, to use another of the psychoanalytic terms often at the centre of this perspective on emotional development; the existence of others must at a deep level be denied, since their otherness as independent agents would constitute a limit to the subject's omnipotence. The acceptance of the reality of others, and the endurance of psychic pain, are opposite sides of the same coin. It is clear here that this psychoanalytic perspective on omnipotence and narcissism is a moral one: it points to a fundamental failure to acknowledge the existence of others with needs outside of oneself, a failure that may underlie or subvert the most apparently adult and sophisticated of our beliefs and actions in later life.

Given this sort of approach, there is one obvious application of psychoanalysis to the analysis of political ideologies and rhetorics. This is the one for which Freud himself is perhaps best known: the critique of utopian programmes as indicative of a failure in coming to terms with reality, of a failure to accept the frustrations, limits and pains of life that are inevitable in any kind of society whatsoever. Chasseguet-Smirgel and Grunberger ([1976] 1986) have written a powerful critique of Freudo-Marxism in just these terms. Many leftist attempts to appropriate psychoanalytic insights have foundered on their refusal to accept this tenet, and there have also been tendencies within psychoanalysis that have, albeit some-times implicitly, encouraged a rejection of it. Lacanianism is, in an ambiguous way, the most important recent example of this. In my reading of it, contrary to these tendencies, psychoanalysis is a fun-damentally anti-utopian way of thinking about human possibility.

In the present era of enterprise culture, something interesting has happened in that the most prominent expressions of the utopian impulse in political culture seem to have moved across the political spectrum. Whereas in the 1960s and 1970s it was almost always the Left that was the architect of utopian futures and that gave voice to utopian impulses in the national consciousness, not it seems as if it is the New Right that has placed before us the most compelling agendas for social transformation.

Omnipotence vs utopian program

I am here anticipating the main thesis of this chapter, that one of the primary questions that psychoanalysis puts to any political discourse is: to what extent can the voice of omnipotence be heard within it? To the extent that it can, then it must be rejected, whatever its manifest objectives and credentials, and however powerful its sentimental appeal. I suggest that this approach provides a valuable criterion for differentiating between varieties of enterprise. Russell Keat (1991) has proposed that a basic distinction can be made between forms of enterprise culture, according to whether or not they conceive of enterprise in terms of market relations. It may be equally important to judge different cultures of enterprise, non-market and market, according to whether or not they give expression to illusions of omnipotence.

I will be focusing here on some neo-liberal or 'Thatcherist' discourse. I do this because Thatcherism has been the central ideological formation on the surface of present British political culture, and there is still a great deal to be learnt about and from it. However, I should stress that this focus is a very selective one, and that there are many other forms of the enterprising spirit, actual and potential ones, to which my analysis does not apply. Even within the particular valorizations of enterprise that are a major part of 'Thatcherism', there are, no doubt, many exceptions to this analysis. There is no single 'enterprising self'; there are as many kinds of enterprising self as there are social locations for their articulation. Rather than proposing a blanket analysis of all such selves, I am trying to find a way of distinguishing some from others, according to a basic criterion of moral–psychological value.

If the moral nature of this criterion seems to be too bound up with an abstract theory of development, then we should consider what happens when fantasies of omnipotence come to dominate action as well as rhetoric, because then disaster is at hand in a very concrete way. It is not difficult to identify the omnipotence at work in fascist programmes of social transformation, in all fundamentalisms, and in some expressions of nuclear militarism. The melting away of the needs and very existence of others behind the bright light of one's own truth, and the ruthless attempt to remake the world in the image of that truth, are – as Ronald Aronson (1983) has argued – the hallmarks of a state of mind that can accurately be called omnipotent. The psychoanalytic scrutiny of political rhetoric is therefore more than a matter of interesting cultural research; it may help to deepen our understanding of the most destructive modern forms of paranoia and grandiosity, and to trace their affinities with more moderate ideologies.

A slogan

To begin with some specific analysis, we will reflect on a slogan: 'There is no alternative', the famous TINA slogan of mid-1980s Conservative Party enthusiasm. At the party political level, the enterprise culture has been unleashed over us because – we have been told, and enough of us have believed – there is no alternative. No alternative to the programmes of deregulation, denationalization, and so on, of sticking to monetary policy and pressing ahead with privatizations, and sitting out the allegedly short-term adversities that may be created. From the receiving end, 'There is no alternative' is a stern admonition. The psychoanalytic question is, what may be its deeper meanings to those who utter it?

And this applies not only to the Conservatives at the time in question; how many of us have not used the same statement when seeking to explain or justify something we have done? 'I had no alternative but to. . .' This form of words is very commonly used, for example, by both sides in industrial disputes. On the face of it, it is an expression of powerlessness: it says that external reality has set our path for us, and that we can do nothing to change it. Thus, it speaks to the sense of helplessness at the core of us all, and draws us into its prescription. However, as we know, it is rarely spoken in a mood of helplessness, but frequently in one of triumphant defiance. There is a mismatch between the spirit and the letter of the statement, and we must look to the spirit of its pronouncement for clues as to its deeper moral–psychological meanings. And the spirit is one of omnipotence. It says: 'We know we are right. There is no possibility here of human error, or of valid opposition, and no need for making choices. We are spared the painful process of decision, the agonies of doubt and regret. We are, in short, elevated above the human condition, free of the pains of guilt and uncertainty. We have no need of the capacity to choose, of potency, because we are omnipotent –

we know how the world is arranged and what must be done to master it.'

So in the simple TINA cliché we can find a powerful resolution of a fundamental anxiety: the intractability of the external world is acknowledged, but fleetingly and in a way that finally subverts the acknowledgement, burying it beneath a surge of self-importance. We get a glimpse here of what may be a major pattern of feeling in the enterprise culture. Before we leave TINA, two other points can be made. One I will not pursue now, which is that the omnipotent outlook is here feminized into a powerful woman. The second, which I have mentioned already and will return to, is also connected, at least incidentally, with the sex of the former premier. This is that there is, of course, an alternative, of a sort, implied by 'There is no alternative', but it is an alternative so terrible in its consequences as to be unthinkable. It is the alternative of returning to the state of infantile dependence upon the mother, as symbolized by the hated and derided apparatus of governmental provision and supervision, especially through socialized welfare. For the omnipotent self this is no alternative at all; it is the catastrophic collapse of omnipotence into the suffocating embrace of the mother.

Elsewhere (Richards 1989: 155–60) I have considered the writings of the leading neo-liberal philosopher Friedrich von Hayek (1967) as another, particularly influential, expression of primitive anxieties of this kind. At first sight Hayek's writings might seem to embody a firm rejection of omnipotence, in his repeated assertion that we cannot hope to know all that needs to be known in order to make effective and rational plans for the overall direction of economic life. Command economies are, he implies, crumbling monuments to the impossibility of controlling the world, and to the moral dangers of trying to do so. Purposive human intervention cannot improve, and indeed must reduce, the efficiency of the spontaneous market.

Although acknowledging the force that recent developments in Eastern Europe and Russia have added to the rational content of such an analysis, we can still inspect the writings of a polemicist such as Hayek for their emotional tone, and for the configurations of unconscious fantasy that inhabit them. Through such an exercise, it is possible to show from Hayek's work that here again, in what is apparently a rejection of omnipotence and an acceptance of limits, there is the illusion of transcending the necessity for compromises with others and for the endurance of guilt. Simply put, there is an omnipotent wish, coupled as usual with a yearning for an all-powerful and omniscient force with which to identify or to which to devote oneself – either way to remove doubt and limitation. While the state socialism with which Hayek is so deeply engaged saw this force in the principles and apparatus of planning and distribution, the neo-liberal sees it in the market and the spirit of enterprise (and, in Hayek's case, explicitly in the power of *evolution*, of which the market and enterprise are the main human expressions).

A speech

Here, to illustrate further the kind of analysis I am proposing, I shall take another text from the enterprise culture, a more recent and local one than the panoramic vision of Hayek. It is an address to the 1990 Annual Convention of the British Institute of Directors (IOD) by its Director General, Peter Morgan. The IOD describes itself as 'The Voice of Business Leaders' in the UK, and this speech attracted considerable media attention. It was delivered at a time (February 1990) when the opinion polls were showing a swift and substantial decline in the popularity of Mrs Thatcher and in the electoral chances of the Conservatives. Although much of this shift in popular opinion has been attributed to the widely disliked 'poll tax', it is also believed to be a result of a slower and deeper movement of feeling against the 'enterprise culture', or at least against some of its works. It is now a cliché of superficial cultural commentary to refer to the coming decade as likely to be the 'caring nineties', in contrast to the 'me' decade of the eighties.

Whatever the accuracy of these predictions, the relevant point here is that, for the first time for a decade, advocates of neo-liberalism in Britain are on the defensive. We might expect that at such a time, a programmatic speech by the leader of an organization that has been closely identified in recent years with the neo-liberal advance would set out the fundamentals of the 'faith' in a particularly clear way. Given also that this particular text has no claim to philosophical subtlety, and is unabashedly passionate, it should therefore be particularly good material for psychological scrutiny.

It begins with the statement that Britain compares poorly with some European countries in its commitment to the enterprise culture. Despite the triumph of the market economy in Eastern Europe, the British people are ambivalent towards it, claims Morgan. Indeed, according to 'a recent survey . . . nearly one person in five feels positive about communism' (Morgan 1990: 1). Worse, the problem exists in the IOD itself; the Director General has 'found that not all our members have a coherent vision of the enterprise culture' (p. 1). The task of his speech is therefore to 'develop a vision which we can all share' (pp. 1–2). This opening is evocative of the sermon: thhe audience is asked to address its unbelief, to look to exemplars of the faith, and to commit itself to a saving vision. Such religious parallels are, of course, commonplace in much political discourse, but their significance here will be returned to later.

There follows a passage of unusually florid and self–congratulatory imagery.

> Successful companies, which regularly make profit and grow, are the flagships of the enterprise culture. Directors who lead those successful companies are heroes of the enterprise culture. Any of our products or services which lead the world, are the pride of the enterprise culture. . .
>
> In an enterprise culture the whole nation understands that we are locked in competition with other nations. We are all soldiers in a global economic war. There is a convention which defines the conduct of the war – it is called GATT, but there is no arms limitation treaty.
>
> A nation is allowed to put into the economic battlefield any number of its citizens that it chooses – there are no restrictions. Nor are there any restrictions on the training or the technology which can be given to our economic warriors (Morgan 1990: 2–3).

No depth-psychological analysis is necessary to notice the language of glorified combat in which economic activity is here described. An 'enterprise culture' is understood entirely in terms of the exclusive interests of the nation-state, and again, in the call to mobilize the entire society for the economic war, there is an implicit warning that, without such a totalization of British society ('UK plc') around a common vision, then we shall suffer – although our precise fate is not specified.

The military language provides an occasion to introduce some more psychoanalytic thinking of relevance to understanding this text. The work of the British analyst Wilfred Bion is currently very popular among some psychoanalysts, whose interest tends to focus upon his later works and his formulations of the mother–infant relationship, his 'alimentary' or digestive model of psychic development, and his suggestions concerning the emotional basis of the capacity to think. Bion is best known to a wider public for his earlier work on the dynamics of groups (Bion 1961), which still has much to offer to the project of making some psychoanalytic sense of large-scale social phenomena (but for a contextualization and critique of Bion's work on groups, see Barham 1984).

Bion's work in small experimental therapy groups (with real soldiers, who were psychiatric casualties in a real war) led him to postulate the notion of a 'basic assumption', an unconscious 'group mentality' that can pervade the interactions between members of a group (and between the group and the outside world). Individuals in the group both contribute to, and are influenced by, the basic assumption. Bion called it by this name to stress that it is a pattern of feeling that seems to focus on a belief about what the group is *for* – that is, it is an 'assumption' about the nature of the group and about what to expect as a member of it, although it is an assumption at the level of unconscious fantasy rather than of conscious or pre-conscious thought.

Groups under the sway of basic assumptions are contrasted with 'work groups', those that are relatively unencumbered by irrational fantasies and can therefore proceed with the task in hand, whatever it might be. In a basic assumption group, a lot of distress is often generated, and very little real work is done (however many formal agendas are completed), because that is not what the members unconsciously believe the group exists to do. Most actual groups alternate between being basic assumption groups and being work groups; the reality–task orientation is intermittently (perhaps chronically) subverted by a basic assumption mentality.

In particular, Bion wrote about three sort of basic assumption, two of which concern us here. One he called 'the basic assumption of unity for fight or flight' (p. 67), referring to those groups in which paranoid feelings about other groups predominate. 'Preoccupation with fight–flight leads the group to ignore other activities, or, if it cannot do this, to suppress them or run away from them' (p. 67). As Freud (1921) had pointed out, one reason for this direction of all hostility outwards is to protect the group from its internal tensions. This creates the illusion of belonging to a perfectly unified and unsullied whole, and averts for all group members a painful confrontation with their necessarily mixed feelings for each other. Thus, a basic assumption is a defence, against painful aspects of psychic reality: in the face of the conflicts and anxieties evoked by the real world, the group omnipotently creates for itself the illusion that it can avoid them, in this case by externalizing conflict.

However, Peter Morgan's speech was not made in a small group setting. It was given for a societal audience, to which the assembled directors were a bridge. Nonetheless, it is still valid to apply Bion's concepts here, as Bion himself did in his suggestions that some large-scale social institutions can be regarded as operating on basic assumption lines. For example, the army has a work task, national defence, which makes it particularly vulnerable to becoming dominated by the fight–flight assumption (and to the extent that it is, it will be less able to see the world realistically, and so be less efficient at its task).

In the opening passage of Morgan's address, the fight–flight assumption (in familiar nationalist livery) is in the ascendant. It is taking possession of the group from and for which he is at that moment speaking. (In an interpretive exercise of this sort, we are taking the text as expressive of some *group* mentality rather than as diagnostic, in some general way, of the individual who wrote or spoke it. A psychological approach to political discourse is not, therefore, a matter of 'character assassination', though it certainly points to those *aspects* of an individual's make-up that are mobilized by the group mentality.)

Characteristically, perhaps, of much nationalist bombast, the appeal is not to the nation as a whole but to a rather small fraction of it. As the speech progresses the 'we' is sharply distinguished from the 'establishment', the 'middle-class salariat' and the 'lumpenproletariat'. These other groups are in fact the problem,

the 'obstacle' that the warriors will have
against them, as well as against other natio⌐.

Overall, Bion's work can be seen as an extens⌐
theory of the group, and both writers belong to th⌐
of liberal thought whereby social processes on all sca⌐
mental life itself) are thought of as constituted by confl⌐
a rational, realistic task-oriented principle and the irratio⌐
of primitive needs and their intellectual expressions. It is fron⌐
kind of theory of the reality principle that the psychoanalytic critiq⌐
of neo-liberalism (and of many other ideologies) most powerfully
proceeds.

This is an important point, given the tendency of many advocates
of 'enterprise' to lay sole claim to 'realism', as does Peter Morgan in
this paper. The realism advanced here is that of 'wealth creation': 'In
an enterprise culture. . .we believe that wealth creation comes first'
(p. 2). Dons, bishops and the whole intellectual 'establishment' are
taken to task for their view that 'the distribution of wealth is a noble
activity – creating wealth is mucky and squalid' (p. 6). Baking the
national cake – as big as possible – is the noblest activity, not
cutting it up.

Setting aside the obvious point, which Morgan omits, about the
role in reality of manual workers as well as company directors in
'wealth creation', what can we find at the underlying fantasy level?
There is a scenario of goods that are arduously provided by some,
and then hypocritically and greedily consumed by others without
thought for their source. This is a common theme in the neo-liberal
castigation of the welfare state – the fear appears to be that the
providers (who are always, in psychoanalytic terms, representative
of the parents) are being ignored or denigrated, and are overrun
and depleted by their arrogant dependants.

This leads to a second fantasy theme or 'basic assumption'. This
one is called by Bion the basic assumption of 'dependency'. Here,
'The group is combining to establish a firm portrait of the object
on which it can depend' (Bion 1961: 83). The assumption is that
the group has formed in order to be nourished and protected by
an omniscient and omnipotent leader. Any teacher who has sat
uncomfortably before a class of passively expectant students has
experienced something of this. It is a defence against separate-
ness, a replacement of the contingencies of actual dependence on

ate attachment to an idealized

y form is the last thing that the
least of all its most pugnacious
erprise culture is one in which
the world does not owe him
The tirade against welfare, in
texts, appears to be a complete
l as well as economic grounds.
l to enterprise.

tacle [to progress]. What do I
salariat'? I mean our vast body
e to worry where the next pay

check [sic] is coming from.

- in nationalised industries
- in central government
- in social security
- in local government
- in schools and universities
- and in health. . .

These groups are the major users of the welfare state and also its principal providers. They therefore have an enormous vested interest in the status quo (Morgan 1990: 7).

Also:

Earlier this month a survey showed that. . .30% [of the general population] did not even know what the basic rate of tax was. I wonder whether these people realise that their taxes pay ambulance drivers' wages, and that government spending increases the cost of mortgages. Business must help the government bring economic commonsense into the affairs of the nation (Morgan 1990: 9).

And further:

We urged him [the Chancellor] to abolish inheritance tax and capital gains tax. Capitalism needs capital. These taxes convert the capital accumulation of generations into the weekly wages of hospital porters (Morgan 1990: 10).

Behind the contempt for health workers and their wages is the implication that welfare provision is wasteful. One wonders who would lift and wheel the sick in an enterprise culture, but it is not Morgan's purpose to specify how a full market in health care would provide ambulance drivers and hospital porters, nor are these reality considerations relevant to our consideration of his rhetoric. His vision is of a parasitic 'salariat' of millions, the 'providers' of welfare only in the secondary sense that they spend others' money to provide it. As 'major users' also, they are doubly responsible for bleeding capitalism of its lifeblood, capital, aided by taxes that destroy the capitalization that could be achieved by prudent individuals and families.

Bion remarked (1961: 124) that 'Whenever a state exists that is likely to activate, or itself to have been activated by, the *baD* [his shorthand for the basic assumption of dependency], there is a fear of dictatorship – a recent example is the often expressed fear that the Welfare State will lead to a tyrannical interference with liberty'. He leaves open the possibility that the desire for the welfare state is itself a product of *baD*, that is, of dependency needs. That is an important question, to which a psychoanalytic perspective may be able to bring something new, but it is beyond the scope of this paper. For the present purpose, Bion's remark raises the question of whether the rhetoric of the enterprise culture is itself driven by dependency longings and the fight against them.

In my analysis of Hayek, and also in a discussion of monetarism and its electoral successes (Richards 1989), I argue that neo-liberalism should indeed be seen in this way. The threat of dependency on the other is countered in two ways: first, actual relations of dependency in the world are attacked, and, secondly, an absolutely dependable, omnipotent other is imagined, as the projection of the subject's own omnipotence – a 'firm portrait of the object on which . . . [to] depend'. These manoeuvres are also to be seen in Morgan's text, as they are routinely in such statements. The first is evident in his comments on welfare and the 'salariat', and the second in his vision of enterprise, a force that needs only release from the burdens of taxation and public sector unaccountability in order to generate wealth for all. (It also needs, he argues, a revolution in education in order to eliminate the massive, unenterprising and dependent 'lumpenproletariat', though it is not clear from his paper what that would entail.)

'Welfare' is thus the screen onto which the hero–director projects some deep fears: of being helplessly dependent on necessarily less–than–perfect others, of submission to a cruel authority, of annihilation in a claustrophobic closeness, and – especially in this text, via an identification with the maternal provider, the 'creator' of wealth – of the source of goodness being crushed by the thankless greed of claimants. The bulwark against these anxieties is the 'enterprise culture', a secular ideal but one enjoying some of the ambience of the sacred. 'The government must keep the faith' (Morgan 1990: 15). The sermon-like quality of Morgan's opening statements, noted earlier, also alerted us to the quality of worship to be found in idealizations of enterprise. Again, Bion's formulation is relevant: he postulated that the social institution to which *baD* was most closely linked was the church. Yet, while the church may have developed specialized techniques for the exploration and management of dependency needs, the predominance of those needs in other, non-therapeutic social settings is likely to result in the eclipse of the reality principle.

There are two jokes in Morgan's address, both worthy of some psychological comment. The first concerns

> a little girl who was asked to prepare a short story which introduced the word frugal. She went home and found that the dictionary meaning gave 'conserve' or 'save' as the essence of being frugal. 'Once upon a time' she wrote 'there was a beautiful princess who was riding her horse beside the river. Then it slipped and she fell into the rushing water. Just then a handsome prince rode by and she called out. 'Frugal me. . . frugal me.' So he got off his horse and frugalled her. . . and they lived happily ever after (Morgan 1990: 4–5).

> . . . and people expect the government to be frugal. I like that word frugal – it sounds right (pp. 4–5).

'Frugality', then, suggests potency; the joke celebrates monetarism as a rather dominative form of male sexuality, displacing more common connotations of it as anti-libidinal and withholding. The second joke, later in the paper, draws on the deeper level of omnipotent fantasy.

> We support the Chancellor's interest rate policy but we can still make jokes about it. There was a summit meeting held between Mr Gorbachev, President Reagan and Mrs Thatcher. Each of the leaders was allowed to ask God one question. Mr Gorbachev started by asking 'When will communism become internationally established as the sole political philosophy?' God, after a few minutes hesitation, replied: 'About the 22nd century' and Mr Gorbachev burst into tears because he knew he would not live that long. President Reagan then asked 'When do you think my star wars research will come to fruition?' Again, God thought for a moment and replied 'Not until the end of the 21st century', at which President Reagan burst into tears because he knew he would not live that long. Finally, Mrs Thatcher asked: 'And when do you think my monetary policy will succeed?' – And God burst into tears (Morgan 1990: 10–11).

In the second joke, the focus is still upon a relationship between a man and a woman, but the woman is now dominant, albeit absurdly. Each leader has an omnipotent design, and hers is the most extreme and unrealistic, the joke tells us. Yet as well as containing an affectionate mocking, it also admires her: she alone has the capacity to project a future beyond God. Welcome (and reassuring) though the joke is as a relief from the deliberately high moral tone of the rest of the paper, it confirms that there is a grandiosity at work in the 'vision' offered here.

As I have argued, the psychic realities against which this vision defends, which it seeks to obliterate, are those of dependency needs. While we cannot make too much of one speech, if the foregoing observations have any validity then this particular text does show us how, by an omnipotent denial of needs for others, these painful realities can be avoided and a stirring cast-list of 'heroes' and 'warriors' be given sole responsibility for society. When this sort of language predominates in any particular depiction of the 'enterprising self', then it is an omnipotent, denying self that is being talked about. Similarly, in so far as the 'consumer' is seen as someone who seeks to gratify all desires, then again an omnipotent way of being is invoked (albeit there, perhaps, in a more passive or regressed mode than in entrepreneurial enterprise).

But if, in contrast, consumption is seen as the source of just *some* degrees of self-expression and of wellbeing, then the psychological meaning of consumption is different. Similarly, if the enterprising self is also a reflective and troubled self, moved as much by its recognition of dependency and guilt and by the wish to make reparation as by its self-reliance and its initiative, then we have the makings of a very different articulation of enterprise.

References: Chapter 12

Aronson, R. 1983. *The Dialectics of Disaster*. London: New Left Books.

Barham, P. 1984. Cultural forms and psychoanalysis: some problems. In B. Richards (ed.), *Capitalism and Infancy*. London: Free Association Books, pp. 38–54.

Bion, W. 1961. *Experiences in Groups*. London: Tavistock.

Chasseguet-Smirgel, C. 1986. *Sexuality and Mind*. New York: New York University Press.

Chasseguet-Smirgel, J. and Grunberger, B. [1976] 1986. *Freud or Reich? Psychoanalysis and Illusion*. London: Free Association Books.

DeMause, L. 1984. *Reagan's America*. New York: Creative Roots.

Ducat, S. 1988. *Taken In: American Gullibility and the Reagan Mythos*. Tacoma, Wyo.: Life Sciences Press.

Freud, S. 1921. Group psychology and the analysis of the ego. *The Standard Edition of the Complete Psychological Works of Sigmund Freud* XVII, 145–59. London: Hogarth.

Fromm, E. [1947] 1986. *Man for Himself*. London: Routledge and Kegan Paul.

Hayek, F. 1967. *Studies in Philosophy, Politics and Economics*. London: Routledge and Kegan Paul.

Hoggett, P. (in press). *Partisans in an Uncertain World*. London: Free Association Books.

Keat, R. 1991. Introduction: Starship Britain or universal enterprise? In R. Keat & N. Abercrombie (eds), *Enterprise Culture*. London: Routledge, pp. 1–20.

Kernberg, O. 1980. *Internal World and External Reality*. New York: Jason Aronson.

Klein, M. 1986. *The Selected Melanie Klein*. Harmondsworth: Penguin (edited by J. Mitchell).

Kovel, J. 1988. *The Radical Spirit*. London: Free Association Books.

Langer, M. 1989. *From Vienna to Managua*. London: Free Association Books.

Morgan, P. 1990. Address to the Institute of Directors' Annual Convention. London: Institute of Directors press release.

Parin, P. 1985. Freedom and independence: on the psychoanalysis of political commitment, *Free Associations*, 3: 65–79.

Richards, B. 1989. *Images of Freud*. London: Dent.

Rustin, M. 1989. Post-Kleinian analysis and the post-modern. *New Left Review*, 173: 109–28.

Volkan, V. 1988. *The Need to Have Enemies and Allies*. New York: Jason Aronson.

Winnicott, D. 1960. Ego distortion in terms of True and False Self. In *The Maturational Processes and the Facilitating Environment*. London: Hogarth Press, pp. 140–52.

Wolfenstein, E. V. 1981. *The Victims of Democracy* Berkeley, Calif.: University of California Press.

PART 4

Religion and enterprise

13 The invisible hand: providence and the market

DAVID NICHOLLS

You may be familiar with the story which is told (in different versions) of the shopkeeper belonging to one of the world's entre-preneurial ethnic minorities: Indians in East Africa, Lebanese in West Africa, Jews in Europe and the USA, or Chinese almost anywhere (except China). The shopkeeper's son comes home from school and asked his father, 'What is ethics?' 'Ethics is like this my son. A customer comes into the shop and gives you a fifty pound note; you and he both think it is a ten pound note and you give him change for ten. Just as he is going out of the shop you see that it is a fifty. Now, this is the question of ethics: do you tell your partner?'

The story draws attention to two aspects of the enterprise culture: human acquisitive tendencies and the need to limit these to achieve a degree of cooperation and common purpose. Here, I shall consider the role played by these values in relation to concepts of divine providence. Versions of the Christian religion have in the past provided and still provide a powerful ideological defence of the enterprise culture, while other versions provoke a searching critique of enterprise values and assumptions. One obvious link between religion and the economy – between God and the market – is ethics. God is thought to lay down moral principles, which may then be applied to economic issues. A more interesting and perhaps more significant connection is at the level of analogy.

Images of God and the state

God's role in the universe is often seen as a model for the government's function in the economy, and economic institutions and
assumptions in turn influence human images of God. Thus, there
is frequently a close, but subtle, connection between economic
and political structures and conceptions of God's relationship to
a universe that he 'governs'. In Britain and in other parts of
the North Atlantic world, the dominant image of both God
and the state during this century has been that of a powerful but
benevolent bureaucrat concerned above all things with *welfare*.
Liberal theology reinforced – and at times inspired – the 'new
liberalism' of the late nineteenth century, which played a major
role in the development of a welfare state in Britain. (The very term
'welfare-state' was probably first used in print by the then Archbishop of York, William Temple, in 1929.)[1] Liberal images of the
welfare god also reflect the political rhetoric of positive state action,
which was seen by many as the only way to avert revolution. This
tendency reached its apotheosis in the celebrated preacher, Henry
Scott Holland, at the turn of the century. He wrote of the people of
London: 'The State, in some far golden day yet to come, may be to
them as a home. . .Its eye will be on them, its arm about them; its
friendly co-operation will ensure them consideration'; be claimed
that the paternal role of the state will remind citizens of a heavenly
father, 'whose eye is ever on them' (Holland, in Wescott, B. *et
al*. 1901: 51–2).[2] In Germany, Bismarck's social legislation was
justified in terms of a 'Christian' paternalism: financial dependence
of the masses on the state would lead to submission. The Iron
Chancellor looked forward to a time when hundreds of thousands
of potentially revolutionary workers would be drawing small
pensions from the government (see Nicholls 1989: i, 81 ff.).

In recent years, however, there has been a reaction against this
model and a return – in some respects – to an earlier picture of
God and the state. Gone is the God of caring and concern. He
is replaced by a more severe figure, who is conceived as having
created a universe that runs according to a set of laws; his role is
to maintain the system in being, with perhaps occasional direct
intervention in emergencies, to keep things going and to avert
collapse. Similarly, the state is seen as maintaining a structure

within which individuals may compete to secure advancement for themselves and their families. The competition is said to stimulate self-reliance and individual autonomy, while forwarding the general happiness. The marketplace where this activity occurs must, however, run according to rules that limit the avarice of participants. Churches, schools and other cultural institutions are to inculcate 'values' that, while celebrating the importance of competition, also prohibit extremes of acquisitiveness and rapacity. Self-interest is thus the engine of the enterprise culture, but must be held in check by moral values – hence the state's concern with education and with maintaining an established church. Despite talk of original sin and human vice, the position is basically an optimistic one, for it concludes that the outcome of all these selfish actions will be the general happiness. In the well-known words of Bernard Mandeville's *Fable of the Bees*:

> Thus every Part was full of Vice,
> Yet the whole Mass a Paradise. . .
> Such were the Blessings of that State;
> Their Crimes conspir'd to make them Great.
> (Mandeville 1723, Vol. 1, p. 9)

Religion and the enterprise culture

The enterprise culture, as envisaged by its apologists, is characterized by an emphasis on freedom of choice, within the context of a market economy. It is contrasted with a welfare state where individuals become dependent on state benefits, being deprived of opportunities for initiative and personal choice. Ideologists of 'enterprise' look back to British theorists of the late eighteenth and early nineteenth centuries, finding inspiration in the writing of economists such as Thomas Chalmers, Robert Malthus and, above all, Adam Smith. Others in this period who consciously related their economic theories to their theology include Archbishop Sumner, Archbishop Whately and William Whewell, Master of Trinity College Cambridge.

These men asserted or assumed a certain theology.[3] A rational creator or 'director' of nature, ruling the universe, provided for them a model of the government's role within the nation. God is conceived as having set up a 'system' or 'machine', which generally runs smoothly according to certain laws although (in some versions) it needs occasional direct action by God, as in Isaac Newton's cosmology.[4] Having set things up, God's role is thus minimal. Similarly, the office of government is rather limited, being concerned largely with protection and regulation. Individuals pursuing their own ends are led, by an invisible hand, unintentionally to promote the public interest. Boyd Hilton points out how, in contrast, those nineteenth-century evangelicals, such as Shaftesbury, Irving and Drummond, who believed that God frequently intervenes in human affairs by a *special* providence, were also those who advocated state action in the social and economic field (Hilton 1988: 15).

Thomas Chalmers

Perhaps the most influential of these theological economists was the controversial Scottish ecclesiastic, Thomas Chalmers. He owed a considerable debt, however, to Robert Malthus, whose own contemporary influence was limited by popular misconceptions of his population theories. 'I consider you as my ablest and best ally,' the English clergyman told Chalmers in 1822 (quoted in Brown 1982: p. 116). Writing at the beginning of last century, Chalmers pictured God as 'a real and living artist, whose fingers did frame the economy of actual things, and who hath so marvellously suited all that is around us to our senses and our powers of gratification' (Chalmers 1833, Vol. ii, p. 269). Having created the universe, God is 'the unseen Legislator', and 'the moral governor of a kingdom' (Chalmers 1835–41, Vol. i, p. 19; 1833, Vol. ii, p. 109). The natural affections of humans are of an ambivalent status. As implanted by God they cannot be simply condemned. Yet all is tainted with sin. Even our best actions reveal selfish motives; yet these are the dynamic by which communities exist and prosper. 'When each man is left to seek, with concentrated and exclusive aim, his own individual benefit,' he declared in this famous Bridgewater Treatise, 'it is then that markets are best supplied. . .and the most free and rapid augmentation takes place in the riches and resources of the commonwealth' (Chalmers 1833: 34).

An exchange of goods and services centred on the market place was for Chalmers the essence of an economic process in which the general interest is forwarded, without being intended by any of the actors. It is by the 'magical chain' of self-interest that the commercial world is held together; if this were removed it would fall apart (Chalmers 1833, Vol. ii, p. 177; 1835–41, Vol. vi. p. 62). This situation, he maintained, 'strongly bespeaks of a higher agent, by whose transcendental wisdom it is, that all is made to conspire so harmoniously and to terminate so beneficially (1833, Vol. ii, p. 34). God is in fact the 'Supreme Contriver', who has ordered the world in such a way that the selfish and indeed sinful propensities of its creatures result in human progress. Chalmers was a Calvinist and saw the economic system as evidence for the sovereignty of divine grace. 'Society is held together', he said, 'only because the grace of God can turn to account the worthless propensities of the individuals who compose it' (1835–41, Vol. i, p. 71).

God's providential action is such that the state may be thought unnecessary. Not so. 'The doctrine of a celestial influence does not supersede, but rather calls for, a terrestrial mechanism, to guide and to extend the distribution of it (1835, Vol. xiv, p. 45). Human government is an emanation or derivation from God's authority and its mode of operation is analogous to his. Governments should respect divine providence as manifested in the workings of the market economy, guiding and regulating – rather than attempting to suppress – human acquisitive propensities.

As Chalmers rejected the paternalistic state, he also criticized those who emphasized the benevolence of God at the expense of his justice, and 'resolve the whole character of the Deity into but one attribute – that of a placid undistinguishing tenderness;. . .holding Him forth as but the indulgent Father, and not also as the righteous Governor of men'. This onslaught on the image of God as 'a universal parent, throned in soft and smiling radiance' is manifestly linked to his attack on the paternal state (1833, Vol. ii, pp. 61–2, 99). This analogy between God's providence and the economic role of the state is also to be found in Adam Smith, to whose ideas Chalmers owed a considerable debt.

Adam Smith

'The Wealth of Nations', it has been said, 'is a stupendous palace erected upon the granite of self-interest' (Stigler 1976: 237). How does the palace stand on foundations so potentially insecure? The answer is to be found in Smith's doctrine of the created order and in his analogy between divine providence and state action. God's relation to political economy is twofold: analogical and univocal. On the one hand, God rules and manages his universe according to the same principles that a good government manages the economy; on the other, God has created the universe in such a way that the selfish propensities of humans when exercised within limits lead to the general welfare. His attempts to discover the general laws of the economy were, indeed, 'directly inspired and shaped by the example of Newton's success in discovering the natural laws of motion' (Hetherington 1983: 497). Smith's recent commentators have insisted that it is in the context of the eighteenth-century Scottish enlightenment, rather than in terms of nineteenth-century liberalism that his theories must be understood. His assault on mercantilism, with its monopolies and state bounties, should not be seen as an unqualified approval of laissez-faire. Indeed, he recognized a positive, if limited, role for state enterprise.

The theology of Adam Smith

The religious ideas of Adam Smith bear the clear mark of eighteenth-century rationalism and at times of deism. God was first and foremost 'the Author of Nature', who wills the happiness of mankind (Smith [1759] 1853: 235). He is also called 'the Director' of nature, who has 'adjusted with the nicest artifice' each part of the universe to the end for which it was created. His work is compared to that of the watchmaker, an analogy later made famous in the writings of William Paley.[5] Smith often spoke of the universe as 'an immense machine', created by 'that great, benevolent, and all-wise Being, who directs the movements of nature, and who is determined, by his own unalterable perfections, to maintain in it at all times the greatest possible quantity of happiness' (Smith [1759] 1853: 345; see also pp. 347 ff.).

Nature's harmony is an important theme in Smith's moral theory, reflecting the influence of Stoic thinkers (see Raphael 1985: 73). Human interposition by rational calculation can have only a limited influence on the course of events. Humans should 'co-operate with the Deity' in forwarding the happiness of rational creatures – the end for which the universe was created. There are, however, occasions when generally benevolent rules will have unfortunate consequences and human initiative is appropriate, though it is rarely rewarded with total success. Only in the context of an after-life will the divine plan be completed and all injustices be removed. Earthly happiness will, thus, depend on an appeal to 'the all-seeing Judge of the world' and on an 'expectation of a life to come' (Smith [1759] 1853: 235, 239 ff., 187).

Reason, sentiment and providence

God has created a universe where the rational and calculated actions of humans, then, play a relatively small part. The idea of 'contrivance' is crucial. 'The economy of nature' reflects a harmony between means and ends. Its author has not left human reason to discover the best means of securing 'the welfare and preservation of society', but has endowed humans with 'an immediate and instinctive approbation' of those things that realize this end (Smith [1759] 1853: 109). They have not only an appetite for the end but also for the means of attaining that end, which are not therefore entrusted to 'the slow and uncertain determinations of our reason' (p. 110). This is evident in the relationship between parents and children, where Smith sees God's providential hand at work. As the future of the human race depends more upon parents caring for their children than children caring for their parents, so parental tenderness is a much stronger sentiment than filial piety. Moralists do not need generally to encourage parents to protect and forward the interests of their children, but rather urge them to restrain their fondness (p. 199). Again, as 'beneficence is less essential to the existence of society than justice' (which is 'the main pillar that upholds the whole edifice'), so nature has implanted in the human breast a powerful consciousness of injustice and a terror of merited punishment which leads people to protect the weak, restrain the violent and punish the guilty (p. 125). Thus, although we may properly speak of Smith's theology as reflecting an eighteenth-century rationalism, he fully recognized the role that non-rational factors do play in human affairs.

This is the context in which Smith's celebrated notion of the 'invisible hand' is to be read. D. D. Raphael, however, pronounces that Smith's invisible hand 'is not a piece of theology' (Raphael 1985: 72). Certainly he did not assume the notion of a God who 'pulls the strings all the time', arbitrarily intervening in the world. This would have implied the kind of polytheism that he rejected: 'the invisible hand of Jupiter'. Nevertheless, the metaphor of the invisible hand, as found in Smith's two principal works, is clearly related to the rational theology that he espoused. Smith's whole doctrine of unintended consequences does not imply a 'god of the gaps' who acts arbitrarily in particular cases to bring good out of evil by a special providence, but assumes an Author of nature who has set up a system in which the social welfare is realized in general by each pursuing his or her own interests. 'Private interests and passions of individuals', he wrote, 'naturally dispose them to turn their stock towards the employments which in ordinary cases are most advantageous to society' (Smith [1776] 1976: 630). He applied this idea to political economy in such a way as to attack excessive governmental regulation.

Cosmic and social harmony

In his early lectures on the history of physics and of astronomy, following Newton again, Smith related the development of the natural sciences to the abandoning of polytheism for monotheistic beliefs. Only when the universe was seen as a single system, could a science acknowledging general laws and a religion recognizing a single rational creator be developed. Polytheism ascribes 'all the irregular events of nature to the favour or displeasure of intelligent, though invisible beings'. The *regular* occurrences in nature are not ascribed to 'the invisible hand of Jupiter', but only the unusual and the unpredictable: thunder, lightning and storms.[6] In the distant past the apparent incoherence of the universe led people to ascribe 'almost every unexpected event, to the arbitrary will of some designing, though invisible beings, who produced it for some private and particular purpose'. They had no idea of a universal God who created and governs the whole according to general laws. But 'as soon as the Universe was regarded as a complete machine, as a coherent system, governed by general laws, and directed to general ends', it came to be seen as the work of a supreme being. 'As ignorance begot superstition, science gave birth to the first theism that arose among those nations, who were not enlightened by divine Revelation' (Smith [1795] 1980: 122 ff.).

Yet Smith did not give unqualified approval to the Stoic belief that all events, including 'the vices and follies of mankind', are necessary parts of one great system.[7] He claimed that such speculations conflict with our natural abhorrence of vice, the immediate and harmful consequences of which must outweigh any remote benefits that might result (Smith [1759] 1853: 47). It is therefore misleading of Donald Winch (1978) to speak of his 'Mandevillian cynicism'. Bernard Mandeville had taught that the public interest may be served by private vices, and this Smith explicitly rejected.[8]

He understood Mandeville to abolish the distinction between virtue and vice and to maintain that all preference of public to private interest is nothing more than the indulgence of vanity. While admitting for the sake of argument that 'the most generous and public spirited actions may. . .in some sense be regarded as proceeding from "self-love"', he insisted that self-love may frequently be a virtuous motive for action. He was here, of course, following the mainstream of British eighteenth-century moral theology, as exemplified in Joseph Butler's notion of 'cool self love' as an acceptable motive for virtuous action. Smith taught that human instincts that lead to a particular affection for ourselves and those close to us are providentially designed to forward the general interest.

> That wisdom which contrived the system of human affections, as well as every other part of nature, seems to have judged that the interest of the great society of mankind would be best promoted by directing the principal attention of each individual to that particular portion of it which was most within the sphere both of his abilities and of his understanding (Smith [1759] 1853: 337).

We shall, in due course, see how he applied these ideas to the historical development of states and to the running of a national economy.

The machine of state

There is thus a natural order in the universe as a whole that is replicated at a lower organic level in 'the mechanism of a plant' and at the political level 'in the great system of government' (Smith [1759] 1853: 126, 265). Smith spoke of the political order as a machine whose end, like that of the universe, is general happiness. From a philosophical standpoint, 'Human society. . .appears like a great, an immense machine, whose regular and harmonious movements produce a thousand agreeable effects.' It is moreover a 'beautiful and noble machine' (pp. 463–4). He believed that the appeal to human imagination and aesthetic sensibilities is more likely to encourage respect for the public interest than arguments based on purely material considerations.

This aesthetic admiration for system and order is characteristic of Smith's cosmology as well as of his political economy. In his essay 'Of the imitative arts', he compared the pleasure of contemplating an ordered system with that of hearing 'a well-composed concerto of instrumental Music':

> In the contemplation of that immense variety of agreeable and melodious sounds, arranged and digested, both in their coincidence and in their succession, into so complete and regular a system, the mind in reality enjoys not only a very great sensual, but a very high intellectual, pleasure, not unlike that which is derived from the contemplation of a great system in any other science (Smith [1795] 1980: 205; cf. p. 105).

Jacob Viner's comment that there is 'a wide divergence between the perfectly harmonious, completely beneficent natural order of *The Theory of Moral Sentiments* and the partial and limited harmony in the economic order of *The Wealth of Nations*' is therefore misleading. The cosmic harmony is not complete and the laws of the universe allow occasional injustice, oppression and wrong; all is not well in a fallen world inhabited by beings in a 'depraved' state (Smith [1759] 1853: 109 n). It is only in a life beyond that true harmony will exist. Thus, in the 'economy of nature' as well as in the civil economy, only a partial order and harmony are to be found. But what are the nature and limits of the political and economic order?

Social order and class distinction

Smith saw a kind of order in human communities and related this to their economic base. He outlined four 'periods of society' based successively on hunting, sheep-rearing, agriculture and, finally, commerce. In this historical process, he saw at work a principle that, as we have seen, operates at other levels: the providential role of unintended consequences. In the agricultural period the increased production of manufactured goods encouraged new wants. The great barons and the higher clergy started spending the whole of their revenue; the only way to increase revenue was to grant leases to tenants, who thereby acquired a significant degree of independence. Thus, the vanity and excessive desire for opulence on the part of the landowning classes led to a strengthening of tenants rights, to the demand for greater liberty and 'the regular execution of justice' (Smith [1776] 1976: 421, 803).

Later social formations are characterized by a hierarchy of orders, ranks and classes. He was ambivalent about the sentiments producing this structure, which includes an obsequiousness to our superiors, arising largely from our admiration for the advantages of their situation. He pointed to the human disposition almost to worship the rich and powerful and to despise the poor, which is a principal cause of the erosion of moral sentiments (Smith [1759] 1853: 73, 84). It is partly for this reason that Smith viewed the development of a commercial system as something of a mixed blessing. He nevertheless insisted on the importance of such divisions.

> Every independent state is divided into many different orders and societies. . .Upon the ability of each particular order or society to maintain its own powers, privileges, and immunities, against the encroachments of every other, depends on the stability of that particular constitution (Smith [1759] 1853: 338–9).

In relation to these social divisions Smith made two points which reflect his doctrine of providence and the invisible hand. First, the 'distinction of ranks', upon which depends social peace, is founded not on 'the often uncertain difference of wisdom and virtue' but on the more palpable difference of birth and fortune, which provides a firmer footing for affective ties (p. 332). Secondly, the partiality that individuals have for the groups to which they belong, 'though it may sometimes be unjust, may not upon that account be useless'. In checking innovation, this tends to preserve a balance among the different orders into which the state is divided and contributes to the stability and permanence of the whole system (p. 339).

This takes up a point made earlier about how general welfare is typically forwarded by persons pursuing their own interests and responding to the limited responsibilities of their station, although Smith also insisted that good citizenship implies a wish to promote 'the welfare of the whole society'. Particular loyalties and appetites must therefore he held in check (p. 339). A good ruler, he declared in Burkean style, will accommodate as well as he can to the prejudices and habits of the people and 'will content himself with moderating, what he cannot annihilate without great violence' (p. 342).

The foundation of government

Following David Hume, Smith rejected any idea that social order or civil authority can be founded in a social contract, exposing the fallacy of 'tacit consent' (Smith 1978: 316–17). In *The Theory of Moral Sentiments* he argued that 'society' is held together and subsists 'as among different merchants, from a sense of utility, without any mutual love or affection; and though no man in it should owe any obligation, or be bound in gratitude to any other, it may still be upheld by a mercenary exchange of good offices according to an agreed valuation' (Smith [1759] 1853: 124). Government also is generally based on 'the principle of utility' in combination with 'the principle of authority'. While republican and democratic governments are based predominantly on the former, monarchies rely greatly on a general respect for authority. This is often reinforced by the divine analogy; the king stands to his realm as God stands to the universe, and disobedience to civil government is understood as 'a sort of sinfulness or impiety' (Smith 1978: 318). Governments, in fact, came into being for the protection of property. A nation of hunters has almost no private property, 'but when flocks and herds come to be reared, property then becomes of a very considerable extent' (Smith [1776] 1976: 709 ff.; 1978: 16). It is at this stage that governments evolve, for they exist to protect the rich from the poor. In his lectures, he is reported as saying:

> Laws and government may be considered. . .as a combination of the rich to oppress the poor, and preserve to themselves the inequality of the goods which would otherwise be soon destroyed by the attacks of the poor, who if not hindered by the government would soon reduce the others to an equality with themselves by open violence (Smith 1978: 208; see also p. 404; [1776] 1976: 710, 715).

Among the generally beneficial effects of manufacturing and commerce was the introduction of order and good government 'and with them, the liberty and security of individuals' (Smith [1776] 1976: 412).

In properly ordered states, the government has a threefold duty of protecting the nation from external threats, protecting each individual from injustice or oppression from fellow citizens (by establishing 'an exact administration of justice') and, finally, 'the duty of erecting and maintaining certain publick works and certain publick institutions' (pp. 687–8). These include especially institutions which 'facilitate the commerce of the society' and which promote education (p. 723). Smith clearly acknowledged that there were enterprises of public benefit, but which 'it can never be for the interest of any individual, or small number of individuals, to erect and maintain'. He recognized, furthermore, the right of governments to raise revenue by taxation, using fiscal policy to deter foolish or anti-social practices (p. 688; pp. 831–2).

Nevertheless, Smith saw the basic role of government as regulating and maintaining conditions for the smooth running of the social system.

> The natural effort of every individual to better his own condition, when suffered to exert itself with freedom and security, is so powerful a principle, that it is alone, and without any assistance, not only capable of carrying on the society to wealth and prosperity, but of surmounting a hundred impertinent obstructions with which the folly of human laws too often incumbers its operations (Smith [1776] 1976: 540).

By the regulation of commerce Smith did not mean the introduction of protection or bounties or the establishment of government subsidies for certain products. These are almost always urged by tradesmen whose interests are different from those of the public and 'who have generally an interest to deceive and even to oppress the publick' (p. 267). In a celebrated passage he denounced the 'sneaking arts of underling tradesmen', which are 'erected into political maxims for the conduct of a great empire'.

Government should thus provide a structure within which individuals and groups can pursue 'their own interest in their own way'. But, as in a game, the competitor must abide by the rules:

> In the race for wealth, and honours, and preferments, he may run as hard as he can, and strain every nerve and every muscle, in order to outstrip all his competitors. But if he should justle, or throw down any of them, the indulgence of the spectators is entirely at an end (Smith [1759] 1853: 120).

Honest competition in the marketplace is, he insisted 'advantageous to the great body of the people', who profit greatly by it (Smith [1776] 1976: 494). Each competitor is thinking primarily of his own interest and the general interest is forwarded. It is not 'from the benevolence of the butcher, the brewer, or the baker, that we expect our dinner, but from their regard to their own interests'. The capitalist who invests in local industry and uses his influence to increase its efficiency does not intend to promote the public interest, but is 'led by an invisible hand to promote an end which was not part of his intention' (pp. 27, 456). The invisible hand is also at work in the distribution of goods. A rich person, despite vain and insatiable desires, is able actually to consume little more than the poor. The prosperity of the rich in a community indeed benefits the poor, by what is sometimes called a 'trickle-down effect':

> [The rich] are led by an invisible hand to make nearly the same distribution of the necessaries of life which would have been made had the earth been divided into equal portions among all its inhabitants: and thus without intending it, without knowing it, advance the interest of the society and afford

means to the multiplication of the species (Smith [1759] 1853: 265).

God the economist

I have looked in some detail at the way Adam Smith drew out the analogy between God's management of the universe and a good government's management of the economy. The notion of general harmony of interest in the state (with only occasional government interventions) is both paralleled, and to some extent legitimated, by the operation of the Divine Providence. In elaborating this analogy, Smith was by no means the only thinker to pursue such a line of inquiry – and this tradition goes back, at least, to Leibniz, and has powerful resonances in the contemporary debates concerning the theological and the economic.

Some years ago Jon Elster (1975) attempted to show how Leibniz's conception of God was a transposition from the economic realm. Leibniz saw God on the model of the capitalist entrepreneur; his theodicy assumed a 'cost benefit' approach of optimizing happiness in the best of all possible worlds (cf. Nicholls 1981: 205–15). More recently, Douglas Meeks (1985) has defended the analogy of God the economist, pointing to the way Christian theologians have from early times used the concept of *oikos* to characterize God's dealings with his 'household'. What kind of economist is God?

Modern ideas of the enterprise culture assume a God who has created a universe to run according to certain laws and has handed over responsibility to humans, who have been given total 'freedom of choice'. But the freedom is in many cases purely formal and lacks content. Miners, made redundant in one part of the country, are free to move to another area, or are free to retrain as computer technicians. There is no external constraint or law preventing them. The fact that the miner owns a house in the village, which he cannot sell owing to the absence of employment opportunities, the fact that he has affective ties with the village, the fact that he cannot afford to live in those areas where there is alternative employment, are seen as irrelevant to the question of freedom. Those who think like this are operating with a formal and inadequate conception of freedom, sometimes called 'negative liberty' (see Berlin 1969: Nicholls 1962).

When the highwayman says 'Your money or your life' he is offering, on this account, a perfectly free choice to his client, who is at liberty to retain his money and accept the consequence. But this is not the kind of freedom that God gives to his people.

Margaret Thatcher's statement to the General Assembly of the Church of Scotland (1988) that 'man has been endowed by God with the fundamental right to choose between good and evil' and that 'we are expected to use all our *own* power of thought and judgement in exercising that choice' is radically Pelagian and calls into question the Christian doctrines of grace and original sin (in Raban 1988: 10). This is curious, because her own Chancellor of the Exchequer practically defined conservatism in terms of commitment to original sin (cited by Atherton 1988: 61). There is a serious incoherence in the theological defence of the enterprise culture. Its critics, of course, like R. H. Tawney, have argued that not only does this culture *recognize* human acquisitive tendencies but it *encourages* them, leaving no scope for cooperative instincts. 'Were a people to become quite disinterested,' observed the eighteenth-century economist, Sir James Steuart, 'there would be no possibility of governing them' (cited by Hirschman 1977: 50). This principle has been exemplified in recent trade union legislation, which permits strikes when the material interests of workers are at stake, but outlaws strikes undertaken in solidarity with others. Disinterested action of this kind is thought to be subversive – altruism walks hand-in-hand with anarchism.

Modern economic theory is based on scarcity; Meeks challenges this assumption that scarcity is a fact of nature (Meeks 1989: 170 ff.). Scarcity is related to demand as much as to supply. God the economist is the author of abundance; scarcity is the result of our sinful acquisitive tendencies and deliberate attempts to create artificial wants. The enterprise culture depends upon a continued stimulation of new desires. A European businessman, James Franklin, resident in Haiti in the early nineteenth century, denounced president Boyer for a policy of keeping his people 'ignorant of artificial wants' (Franklin 1828: 240). Acquisition and consumption are in truth the engines that keep the machine going. One Conservative MP has even modified the Cartesian dictum to read 'I consume therefore I am'. In his recent Hibbert Lecture on 'The love of money', Andrew Phillips illustrates this aspect of the enterprise culture by quoting the head of an international recruitment agency, who writes of the new breed who are 'aggressive, restless, greedy urban techno-crats. . .interested in money to the point of obsession. . .that's the way they are, and that's the way we want them' (Rowlinson, cited by Phillips 1988: 8). The Christian can thus detect several heresies at work in the enterprise culture: idolatry; animism (*'make your money work for you'*) or that 'fetishism of commodities' scrutinized by a nineteenth-century secular theologian; and the identification of the human person with his or her possessions.

There is today evidence that some defenders of the enterprise culture see dangers in the emphasis on ruthless accumulation at the expense of communal values, interdependence and responsibility. Douglas Hurd told a meeting of Anglicans, 'We need to work together, in Church and State, to rebuild the moral standards and values which should form the sure foundation of a cohesive and united nation' (Hurd 1988). It is the job of the church and of the education system to foster these values, which form a necessary framework within which the enterprise system may operate. Some of the writers we discussed earlier were fully aware of the need for limits. 'Everything is now made a question of finance', wrote Chalmers, 'and science with all which can grace or dignify a nation, is vulgarized and brought down to a common standard – the standard of the market and of the counting-house' (Chalmers 1835–41, Vol. xix, p. 184). He might have been reflecting on Thatcherite Britain.[9]

As theories of laissez-faire in the early nineteenth century devel-oped, in reaction to the corrupt and stifling results of the bounties, monopolies and restrictions of a mercantilist age, so the enterprise ideology of Thatcherite Britain should be seen against the back-ground of the omnicompetent paternalism of the welfare state. In both cases the reaction was partially justified. The market has generally proved the most effective way of matching demand with supply; attempts to replace it with central planning have failed dismally. The recognition of self-interest as a major factor in human action and of the need for initiative and entrepreneurship is to be welcomed. The maternalistic 'grandmother' God of welfare has, however, been replaced by an equally unattractive and unbalanced image of the severe and detached despot of deism. There is, however, another image in scripture and tradition, which sees

God as supporting, leading and guiding, without imposing on
his people. A God who calls them to justice and to cooperation with each other and with God; a trinitarian God where
differences are recognized as the basis for a true harmony – a
community of persons in which 'none if afore, or after other:
none is greater, or less than another'. Perhaps the ethical question
should not be 'do you tell your partner?' but 'do you have a
partner to tell?' I conclude with some words from a sermon
in 1978:

> Whether we are likely to get very far in convincing others of
> this, of 'God as community' in the present social and political
> situation is doubtful. There is today so little experience of true
> community life that the image of God as community is hardly
> understood by the majority of our population. . .Only in a state
> based upon ideas of justice, co-operation and community will
> it be possible for people properly to understand God the Holy
> Trinity. This is at least one reason why orthodox theologians
> must be committed to social action.[10]

Notes: Chapter 13

1 *Christianity and the State* (1929: 169–70); the new *Oxford English
   Dictionary* mistakenly gives 1940 as the first date for the use of
   this term.
2 This notion of welfare as characteristic of God and the state is
   elaborated in David Nicholls (1989), Chapters 2 and 3.
3 For the relation between theology and political economy in the early
   nineteenth century, see particularly Waterman (1983: 231; 1986: 99
   ff.), Rashid (1977: 147), Soloway (1969) and Hilton (1988).
4 The Newtonian theologian, Samuel Clarke, defended Newton's
   divine interventionism against the criticisms of Leibniz by a political
   analogy. Would a king who never did anything really rule? God's
   government is a real government, therefore he acts directly from
   time to time. Leibniz, of course, replied that a perfect king sets
   up such a legal framework that he does not need to intervene. See
   Nicholls (1981: 205 ff.).
5 See Adam Smith ([1759] 1853: 110, 126); see also his reference to
   God as 'the great Conductor of the universe' (pp. 346–7).
6 See also A. Macfie (1971: 595 ff.). It is particularly in the context of
   weather forecasting that modern scientists have developed ideas of
   the so-called 'butterfly effect', according to which the most minute

change (which some would say is inherently unpredictable, because in principle unmeasurable) can have huge effects on weather systems. They are less likely to see the universe as a closed system than Smith was, and to acknowledge that perhaps, after all God does play dice (see Polkinghorne 1989).

7   Macfie suggests that Smith 'seems to accept, and interpret in his own way, the broad outline of the "ancient stoics"' (Macfie 1971: 599).

8   Winch (1978: 80, 172) ascribes a Mandevillian position to Smith. Curiously, however, he fails to note the paragraphs in *The Theory of Moral Sentiments* where Smith describes Dr Mandeville's system as having a tendency that is 'wholly pernicious' (Smith [1759] 1853: 451).

9   See Chalmers (1835–41, Vol. xix, p. 184; see also Vol. xvi, pp. 285 ff.), where he defended community values against the individualism of Smith.

10 See Nicholls (1979). There is a good deal written on the relationship between Trinitarianism and politics, going back to the poet and preacher John Donne. Much of it, however, assumes that if we get our theology right our politics will follow from it, but the relationship is more dialectical. There is no chance that we will 'get our theology right' in an ideological vacuum. See my *Deity and Domination* (1989).

References: Chapter 13

Atherton, J. 1988. *Faith in the Nation: A Christian Vision for Britain.* London: SPCK.

Berlin, I. 1969. *Four Essays on Liberty.* Oxford: Oxford University Press.

Brown, S. J. 1982. *Thomas Chalmers and the Godly Commonwealth.* Oxford: Oxford University Press.

Chalmers, T. 1833. *On the Power, Wisdom and Goodness of God*, Vol. ii. London: W. Pickering.

Chalmers, T. 1835–41. *Collected Works of Thomas Chalmers*, Vols i, vi, xiv, xvi, xix. Glasgow: William Collins.

Elster, J. 1975. *Leibniz et la formation de l'esprit capitaliste.* Paris: Aubier-Montaigne.

Franklin, J. 1828. *The Present State of Hayti.* London: J. Murray.

Hetherington, N. 1983. Isaac Newton's influence on Adam Smith's Natural Laws in Economics. *Journal of the History of Ideas*, 44, 3: 497–505.

Hilton, B. 1988. *The Age of Atonement: The Influence of Evangelicalism on Social and Economic Thought, 1785–1865.* Oxford: Clarendon Press.

Hirschman, A. 1977. *The Passions and the Interests.* Princeton, NJ: Princeton University Press.

Hurd, D. 1988. Speech by the Home Secretary to a Fringe Meeting of the General Synod of the Church of England, Church House, London, 10 February 1988.

Macfie, A. 1971. The invisible hand of Jupiter. *Journal of the History of Ideas*, 32, 4: 595–9.

Mandeville, B. [1714] 1723 (2nd edn). *The Fable of the Bees, or Private Vices, Public Benefits*. London: E. Parker.

Meeks, D. (1989), *God the Economist: The Doctrine of God and Political Economy*. Minneapolis, Minn.: Fortress Press.

Nicholls, D. 1962. Positive liberty: 1880–1914. *American Political Science Review*, 56, 1: 114–28.

Nicholls, D. 1979. *Principalities and Powers*. London: Jubilee Group.

Nicholls, D. 1981. Images of God and the state: political analogy and religious discourse. *Theological Studies*, 42, 2: 202–15.

Nicholls, D. 1989. *Deity and Domination*. London: Routledge.

Phillips, A. 1988. *The Love of Money*. London: Hibbert Trust.

Polkinghorne, J. 1989. *Science and Providence: God's Interaction with the World*. London: SPCK.

Raban, J. 1989. *God, Man and Mrs Thatcher*. London: Chatto & Windus.

Raphael, D. 1985. *Adam Smith*. Oxford: Oxford University Press.

Rashid, S. 1977. Richard Whately and Christian political economy at Oxford and Dublin. *Journal of the History of Ideas*, 38, I: 147–50.

Smith, A. [1759] 1853. *The Theory of Moral Sentiments*. London: H. G. Bohn.

Smith, A. [1776] 1976. *An Inquiry into the Nature and Causes of the Wealth of Nations*. Oxford: Clarendon Press.

Smith, A. 1978. *Lecturers on Jurisprudence*. Oxford: Clarendon Press.

Smith, A. [1795] 1980. *Essays on Philosophical Subjects*. Oxford: Clarendon Press.

Soloway, R. 1969. *Prelates and People: Ecclesiastical Social Thought in England, 1783–1852*. London: Routledge.

Stigler, G. 1976. Smith's travels on the ship of state. In A. S. Skinner and T. Wilson (eds), *Essays on Adam Smith*. Oxford: Oxford University Press.

Temple, W. 1929. *Christianity and the State*. London: Macmillan.

Waterman, A. 1983. The ideological alliance of political economy and Christian theology, 1798–1833. *Journal of Ecclesiastical History*, 34, 2: 231–44.

Waterman, A. 1986. Christian political economy: Malthus to Margaret Thatcher. In W. Block and I. Hexham (eds), *Religion, Economics and Social Thought*. Vancouver: Frazer Institute, pp, 99–124.

Wescott, B. *et al.* 1901. *The Church and New Century Problems*. London: Wells, Gardner, Garton & Co.

Winch, D. 1978. *Adam Smith's Politics*. Cambridge: Cambridge University Press.

14 Critical reflections on Michael Novak's The Spirit of Democratic Capitalism

ALAN SUGGATE

Novak's influence is international. His writings have been translated into every major western language, and into Korean and Japanese. *The Spirit of Democratic Capitalism* (1982) was published underground by Solidarity in Poland. A frequent visitor to Britain, Novak has been an important source of encouragement and inspiration to the advocates of the enterprise culture here and has developed links with the Establishment in this country. At present, he is a Professor of Religion and Public Policy at the American Enterprise Institute in Washington, DC.

Novak is an American Roman Catholic with ancestral roots in Slovakia. He has abandoned a position very critical of capitalism, and is now one of the the the most eloquent defenders of it, or at least of the version of democratic capitalism that he sees embodied in the United States. I have concentrated on *The Spirit of Democratic Capitalism* because it is a seminal treatise on the enterprise culture. I have also taken account of some of his more recent writings, *Free Persons and the Common Good* (1989a) and *Catholic Social Thought and Liberal Institutions* ([1984], 2nd edn, 1989b).

The yardstick for my critique is primarily the English tradition of Christian social ethics, represented by William Temple, R. H. Tawney and, more recently, Ronald H. Preston. In the last sixty years it has been strengthened by contact with the Ecumenical Movement, and notably the thought of Reinhold Niebuhr, and it has strong points of affinity with post-Vatican II Roman Catholic social ethics. Its procedure is to operate with a broad understanding of the Christian faith under the rubric of the Kingdom of God, from which are inferred certain social principles, such as the freedom and dignity of human beings and their sociality. These principles are brought alongside an analysis of the social situation, so that a critique can be made of the status quo. From this interplay of situation and principles, suggestions can then be made about the broad directions in which society should move in order to be more in conformity with the Christian faith. I recently proposed a particular variant of this procedure (Suggate 1987). I am now testing it out by reference to issues such as the New Right and by taking more thorough account of liberation theology.

A good deal of what I am going to say can also be said on non-Christian grounds, and I firmly believe in finding as much common ground with non-Christians as possible. Our pluralistic society pushes us in that direction in any case. But Christianity has, I believe, its own coordinates, which form a base for social ethics. What Christianity has to offer to social ethics is much disputed among Christians themselves, from the foundations to the practical implications, but that is not a sufficient reason to abandon the quest for a Christian social ethic.

Novak's 'Theology'

A central concept in Michael Novak's *The Spirit of Democratic Capitalism* (1982) is that of emergent probability, which he takes and adapts from Bernard Lonergan's *Insight, a Study of Human Understanding* (1958). Lonergan, he believes, holds certain assumptions, which most people in democratic capitalist societies take for granted, and which some relate to religious images of creation, providence, sin and history. Events in the world process do not happen by cold logical necessity, but neither are they perfectly random. They occur in accord with schemes of probabilities. The world process is open to events and schemes of recurrence that have never before emerged, subject to the fulfilment of their preconditions. It is also open to breakdowns and reversals. A world of emergent probability requires constant changes in our understanding, but understanding is not easy. 'There are meanings to be discerned, breakthroughs to be achieved, possibilities to be grasped and realised, riches to be wrested from silent nature. Nature is not regarded as achieved, complete, finished. Creation is unfinished.' Novak picks up Lonergan's emphasis on the capacity of human beings for insight. It is, for example, through insights and their verification that science advances (Novak 1982: 72–5).

In Novak's view, such a belief about the world process is crucial to the habit of mind designated by the term 'enterprise'. An entrepreneur knows that the world is open to human intelligence and intervention. The application of intelligence affects the probabilities of success and failure, but events are complex, the schemes of probabilities are uncertain, and so decisions are hazardous. 'The most intelligent of efforts can end in failure. Sheer luck can sometimes bring success. But over the long run humans face a world of risk to which intelligence is sufficiently matched to wrest significant successes' (Novak 1982: 76).

Democratic capitalism itself did not emerge either by cold logical necessity or by random accident. Crucial was the insight of Adam Smith, who hit upon the bold and original ideal of sustained economic development produced as a matter of intelligence. His probability of success was high, for many of the assumptions he needed to draw on, especially the moral–cultural values that Max Weber later codified under the name 'the Protestant ethic', were taking hold. Smith was counter-intuitive in that he did not put his emphasis upon the possession of great natural resources, or upon political status, or upon underpopulation or overpopulation, or upon ownership of the means of production by the state, or upon better and more detailed planning, or upon religious rules of justice and charity, or upon the organization of states by the military. He grasped the importance of system as a good basis for order, and had the intelligence to devise a system designed as closely as possible to fit human character. That was the best way to unleash human creativity. The key to the wealth of nations lay in human creativity more than in any other source, and that key lay in the natural system of liberty, which fostered practical intelligence and the organization of personal life (Novak 1982: 76–78, 102 ff.).

It is essential to agree with Novak that emergent probability and the creative use of intelligence are features of the world that God has chosen to create, and those who dwell upon visions of justice and charity cannot afford to bypass them, or the disciplines that handle these phenomena, notably economics. As Novak rightly affirms, 'In the real world, moral motives do not suffice. The bafflements of emergent probability do not yield their meaning to good intentions' (1982: 80). The English tradition of Christian social ethics has generally been very strong on moral ideals and prophetic critiques, on the evils of maldistribution of goods and services, rather than the creative use of intelligence for economic development. It has tended to back off from giving any serious attention to the discipline of economics. This is true of most of the earlier groups devoted to Christian socialism, and also of the Christendom Group. One of the few exceptions to this tendency is Ronald Preston, who has never ceased to insist that Christians must get to grips with the discipline of economics and face up to the fundamental problems with which economics is concerned: centrally, the allocation of scarce resources (Preston 1979: 24; cf. 16). To harp on visions as if they could of themselves solve our problems is to retreat into an unreal world of idealism. Liberation theology is also woefully weak at this point. Rightly scandalized by mass poverty, exploitation, oppressions and neo-colonialism, it tends to ally a discredited Marxist interpretation of economics with utopian ideas about the emergence of a new man on the other side of the revolution. Liberation theologians excuse themselves from the hard questions of what system of economics would be required in the new era. Unless they turn their backs on science and technology altogether, they will need to have some system that takes account of this feature of emergent probability and encourages creativity in economic development.

There are, however, serious questions to raise about Novak at this point. He seems intoxicated with the idea of emergent probability and intelligence, grounded in a doctrine of creation. In a later chapter, entitled 'Providence and practical wisdom', he contrasts the image of God as *nous*, the all-seeing God of harmony, with Aquinas's metaphor of God as Providence, stressing the respect of God for a world of concrete contingencies, secondary causes, liberties and sin (Novak 1982: 96 ff.). In so far as God features in the pages of Novak, it is chiefly this dimension of God that is prominent. The critical question is whether it should have that prominence.

Most English social ethics and liberation theology would argue that the dimension of God as Providence needs to be set within the context of a God of the Covenant. One basic point is that the exercise of intelligence and creativity is ambiguous. Practical intelligence and organizational ability were used to excellent effect in the extermination of the Jews (see Haas 1988). They are instrumental values, whose use is crucially dependent upon the ends to which they are put, ends like the dignity of the human person and the development of persons in community. Liberation theology stresses God's concern for the vulnerable and the poor as members of the community. Novak would agree that the values associated with enterprise, chiefly rational self-interest, are not sufficient for social life, or even for the economic system itself. He goes on to say much about human dignity and human communities, both here and in *Free Persons and the Common Good*. Yet his stress on creation (repeated in *Catholic Social Thought and Liberal Institutions* and in the riposte to the American Catholic Bishops on the US Economy) acquires too great a prominence.[1]

At first sight, what Novak says about human frailty meets this problem. A system designed to fit human character, says Novak, will on the one hand give maximum scope to human intelligence and creativity, but it also firmly recognizes human frailty and sinfulness. Adam Smith was not optimistic about the human capacity for reasonableness or virtue. Democratic capitalism's *bête noire* is political tyranny. It is highly sceptical of any revolution which promises a new type of moral man, which is almost always to be guaranteed by the coercive power of the state. In contrast, it looks on sin as rooted in the free personality, beyond the reach of any system, 'an ineradicable given from which all realistic thinking about political economy must begin'. It agrees with Aristotle that in systems one must be satisfied with 'a tincture of virtue', even though rather more than that may sometimes be obtained (Novak 1982: 82–8).

Novak's considerations are valid against certain romantic utopian views, to be found both in the English tradition of Christian social ethics and in liberation theology. R. H. Preston has criticized R. H. Tawney for being too utopian in his theology (Preston 1979: 107–10). Liberation theologians often have romantic views about the virtue of the people. It is true that they generally add a rider that the people are also sinful, but this is no sooner mentioned than it is dropped. As Novak says, one reads them in vain for descriptions of the exact institutional structures by which their dreams of equality, justice, autonomy and brotherhood will be realized (Novak 1982: 87).

Yet Novak's work exudes an air of intolerable complacency. On the one hand, he seems to have great confidence that minimum standards in a free society are assured. 'A free society can tolerate the public display of vice because it has confidence in the basic decency of human beings, even under the burden of sin' (Novak 1982: 351). On the other hand, he never loses an opportunity to warn us of the blight of sin. In his final chapter, 'A theology of democratic capitalism', even his section on the Incarnation instantly turns to the question of sin. 'One of the most poignant lessons of the Incarnation is the difficult teaching that one must learn to be humble, think concretely, face facts, train oneself to realism. . .The point of Incarnation is to respect the world as it is, to acknowledge its limits, to recognise its weaknesses, irrationalities and evil forces, and to disbelieve any promises that the world is now, or ever will be, transformed into the City of God. If Jesus could not effect that, how shall we?' (Novak 1982: 341).

These trenchant remarks are somewhat qualified by the assurance that the Incarnation is a doctrine of hope. However, Novak seems to miss almost entirely the sense that the Incarnation involved the inauguration of a New Age, which deeply challenges the old. The Kingdom of God is present in the life of Jesus himself, and through his death and resurrection (and Novak has scarcely any reference to the resurrection) the new Age of the Spirit is inaugurated. Novak seems to me to miss the dramatic quality of the Christ event. He writes, 'The single greatest temptation for Christians is to imagine that the salvation won by Jesus has altered the human condition. Many attempt to judge the present world by the standards of the Gospels as though the world were ready to live according to them. Sin is not so easily overcome' (Novak 1982: 343). Novak shares Smith's urbane blend of optimism and pessimism. I believe we need a more dramatic reading of the human situation, which, on the one hand, does not count upon the basic decency of human beings as a springboard for cautious further advance and, on the other, captures that sense of hopeful urgency, which is the pressure of the Kingdom of God upon humanity. It is possible that Novak's enthusiasm for Adam Smith is related to the rather old-fashioned Roman Catholic two-tier view of natural law. It is noticeable how enthusiastic Novak is for Aquinas, and how little he enters into more radical currents of Catholic thought in the post-Vatican II era: for example, Charles Curran.

Reinhold Niebuhr criticized two-tier natural law in a double way. According to Thomistic doctrine, the Fall robbed human beings of the capacity for faith, hope and love, but left their nature intact. Fallen human beings, therefore, need sacramental grace for the restoration of these supernatural virtues. But the capacity for natural justice is not seriously impaired. For Niebuhr, this is doubly wrong. It ignores the fact that all statements and definitions of justice are corrupted by the most rational of people through the power of self-interest. On the other hand, the potentialities of human beings for freedom and love are sustained after the fall. Niebuhr himself often speaks of common grace: the possibilities of love do not depend on explicit Christian belief and practice, but are maintained by God for all in the very structure of their existence. Niebuhr, therefore, arrives at a more dynamic blend of suspicion yet hopefulness about the possibilities in human existence for love and justice (Niebuhr 1976: 46 ff.).

Unintended consequences and virtuous self-interest

Novak's complacency shows up further in what he says about unintended consequences and virtuous self-interest. For him, the doctrine of unintended consequences is central to the theory of democratic capitalism. It turns the eyes of the political economist away from the moral intentions of individuals towards the final consequences of their actions and towards systems as systems. Novak follows Smith in a deep suspicion of those who would aim directly at social improvement. The best way to defeat sin or at least transform its energy into creative use (and thus take the best revenge on Satan), is offered by the workings of unintended consequences. The intentions of businessmen may be quite self-interested, but that does not matter. It is the structure of business activity that is decisive. Business activity depends upon the

stability of the law, because businessmen must make investments
long before they receive any fruits in return. They must practise
trust and contract. Many in manufacturing and commerce have an
interest in small aggregate increments and marginal savings. Their
habits of mind incline them to productivity and moderation. They
also have an interest in expanding prosperity, reaching out to other
nations, and in maintaining ties of peace and order abroad. The
structure, therefore, is favourable to the rule of law, liberty, habits
of regularity and moderation, a healthy realism and demonstrated
social progress. The consequences are therefore beneficial (Novak
1982: 82, 89–91).

It is clear enough that Adam Smith had a very important insight
in his doctrine of unintened consequences. In general, it may be said
that the doctrine has worked with moderate success in the West,
though we must not forget colonial exploitation. But Novak surely
overcalls his hand. He does not seem to recognize as clearly as Smith
the conflicts of interest and the inequalities of power in the system,
and correspondingly says little about the restraints on economic
power to be imposed by the political and moral–cultural system
in defence of the weak. The English experience is that it has been
necessary for countervailing power to be built up (an important
motif in Tawney), in order to exercise any effective control of economic power. And it has never been easy to establish any effective
control. The trade unions had great difficulty in building up real
countervailing power, and it is very doubtful whether a succession
of Labour governments exercised an effective check. In the last ten
years many of the defences of the workforce have been removed.

From the standpoint of liberation theology, economic power
exploits the weak bargaining position of the Third World in order
to achieve an endless supply of cheap labour, tax concessions
and the like. Élites in third-world countries provide no effective
countervailing political power. And the situation is compounded
by the huge debt crisis. The burden of repaying the interest on the
loans falls upon a largely poor population, depriving them of the
few welfare services they have, and the priorities of the country are
skewed by the stringent requirements of the International Monetary
Fund and the World Bank. One theologian has called high interest
rates the gas chambers of today.[2] It is just possible that within
the European Community (EC) the political will may be there to

exercise a restraint upon economic power after the removal of trade barriers in 1992. But the chances of any effective political control over transnational economic forces seem to be remote indeed. The issue here is essentially empirical: how does the doctrine of unintended consequences work? The contribution of theology is that it knows from its prophetic tradition about the pursuit of power, including economic power, and the need to defend the weak. It will therefore scrutinize the doctrine with special care.

These considerations need to be related also to what Novak says about virtuous self-interest. He notes that capitalism is savagely indicted for institutionalizing selfishness and greed. This has been the stock-in-trade of Christian socialists. Novak advances certain considerations that have a limited validity. He is right to say that, on the whole, rational long-term interest is what is required by capitalism. Furthermore, the real interests of individuals are seldom merely self-regarding. 'To most persons their families mean more than their own interests; they frequently subordinate the latter to the former. Their communities are also important to them. In the human breast commitments to benevolence, fellow-feeling, and sympathy are strong. Moreover, humans have the capacity to see themselves as others see them, and to hold themselves to standards which transcend their own selfish inclinations. . .Understood too narrowly, self-interest destroys firms as surely as it destroys personal lives. Understood broadly, as a set of realistic limits, it is a key to all the virtues, as prudence is' (Novak 1982: 92 ff.)

Novak falls far short of Reinhold Niebuhr in his recognition of the acute difficulty of harnessing self-interest. A strong card that Niebuhr used to play was that of alter-egoism, where our altruism brings benefit to ourselves. Patriotism is a good example. Novak's model seems to be an extension of interest into ever-widening circles, but at the centre of the circles remains the self. If the problem of the self is as easy to cope with as Novak seems to think it is, one is at a loss to make any sense of Jesus's call for self-denial, or his warning about God and Mammon. I cannot agree with the demands of many liberation theologians that capitalism be simply branded as idolatry, nor can I accept the view of Ulrich Duchrow, resting basically on those grounds, that capitalism brings the church into the *status confessionis* in the way that Nazism did (Duchrow 1987: 126 ff.). I do believe, however, that the Gospels encourage a relentless suspicion about any claim that we can successfully handle the phenomenon of self-interest. Novak approves of Smith's hope that by granting human self-interest its due it can be transmuted into a system of order, imagination, initiative and progress for all, and would evolve interests larger than those of self-love. 'The work of democratic capitalism will not be done until a sound material base has been laid beneath every human life on this planet' (Novak 1982: 149; cf. 1989a: 64).

A very worrying feature at present is that the market can generally flourish without paying the least attention to those who do not have the resources to constitute a market. They represent in Britain between 5 and 15 per cent of the population (termed by Ralf Dahrendorf an underclass); but the percentage is far higher in the Third World. Not only does the First World have no incentive to create competition with itself from the Third World, it also has no need for the foreseeable future to start creating mass markets for its goods in the Third World, and, as Novak himself remarks, getting people into markets is the hardest task (Novak 1982: 109). It seems to be one of the unintended consequences of capitalism that sizeable proportions of populations are left outside the market.

Community

These reflections on self-interest lead into the last theme, community. Novak is strongly aware that philosophers of democratic capitalism have been preoccupied with the concepts of individual and state, and have neglected the mediating structures of community. He compensates by returning time and again to this concept of community. He thus immediately undercuts the stock-in-trade accusation of Christian socialists against capitalism: that it is rampantly individualistic. What is more, he is a good deal more precise than many Christian socialists about what he has in mind by community. He dismisses the nostalgic sense of *Gemeinschaft*, and points to a community of free persons in voluntary association. He identifies four fundamental elements in the structure of democratic capitalism that lead to community, elements that belong to the system as system, independent of the attitudes of those who participate in it.

First, 'the dynamics of the economic system are aimed – in the phrase of Adam Smith – not at the wealth of individuals, and not at the wealth of Scotland or Great Britain, but at the wealth of all nations. The intention of the system *qua* system is to raise the material base of the life of every human being on earth.' Secondly, democratic capitalism brought into prominence the corporation, a voluntary association committed to business enterprise. The corporateness of the corporation is not what the ideology of the rugged individual leads one to anticipate. Managers spend most of their time dealing with human problems, and a successful corporation is frequently based upon the principle of subsidiarity, whereby concrete decisions are made at the level closest to concrete reality. As Novak wittily remarks, corporate managers appear to meet together more often to discuss common strategies than parish priests and bishops, and by comparison with corporate managers, professors of theology, philosophy and literature seem to be rugged individualists indeed. Thirdly, commercial civilization is inescapably interdependent. And, fourthly, the system *qua* system depends upon a community of values, which encourages cooperation, compromise and discipline for practical communal tasks (Novak 1982: 129–34).

Novak maintains that these four elements are the backbone of the forms of community that democratic capitalism has invented. 'They have made possible a new type of human being, neither an individualist nor a collectivist.' Focusing on Great Britain, he maintains that its individualism is not what it appears. We should not underestimate the capacities of the British for organization and sociality. The underlying practice of British society should be distinguished from its public emphasis on the individual. Returning to the works of Adam Smith, Novak correctly refutes the erroneous notion, repeatedly advanced by Christian socialists, that Smith was a rampant individualist, who made a god out of self-interest. *The Wealth of Nations* (1776) must not be read in abstraction from *The Theory of Moral Sentiments* (1759), which he revised just before his death in 1790. The emphasis on self-interest and the invisible hand in *The Wealth of Nations* is to be set in the context of his emphasis on fellow-feeling, common sympathy and benevolence, which is so prominent in *The Theory of Moral Sentiments* (Novak 1982: 134, 145).

So strong is Novak's accent on community, that when he comes to expound six theological doctrines at the end of his book, he assures us that community is essential to our notion of God. God is more to be conceived of as a kind of community than as a solitary individual. 'From human experience, human beings have learned to place highest value upon communities of love, however humble and flawed. The image of the solitary loner, however noble and heroic. . .somehow rings false as a representation of the highest of human experiences. What is most valued among humans is that community within which individuality is not lost. To build such a community is to share God's life. . .I do not think it wrong to hold that this lesson of experience is consistent with the teaching of Scripture.' His final vision is that of 'a republic of independent, self-reliant, fraternal and co-operative citizens, each of whose interests includes the interests of all in brotherhood from sea to shining sea' (Novak 1982: 337 ff. 357).

The sober issue is whether democratic capitalism really functions in a communitarian way or is destructive of community. I wish to call Novak's optimism in question by appeal to two works.

Fred Hirsch's *Social Limits to Growth* (1977) was published as long ago as 1977, and has not yet been refuted. He severely criticized the conventional economic wisdom, which urges us to go for compound economic growth instead of redistribution. As long as we adjust our expectations downwards, screw our performance up, and exercise patience effort and restraint, then competitive individualistic advance, it is claimed, can deliver economic goods for all. In Hirsch's view, this can work only in the case of purely private goods. Most cases in real life are neither purely private nor purely public. In this majority of cases, the satisfaction of a good or utility I have is affected in its essence by the consumption of the same goods or services by others. For example, the satisfaction to me of a car or a country cottage depends on the conditions in which they can be used, which will be strongly influenced by how many other people are using them.

Economists focus on the valuations individuals put upon goods and opportunities. But this worm's-eye-view leads to the situation where each individual gets a worse bargain than was reckoned on when the transaction was undertaken. It is similar to the situation in a crowd: if everyone stands on tiptoe, no one sees any better.

The social environment has a restricted capacity to extend use without deterioration in quality. And where it does, it imposes social limits to consumption. Those later in the queue for these positional goods, as Hirsch calls them, find that they are excluded from them by their increasing scarcity and cost. It is as if there is an imposed hierarchy that confined social goods to those on the highest rungs of the distributional ladder. This precipitates a distributional struggle, which is heightened by the dynamic process of growth – the very reverse of what economists and politicians have come to expect growth to deliver.

Viewing this matter historically, Hirsch claims that economic liberalism is a victim of its own success. Its efficiency resided in its capacity for decentralization of knowledge and decision-making, by harnessing the ancient individual instinct of maximization of personal advantage. Socially beneficial results have thereby been obtained without the necessity of socially oriented motivation. Good has been done by stealth. Hirsch thinks that the invisible hand was a favourable inaugural condition of liberal capitalism. Full participation was confined to a minority, who reached material affluence before liberal capitalism had set the masses on the path of material growth. The system operated on social foundations laid under a very different social order.

Economic liberalism tends to undermine these supports. It spreads the demand for participation to all and erodes social foundations. Hirsch traces the impact of this economic scramble to people's attitudes and, therefore, to the moral–cultural system. The scramble for positional goods makes people more money-minded. There is an excessive creation and absorption of commodities, and an excessive proportion of economic activity is channelled through the market. This is what he calls the commercialization effect. People become more and more contractually minded, and less is taken on trust. And where conventions cannot be counted on and people pursue maximum private benefit, then that change feeds upon itself. Hirsch quotes H. G. Johnson: 'We live in a rich society which nevertheless in many respects insists on thinking and acting as if it were a poor society' (Hirsch 1977: 1, 71, 84, 88–9, 110).

Perhaps the greatest poverty is in human relationships. The scramble for positional goods ensures that time is always at a premium. When your material goods increase you need more time to consume and, therefore, in defence you go for more time-saving goods. The needs of individuals created by positional competition have a cost in time that is represented by the additional money that has to be earned to pay for the additional needs. 'This is the rat-race at the societal level.' A casualty in this scramble is friendship. For friendship is time-consuming. One of the basic points about friendship and love is that, though they have elements of a private economic good, they are much more than implied contracts of long-term exchange. The well being of the other is integrally merged with one's own wellbeing (Hirsch 1977: 73–8).

In short, Hirsch is arguing that the way capitalism actually works erodes the moral cultural stock of the country. He is primarily concerned with analysis. In so far as he looks at inferences from that analysis for policy, he does not believe that we can continue along the same road, introducing merely correctives through technographic management. If we cannot proceed in a purely altruistic manner (and this he accepts), then at least we have to throw much more accent on the pursuit of social good, as if in an altruistic way, and he recommends that we should remove many positional goods from the commercial sector by making them more available through public access and public allocation on a non-market basis (Hirsch 1977: 111, 117 ff., 143, 178 ff.).

The strength of Hirsch lies in the form of his analysis, which is all too rare, where his expertise as an economist is located within a wider cultural context. In fact his work relates economics, social psychology and morality. He also relates to liberation theology in the sense that, in his sections on the commercialization bias and new commodity fetishism, he gives some concrete substance to the wilder accusations of liberation theologians, that capitalism is idolatrous. Novak, by contrast, fails to relate his economic vision to powerful destructive forces at work in the world, which are intimately related to economic processes.

In the tradition of English Christian social ethics, R. H. Tawney used to say that the acid test of a society was the way in which it cared for those who had fallen by the wayside (Tawney [1926] 1938: 184). Liberation theology treats God's concern for the poor as an axial theme of the Bible. The phrase, 'the preferential option for the poor' is in effect a critical question put to those who, like

Novak, advance an optimistic vision of the capacity of capitalism to bring wealth to all.

A recent publication, edited by Ulrich Duchrow and others, is *Totaler Krieg gegen die Armen* (1989). This is a collection of leaked documents of the secret services of the armed forces of the United States and the élites of Central and South America. It is refreshingly frank. The axiom is that there is already a war 'between powers which strive for the domination and distribution of natural resources and strategic raw materials'. It is between the good capitalist West and the evil communist East. It documents every organization in Central and South America that does not fall clearly within the capitalist camp, and it suggests that they are all part of a coordinated plot by Moscow to take over the area. It urges low-intensity conflict, which really means low-profile high-intensity conflict, against these organizations on every level: psychological, educational, economic, social and military. It devotes several pages to liberation theology, attempting to drive a wedge between what it takes to be mainline Roman Catholicism, led by the Pope and Cardinal Ratzinger, and liberation theologians.

In short, we are confronted with the propagation of a holy war in defence of an ideology that has at its heart the free market economy. 'Democracy' is a term used to denote the privatization of economic activity and the establishment of the instruments to enforce it: juridicial, bureaucratic and military. It has nothing to do with popular choice of government. In the document of the secret services the poor do not count at all, except as minds to be won over to support the free market as the only way out of poverty, or to be 'minimized', that is, battered into total submission. Behind Novak's urbane reasonableness lies a grisly scenario. Is Novak's work finally, one asks, little more than a moral front for the naked or clandestine imposition of an economic ideology?

Notes: Chapter 14

1 Lay Commission, 1984. *Towards the Future*. Lanham, Md: University Press of America, discussed in Duchrow 1987, p. 169 ff.
2 Altmann, W. 1984. Hohe Zinssätze: 'Gaskammern' von heute, in epd-Entwicklungspolitik, 16/84, f-h. I owe the reference to Ulrich Duchrow, in a paper to be published in *Studies in Christian Ethics*.

References: Chapter 14

Duchrow, U. 1987. *Global Economy: A Confessional Issue for the Churches?* Geneva: WCC.

Duchrow, U., Eisenbürger, G. and Hippler, J. (eds), *Totaler Krieg gegen die Armen*. München: Kaiser Verlag.

Haas, P. J. 1988. *Morality after Auschwitz: The Challenge of the Nazi Ethic*. Philadelphia: Fortress Press.

Hirsch, F. 1977. *Social Limits to Growth*. London: Routledge.

Lonergan, B. 1958. *Insight: A Study of Human Understanding*. New York: Philosophical Library.

Niebuhr, R. 1976. Christian faith and natural law, in D. B. Robertson (ed.), *Love and Justice: Selections from the Shorter Writings of Reinhold Niebuhr*. Gloucester, Mass.: Peter Smith.

Novak, M. 1982. *The Spirit of Democratic Capitalism*. New York: American Enterprise Institute/Simon and Schuster.

Novak, M. 1989a. *Free Persons and the Common Good*. New York: Madison Books.

Novak, M. 1989b. *Catholic Social Thought and Liberal Institutions*. New Brunswick, NJ: Transaction Publishers (first published as *Freedom with Justice*. New York: Harper and Row, 1984).

Preston, R. H. 1979. *Religion and the Persistence of Capitalism*. London: SCM.

Smith, A. [1759] 1853. *The Theory of Moral Sentiments*. London: H. G. Bohn.

Smith, A. [1776] 1976. *The Wealth of Nations*. Oxford: Clarendon Press.

Suggate, A. M. 1987. *William Temple and Christian Social Ethics Today*. Edinburgh: T. and T. Clark.

Tawney, R. H. [1926] 1938. *Religion and the Rise of Capitalism*. Harmondsworth: Penguin.

15 Individual and community in religious critiques of the enterprise culture

KENNETH THOMPSON

It may still be too soon to write a definitive history of the most significant changes in the ideological climate of Britain in the 1980s. However, a glance at some of the newspaper headlines during the second half of the decade would reveal one rather odd and striking recurrent theme: the bitter conflict between the Church of England, which was once known as the 'Tory Party at Prayer', and the Conservative Government of Mrs Thatcher. At times the conflict has become so bitter that the Prime Minister took to referring to bishops as 'cuckoos' and one of the most prominent of her episcopal critics, the Bishop of Durham, received death-threats.

The question that needs answering is: where does the conflict spring from and why does it run so deep? It is clearly more than just a case of some of the present bishops being rather ideologically 'pink' or 'leftist', as that would be nothing new (as Edward Norman and other contemporary church historians have shown; see Norman 1976). Nor is it anything new for the church to pronounce views on socio-economic issues. What is experienced by each side from a different angle, has to do with the boundary between the sacred and profane (see Thompson 1989 for a development of this Durkheimian theme). The bishops accuse the politicians and economists of idolatry in seeming to raise their secular doctrines to the status of moral and religious truths. The politicians accuse the bishops of pontificating on secular matters where they have no expertise or legitimate authority. The point has been made, rather colourfully and partisanly from the Left, by one of the bystanders to the quarrel, Jeremy Seabrook, who suggests that 'what we are witnessing is the reaction of the church to a process whereby the secular is being sacralised':

> The division between the Church and the Conservative Party goes far deeper than most comment has suggested. The conflict exposes the very core of the values by which we live. It is a profoundly ideological struggle, in which the Left – as in so many other areas of experience in recent years – has been sadly by-passed. It seems that there is really no such thing as a secular society. The language of religion invades even the most crassly and rigorously materialistic structures. But economic growth is a pitiful surrogate for meaning, the magic of the markets a primitive superstition, the unseen hand a phantom to frighten children with. What we are seeing is the re-assertion of the Church against those who would plunder its symbols to dignify their shallow ideologies (*The Guardian*, 26 November 1984).

Seabrook is wrong in depicting this use of sacred symbols as a case of simply dressing up 'shallow ideologies'. The basis of the conflict is far more profound, and relates to opposing elements in the national culture – the values of individualism and communitarianism – which are deeply embedded. The attempted compromise between these two ideological strands can be traced back several centuries to the Establishment of the Church of England itself as a religious *via media* in the sixteenth century. The uneasy balance between the two ideological strands has been upset on several occasions, most notably as a result of the reas-sertion of individualism in eighteenth-century liberalism, again in the nineteenth century when it was linked to the process of industrialization, and in the 1980s by the importation of American 'neo-liberalism' as an aid to economic restructuring and attempted revival of successful entrepreneurship.

The current ideological crisis

The focus of this analysis is on the disruption of the balance between individualism and communitarianism in the prevailing ideological climate of Britain in the 1980s. This has gone against the grain of the main tendency of the English religious tradition, although it derives its missionary force from America and finds some support in the minority dissenting tradition deriving from Calvinism and the Puritan movement of the seventeenth century. There was a similar disruption as a result of the evangelical movement in the nineteenth century, when there was a pronounced expansion of individualism linked to the processes of industrialization.

The conflict over the ideological shift in favour of individualistic and against communitarian values echoes the debates in social philosophy – between, on the one side, liberal philosophers (Rawls 1971, Dworkin 1977, and Nozick 1974) and libertarian free-market economists (Hayek 1944 and Friedman 1962), and on the other side communitarians in various disciplines, such as the social philosophers Alasdair MacIntyre (1984) and Michael Walzer (1983), the economic sociology of Amitai Etzioni (1988), and the work on business ideologies by George Lodge and his associates studying international competitiveness at Harvard Business School (Lodge and Vogel 1987), While each side is made up of diverse positions, the debate is joined over the communitarians' call for a fuller expression of the claims of community and the common good (including moral values, shared understandings, the public interest and citizenship) than is allowed for by liberal individualism. In the economic sphere, the shift towards liberal individualism finds its ideological expression in the attempts to construct or revive an 'enterprise culture'. This ideological project, which in Britain is associated with 'Thatcherism', has run up against a certain amount of resistance: not least from representatives of the Christian churches.

While we avoid being drawn into a much too theoretical discussion, it may be useful to offer a few signposts to the approach being taken to the relationships between religion and ideology (for fuller discussions, see Thompson 1987, and Bocock and Thompson 1985). They can be summarized in the following brief propositions.

Shifts in ideology are always related to changes in material social relations, particularly economic and power structures. Ideological shifts are partly determined by such structural changes and yet also contribute to such changes. However, it is clear that ideology enjoys a relative autonomy. It is not fully determined by structural changes and the field in which it operates is a contested terrain. Ideological change is subject to contestation and resistance. This is partly because ideologies are embedded in cultures that are 'layered'. The symbolic chains and discourses that constitute culture reflect their historical formation. More traditional elements, such as religious symbols and discourses, tend to form a deep and long-lasting layer. They are deeply implicated in the formation of a national culture and articulate with other discourses to constitute the 'imagined community' of the nation. Any attempt to redirect culture and ideology in a particular direction is likely to run up against religious resistance, especially if the redirection appears to draw selectively on religious symbols and discourses for support in the fashion of Thatcherism.

The reassertion of 'enterprise values' in recent years is not a uniquely British phenomenon tied to the hybrid ideology of Thatcherism, which has been described as 'a mixture of charisma, market philosophy, populism and "common sense" homilies'. Certainly, 'enterprise values' do form part of the political project of Thatcherism, particularly that part concerned with rolling back the Keynesian welfare state and the restructuring of the economy. However, the phenomenon is not confined to Britain and is related to broader trends in mature capitalist economies, which have sought to arrest their declining competitive position with a variety of strategies: encouraging new enterprises, particularly small businesses where the entrepreneur risks some personal capital as well as playing an innovative role; instilling a great sense of commitment and motivation to effort in workers; dismantling alleged barriers to competitive market forces, such as the defensive practices of trades unions and professions; overcoming resistance to restructuring and relocation, as represented by sentiments in favour of preservation of communities or jobs; switching from mass manufacturing to customized production or into services, both of which require increased sensitivity and dedication to customer satisfaction; restructuring the labour force in the direction of self-employment, sub-contracting, part-time employment, etc. All of these structural changes require cultural changes and ideological reinforcement and legitimization. The reassertion of 'enterprise values' can be seen as aimed at fulfilling these functions. The peculiarity of Thatcherism is that it has tried to impose a hyper-individualist version of enterprise values that runs up against resistance from the challenge of deep-rooted elements in the national culture.

The general thesis – that the assertion of an individualist version of enterprise values has upset the communitarian–individualist symbiosis that has characterized British (predominantly English) ideology – is now explored in greater detail.

Individualism and communitarianism

The recent surge of interest in the subject of ideology and culture throughout management literature has been traced to the need to introduce organizational changes as a response to the intensification of global economic competition in the 1980s (Lodge and Vogel 1987). Those western countries that have responded to the crisis of deteriorating economic position by further emphasizing individualistic liberal enterprise values still have difficulty in competing with Asian societies (e.g. Japan, South Korea and Taiwan) with more evident communitarian values. Consequently, some comparative studies of economic performance have reached the conclusion that the main ideological competition today is not between capitalism and socialist collectivism but rather between various models of the relationship between individualism and communitarianism. A good illustration of the difference between the two ideologies is with regard to the concept of 'community need'. According to liberal individualism, the public interest emerges *naturally* from the pulling and shoving of interest groups and from the free and vigorous competition among numerous aggressive, individualistic and preferably small companies attempting to satisfy consumer desires. This contrasts with the view of communitarian ideology:

> Business purpose, according to communitarian ideology, is fixed by community need as defined by the community, generally through government or with its participation. Once community need has been determined business activity can be harmonised with it in four ways: prescribed or ordered marketplace competition; regulation of business by government; partnership between government and business; and the corporate charter through which government gives business its license to exist (Lodge and Vogel 1987: 20).

A similar contrast can be drawn with regard to the importance that communitarians give to the idea of consensus in the government of relationships between individuals, rather than the individualists' stress on contract. In some European countries, consensual arrangements take the form of industrial democracy, code termination and workers' councils, and other forms of worker participation in management. In the USA, consensual practices tend to fall under the headings of employee involvement and organizational development as part of human resource strategies, or they feature in quality-of-work-life programmes. Whichever form they take, the intention is to replace the adversarial contractual relationship between managers and managed with a more consensual one. In countries with a tradition of adversarial, bargained contracts, trades unions and managers are unwilling to give up their old bases of authority in the context of an ideological reassertion of individualism and market competition. The problem for Britain is that the prominence of individualistic values in the enterprise culture offensive has left the country more ideologically divided and conflict-ridden. This is shown by the fact that foreign firms in Britain, particularly the more communitarian Japanese, appear to have an advantage when it comes to designing and implementing effective human-resource management strategies, because they are not part of the conflicted establishment.

As part of the comparative study of ideology and national competitiveness in nine countries, Krieger has charted the historical evolution of British ideological traditions from organic communitarianism to the Conservative–Labour consensus that oriented Britain's classic postwar synthesis, to the decline of ideological symbiosis in the 1970s, and the acceleration of that decline in the 1980s (Krieger 1987). As we shall see, religious ideas have provided a major strand throughout that historical evolution.

Religion made a major contribution to the organic communitarianism that has oriented a powerful value scheme in British society from the time of the medieval estates. Organic corporatism involved the idea of the social allocation of rights and duties in accordance with a dominant vision of community need. It began from the premise that harmony among economic interests and organic unity were essential to society and that these ends could be secured only if the various producer groups, notably capital and labour, were imbued with a conception of natural rights and obligations. The principle of organic unity – the sovereign as the 'head' of the 'body politic', including the established church – came to prominence in the sixteenth century. It was challenged in the seventeenth century by Hobbes and Locke, who insisted that sovereignty should derive from contract, arguing that legitimacy of the state should be limited and rest on its ability to represent the individual needs of persons in a competitive society. The result, according to Krieger, was that:

> By asserting individualist ideology, Hobbes and Locke encouraged an individualist–communitarian symbiosis that would help unify Britain's political community and orient its economic behaviour from the eighteenth until well past the mid-point of the current century (Krieger 1987: 32).

In the nineteenth century, economic policy in Britain developed from below as a consequence of market competition and interest-group pluralism, both associated with individualism, and not, as in later industrializing nations, as the planned consequence of community-based and state-enforced design. However, although laissez-faire individualism in economic affairs was prominent in Britain up to the First World War, this was counterbalanced by the evolution of political rights and associated economic tendencies. Citizenship rights expanded from negative freedoms to positive social rights, including economic welfare. Thus, while British ideology held a mix of the two strands of individualism and communitarianism, there was always a real or potential possibility that the balance could be upset.

Whatever may be said about the impact of Calvinism on social thinking in Scotland, where Mrs Thatcher delivered her address to the General Assembly of the Church of Scotland in 1988, in England the prevailing organicist ideology has traditionally sought to balance communitarian and individualist values. The ideological legacy of Anglicanism is deeply sedimented within that organicist ideology. It is this ideological symbiosis that has been in decline since the 1970s – a decline that Thatcherism's assertion of individualist enterprise values has accelerated. As the leader of a party once associated, like the Church of England, with organic symbolism,

Mrs Thatcher signalled the change of course in her statement to
Anthony Sampson that, 'I've always regarded Conservatism as the
party of the individual'. As Jonathan Raban points out, although
an Anglican churchgoer now, Margaret Thatcher seemed to have
remained true to her childhood Methodism and its more Calvinist
strand. In practice, she appeared impatient of mediating institutions
(such as the church, trades unions, local authorities, the BBC or the
universities). Her emphasis was on individual conversion. In 1979
she told Kenneth Harris, 'You can only get other people in tune
with you by being a little evangelical about it'; in 1988, talking
on 'The Jimmy Young Programme' she said of Thatcherism, 'It's
because it strikes a chord in the hearts and minds of men and
women that they say yes and believe it' (Raban 1989: 27).

It is clear that the Thatcher government had significantly recast
the ideological orientation toward neo-individualism and away
from communitarianism. It was this ideological thrust, and its
attendant economic policies, that had brought the government
into conflict with the Church of England and other mediating
institutions. The sharp economic downturn in the 1970s, and
the sustained attacks on the welfare state consensus, brought the
already fragile ideological symbiosis of communitarianism and
individualism – as manifested in the Keynesian and corporatist
traditions – into crisis. But Thatcherism's enterprise policies aimed
at sweeping it away completely. This was evident in the policies
towards industrial relations, which were heavily individualist and
confrontationist, as a result of which the Church of England had at
times been brought into direct conflict with the government. The
most prominent example was during the Miner's Strike of 1984–5,
when the Bishop of Durham used his enthronement sermon to
accuse the government of being confrontationist and said that,
'Such a government cannot promote community. . .' (quoted
in Harrison 1985: 96). The Bishop of Birmingham, similarly,
attacked the government's 'policies of confrontation', while the
Archbishop of Canterbury challenged its whole economic policy
which led, he claimed, to unemployment, poverty and despair
(Harrison 1985).

Within the area of industrial relations, it is clear that the 'values
of the enterprise culture', as interpreted by Thatcherism, involved a
deliberate effort decisively to shift the balance towards individualism

and away from communitarianism, particularly tripartite corporatism (unions–employers–government). As Huw Beynon and Peter
McMylor observed:

> From the beginning, Thatcher has been anxious to break the old
> consensus. . .the old class compromises were not for her, neither
> were collective forms of life and relationships. With all corporate
> forms apparently in crisis (such as incomes policies, etc.), the
> powerful articulation of individualism was made to seem both
> fresh and plausible. In this way of thinking, the phrase 'right
> to work' became deflected from its original social-democratic
> meaning of a public commitment to full employment, towards
> a citizen's right to sell, unhindered, one's labour as individual
> in the market-place (quoted in Krieger 1987: 43).

Trades unions and their members are now in the individualist
position of adversaries, encouraged to engage in competition as
self-interested bargaining units. They are not encouraged to participate in triparite neo-corporatist bodies to arrive at compromises.
Instead, the individualist values of the enterprise culture suggest
that market mechanisms can be trusted to work out the most
efficient solutions. But the problem remains that these may not
be the most 'moral' solutions. Consequently, when the government
sometimes makes moral appeals to people to consider the national
community interest, this rings hollow in the face of the realities of a
competitive market that transcends national boundaries and where
it is the most powerful interests that prevail. The communitarian
and consensualist solution of seeking to ameliorate the 'immoral'
effects of the market through restraining mechanisms, such as the
'Social Contract' and the redistributive efforts of the welfare state,
runs agains the individualistic values of Thatcherism's version of
the enterprise culture. But church leaders such as the Bishop of
Durham condemn these immoral effects of the market. In his
Hibbert Lecture in 1985 he proclaimed:

> To give up the central concerns of the Welfare State and the
> Beveridge Report because we have run into difficulties is sheer
> faithlessness and inhumanity. To return to the ethos of 19th
> century entrepreneurial individualism is either nostalgic nonsense

or else a firm declaration that individual selfishness and organised greed are the only effective motivations for human behaviour. Of course we must be realistic about sin. . .But to promote a materialistic market-orientated individualism as the key to human and social progress is to make an equally destructive mistake about the possibilities and needs of men and women and to turn one's back on real political and social progress which has been made. Realism about sin should not lead to cynicism about altruism and justice, or pessimism about the possibilities of collective organisation and communal caring (The Bishop of Durham, quoted in Harrison 1985: 123).

Enterprise values and religion

It seems to be a common assumption among advocates of the values of the enterprise culture that there is no inherent opposition between individualistic entrepreneurship and religion, at least as far as Judaism and Christianity are concerned. Indeed, even those among them least sympathetic towards sociology are likely to insist that it was the sociologist Max Weber who showed that there are good grounds for giving credit to Judaism and Christianity for providing some of the ethical motivation and commitment, as well as habits of self-discipline, that were conducive to the rise of capitalist enterprise. Weber's thesis of the elective affinity between the protestant ethic and the spirit of capitalism, has stuck in the popular imagination and no doubt informed some of the 'common sense homilies' of Mrs Thatcher. In her address to the General Assembly of the Church of Scotland, on the basis of her selection of key elements from the Old and New Testaments she stated that we gain:

'a view of the universe,
a proper attitude to work,
and principles to shape economic and social life.'
In keeping with these 'we are told we must work and use our talents to create wealth' and that 'it is not the creation of wealth that is wrong but love of money for its own sake. The spiritual dimension comes in deciding what one does with

the wealth' (from the text of the address given in Raban 1989: 12–13).

However, the history of religious debate about enterprise values suggests that the issue is more complicated than a simple commendation of wealth creation and the restriction of the spiritual dimension to decisions about what to do with money. Religion has had a great deal to say about the relation between individual economic activity and community values, including the morality of the methods adopted to create wealth and the extent to which wealth creation takes precedence over other forms of activity and identity. The best summary of that history, in the Weberian tradition, is still Tawney's *Religion and the Rise of Capitalism* (Tawney [1926] 1938).

Tawney's book was based on his Holland Memorial Lectures, the first in that series devoted to the memory of the Christian socialist Henry Scott Holland, having as their subject 'the religion of the Incarnation in its bearing on the social and economic life of man'. They are an outstanding example of the Incarnational theology that inspired the social gospel movement and many of the religious critics of Thatcherism. Such critics have been attacked by some supporters of Thatcherism for straying over the border separating the sacred and profane spheres, as if this were a dangerous innovation (Thompson 1989). But, as Tawney made clear:

> The criticism which dismisses the concern of Churches with economic relations and social organization as a modern innovation finds little support in past history. What requires explanation is not the view that these matters are part of the province of religion, but the view that they are not. . .Religion has been converted from the Keystone which holds together the social edifice into one department within it, and the idea of a rule of right is replaced by economic expediency as the arbiter of policy and the criterion of conduct (Tawney [1926] 1938: 214).

The concluding points in Tawney's book are relevant to current questioning of the primacy of the goal of economic efficiency and to debates between proponents of liberal individualism and their communitarian opponents. Having praised the achievements of capitalist enterprise, Tawney warns:

> Economic efficiency is a necessary element in the life of any sane and vigorous society, and only the incorrigible sentimentalist will depreciate its significance. But to convert efficiency from an instrument into a primary object is to destroy efficiency itself. For the condition of effective action in a complex civilization is co-operation. And the condition of co-operation is agreement, both as to the ends to which effort should be applied, and the criteria by which its success is to be judged. Agreement as to ends implies the acceptance of a standard of values, by which the position to be assigned to different objects may be determined. In a world of limited resources, whose nature yields a return only to prolonged and systematic effort, such a standard must obviously take account of economic possibilities. But it cannot itself be merely economic, since the comparative importance of economic and of other interests – the sacrifices, for example, of material goods worth incurring in order to extend leisure, or develop education, or humanize toil – is precisely the point on which it is needed to throw light. It must be based on some conception of the requirements of human nature as a whole, to which the satisfaction of economic needs is evidently vital, but which demands the satisfaction of other needs as well, and which can organize its activities on a rational system only in so far as it has clear apprehension of their relative significance (Tawney [1926] 1938: 218).

It is this communitarian requirement of common values, on which to base criteria for judging ends and means, that seems to be denied by liberal individualism, particularly in its advocacy of the market economy. For example, a follower of Hayek and Friedman, the economist and Thatcher supporter, Lord Harris, has attacked Church of England bishops for attempting to intrude moral considerations into economic matters that should be left to the market, which he claims is 'morally neutral' (*Sunday Telegraph*, 3 April 1988). He and other contemporary proponents of economic liberalism quote with approval Adam Smith's apparent paradox, that the public good may be better served if individuals pursue their own interest in the market: 'it is not from the *benevolence* of the butcher, the brewer, or the baker that we expect our dinner, but from their regard to their own *interest*' (Smith [1776] 1937: 14). In America, this kind of thinking has been even more fashionable than in Britain during the recent period of economic restructuring to increase national economic competitiveness by freeing-up markets and encouraging the pursuit of profit. However, some American social scientists have begun to discern a turn in the tide against this intellectual fashion. Among the reasons given for this turn are:

> For one, the paradigm about self-interest leading to a work-able and even optimal social order without any admixture of 'benevolence' has now been around so long that it has become intellectually challenging to rediscover the need for morality. To affirm this need has almost the same surprise value and air of paradox which the Smithian farewell to benevolence had in its own time. Second, and more important, it has become increasingly clear that, in a number of important areas, the economy is in fact liable to perform poorly without a minimum of 'benevolence' (Hirschmann 1981: 299).

As an example, it is argued that, at the level of microeconomics, the rehabilitation of benevolence results from a more realistic appraisal of the actual conditions of the competitive market, where there is seldom the 'perfect' information among buyers and sellers that is required for their proper functioning. Buyers often have less knowledge than sellers and will be exploited unless restrained by government or by some other device. One such device is that of voluntary restraint, such as through a code of professional ethics, as in medicine and other professions. Nor is this just a matter of allowing a minimum level of morality and trust in order to allow markets to function. In most services and organizations, experience teaches us that a higher level of morality and benevolence improves output and performance over what can be achieved by encouraging a single-minded pursuit of self-interest. With the switch in employment to increasingly competitive service industries, organizations are tending to make almost quasi-religious demands on employees with regard to their identity and commitments, encouraging them to identify totally with the organization's goals and values, which are given a moral character and not treated just as matters of commercial interest. An example, featured in *The New York Times* (27 August 1989), was the Nordstrom retail chain, which promulgated what a Los Angeles clergyman described as 'the Gospel according to Nordstrom'. An even more striking example is that of direct-selling organizations in America, which have been found to combine religious and patriotic ideas with entrepreneurial values in a potent organizational ideology (Biggart 1989).

Clearly, it is not necessary to be religious in order to see the deficiency of individualistic liberalism's overemphasis of the merits of competition and the market to the neglect of such factors as cooperation deriving from moral community. The point is evident to those who attempt to build up cooperation and commitment by developing a sense of community within an organization; who argue that a moral basis is required to ensure fair dealing in the market. It is also evident when representatives of the national community appeal to individuals to sacrifice their self-interest to a larger cause. Durkheim pointed out that societies treat certain acts and considerations as 'sacred', which need not mean religious in the narrow sense. One characteristic of these 'sacred' moral principles (or 'meta-preferences' as Etzioni calls them) is that they repudiate the instrumental rationality that is exclusively concerned with costs and benefits (Etzioni 1988: 42). A person feels *obligated* to save a life, make a voluntary contribution to a cause, or uphold a basic freedom. These are 'sacred', non-negotiable commitments, even though the people holding them may subsequently make rational calculations about the best means to fulfil those values. To the extent that liberal, 'neo-classical theory' subverts these 'sacred' areas, making the public think about them solely in terms of costs and benefits, it 'secularizes' them, stripping them of their special moral standing. A paradox arises to the extent that it is true that the market is dependent on normative underpinning (to provide what Durkheim called the pre-contractual foundations such as trust, co-operation and honesty):

> The more people accept the neoclassical paradigm as a guide for their behaviour, the more the ability to sustain a market economy is undermined. This holds for all those who engage in transactions

without ever-present inspectors, auditors, lawyers and police: if they do not limit themselves to legitimate (i.e. normative) means of competition out of internalized values, the system will collapse, because the transaction costs of a fully or even highly 'policed' system are prohibitive (Etzioni 1988: 251).

There is, therefore, a strong case to be made for the necessity for a moral community if the market is to operate at all, and that the moral community actually enhances the efficiency of the economy. In this light, perhaps one of the most damaging aspects of the revived economic liberalism is the conceptual opposition it sets up between government and the free market, disregarding the importance of the third realm, that of community, in which cooperation and values find their support. In this context, we can see that Mrs Thatcher's view that 'there is no such thing as society' echoes Bentham's Utilitarian assertion that 'community is a fiction'.

Morality, community and economics

Despite the surface Utilitarianism of Mrs Thatcher's view of society as a fiction, there are good grounds for believing that she did wish to place economic activity within a moral context, as illustrated in her speech to the General Assembly of the Church of Scotland. The problem with this aspiration was that it required a solution that reconciled the opposed principles of individualism and communitarianism (as distinct from state collectivism). This reconciliation has yet to be achieved by the religious new Right, even though the the head of Mrs Thatcher's Policy Unit, Professor Brian Griffiths, had begun to show more awareness of the issue.

This is evident in the new edition of Griffiths's *Morality and the Market Place* (1989). The book is the text of a series of lectures which Griffiths gave in the spring of 1980 at a church in the City of London, and which he describes as a response to a challenge from Milton Friedman: 'How can you be a Christian and advocate the market economy?' (Griffiths 1989: 7). Griffiths's answer attempts to rescue the market economy from the libertarian individualism philosophy of Friedman and Hayek, while rejecting what he sees as the only other major theory – that of state socialism. While emphasizing the biblical legitimization of wealth creation and private property, he also stresses the importance given to justice and stewardship. However, he runs into some problems in reconciling his advocacy of private property with the biblical stress on the virtues of community. He states that 'even though the idea of community was so strong in the Pentateuch, and even though society was organized along tribal lines, it is important to notice that property rights were not communal, they were private' and 'this was not accidental'. Consequently, 'private property rather than the state, social or collective ownership is the Christian norm for society'. However, he also puts forward the Biblical concept of 'trusteeship' and it is not clear why personal responsibility and stewardship associated with trusteeship cannot be exercised as effectively on behalf of a community as it is for private property. The record of charities and voluntary associations, including religious communities, suggests that stewardship according to moral principles is higher in these institutions than in commercial corporations. Indeed, he admits there is a 'certain validity' in the criticisms of limited liability corporations 'which are still the major institutions responsible for the creation of wealth in the Western world' and in the argument 'that the system of property rights in which ownership and control are in the hands of shareholders violates the Christian concept of trusteeship and is contrary to the Biblical ideal of community' (Griffiths 1989: 107–10). His solution is very timid and half-hearted. It consists mainly of exhortation:

It is important that as Christians we conceive of the corporation as a community which has an objective more than just profit maximization. The directorate of a company has a responsibility to those with whom they deal as people rather than just as instruments of profit. It is therefore important that management accept a responsibility to communicate the prospects, plans and performance of the organization to the whole of its work force. A directorate and management will succeed only if they have the trust of those with whom they work – the need to develop a common involvement is important' (Griffiths 1989: 120).

Griffiths rejects any involvement of worker representatives on the board, such as occurs in some other European countries, on the supposed empirical grounds that 'while they help ease labour-management tensions they slow down decision-making and reduce management flexibility' (Griffiths 1989: 121). But even if this is true (and the success of German firms throws doubt on it), these seem flimsy grounds after his strong advocacy of maximum personal responsibility and involvement in the corporation as a community. His objection to workers sharing the responsibility for stewardship in corporations seems to stem in part from his ideological reluctance to interfere with the rights of private ownership and from British élitist reluctance to trust the workers, while assuming that they have an obligation to trust the bosses.

The attempts by the authorities of the Church of England to grapple with the moral problems raised by economic restructuring have frequently met with charges of 'collectivist bias' or even 'Marxism' from the new Right. The *Faith in the City* (1985) report of the Archbishop of Canterbury's Commission on Urban Priority Areas was branded as 'Marxist' in government circles. It is easy to see why its questioning of the morality of government policies might have struck a sensitive nerve. Not only did the report marshall damning evidence about the unequal burden of suffering being borne by the poorer sections of society as a result of economic restructuring, but it also raised questions about basic concepts and philosophies behind Thatcherite ideology. For example, it questioned why the enterprise value of 'wealth creation' seemed to apply only to private market transactions but not to public investment in services such as education or health (p. 212). As for the moral philosophy behind the government's policies, the report questioned whether the balance had swung too far towards individual self-interest and away from collective obligations. It noted that:

> No less an advocate of the market economy than Adam Smith accepted in his *Theory of Moral Sentiments* that economic individualism could not be divorced from moral, religious and social obligations (*Faith in the City* 1985: 209).

Finally, the report insisted that there must be explicit debate about the moral basis for, and implications of, policy decisions taken on economic grounds. Judged by their outcomes, it found unacceptable that the costs of transition during economic restructuring under present government policies should fall hardest on those least able to bear them.

The *Faith in the City* report feared that the government was failing to maintain a balance between wealth creation and wealth distribution, efficiency and compassion, personal initiative and collective provision. There was too much reliance on appealing to economic self-interest and individualism and freeing market mechanisms from interference. In the absence of a spirit of collective obligation, or the political will to foster it, there was no guarantee that the pursuit of innumerable self-interests would add up to an improvement in the common good.

A subsequent report *Changing Britain: Social Diversity and Moral Unity* (1987) was produced by a distinguished group headed by the Archbishop of York, which responded to the many submissions made to the Church of England's Board for Social Responsibility after it released a consultative document, *Goals for our Future Society*. The new report concentrated on the issue of balancing the competing values of individualism and collectivism by reasserting as the new touchstone for the value on which British society ought to be based *koinonia*, or persons-in-interrelationship (community, communion). It traced some of the implications of this for various enterprise values, such as efficiency and managerial leadership or authority. The conclusion was that the bounds of competition must lie at the point where the advantages it bestows in terms of efficiency are outweighed by the damage it causes in undermining community and relationships based on cooperation. Competition should not be seen as a basic value in itself, but simply as a strategy or tool. With regard to leadership, the report maintains companies have a choice over the ethos they adopt, and they should be prepared to talk publicly about their philosophy, even though they may be challenged by reference to their day-to-day management practice.

Morals and values within organizations

These religious views on enterprise values as they relate to organizational functioning – morality within enterprises – are somewhat rare in the correct period of economic restructuring. Most religious criticisms of enterprise values have been concerned with their societal effects with regard to distribution of wealth, the effects of unemployment on communities, the burden being borne by poorer people, and the rolling back of the welfare state. Although Griffiths has insisted that 'a business decision must be capable of being defended on grounds of morality as well as profitability' (Griffiths 1984: 111), he provides little guidance as to how this might affect the structure and functioning of an enterprise. The more fundamentalist Christian new Right largely ignores this question. And yet many trends within business, particularly service industries, tend towards elevating enterprise values to a quasi-religious status, demanding an almost total commitment to organizational goals and roles to an extent that a Christian moral judgement might find almost idolatrous. The phenomenon in one of its most extreme American forms has been described as 'charismatic capitalism' (Biggart 1989).

On the basis of her study of direct-selling organizations, such as Tupperware, Shaklee Corporation, Amway, and Mary Kay Cosmetics, Biggart shows how the flamboyant (at times evangelical) leaders of these companies profitably organize the economic activity of millions of independent contractors by marketing a peculiarly American blend of the ideologies of individualism, entrepreneurship, meritocracy, family and community. Her research is prompting sociologists to revise the standard contention that the rationalization of social institutions is an inevitable consequence of advanced capitalism. It seems that the less rational organizations built on social networks may actually be more economically viable: direct-selling executives create and manipulate family-like bonds in the pursuit of profit. Her findings challenge existing economic ideas – that under capitalism social and economic realms become separated. She shows that private beliefs and emotional social relations are not necessarily impediments to worker discipline, but may be the very means by which management creates commitment to work.

Such enterprises are 'greedy organizations' in that they demand from their members a total commitment to the organization's values and goals, and complete identification with the organizational role. The direct-selling organizations studied by Biggart are perhaps an extreme example of one of the most successful organizational

control strategies: that of using communitarian values to induce
workers to become self-motivated and self-controlled without the
need for close supervision or constant financial inducement. Whereas
bureaucratic firms seek to exclude non-work social relations and
attachments in order to control workers, the direct-selling industry
pursues profit in the opposite way, by making social networks and
value commitments serve business ends. Perhaps more than any
other industry, the direct-selling industry illustrates that 'affective
and ideal bonds can be powerful motivators of economic action,
not necessarily impediments' (Biggart 1989: 12). All business
organizations are based on beliefs, often consisting largely of
an economic ideology of efficiency and profits. Direct-selling
organizations, however, illustrate that they can also incorporate a
substantive or value-based belief system. In their case, this usually
takes the form of belief in the moral virtue of entrepreneurship
sometimes combined with a product-related ideology espoused
by the leadership. According to Biggart, 'For some, direct selling
functions as an extension of worship or as a secular religious
substitute.'

Direct-selling organizations, particularly their American version,
and their apparent reconciliation of the opposed principles of
individualism and communitarianism, may seem a far cry from
Mrs Thatcher's concern to place economic activity within a moral
context. However, this extreme example is useful in showing how
acute are some of the moral issues raised at the organizational level
by current economic restructuring.

It should not be surprising that the church is taking an increasing
interest in such developments and that it resents the politicians'
charge that it is trespassing on their ground. One version of
the ideological offensive of the advocates of enterprise values
– that of Hayek and Friedman – seems to promote an amoral
view of economic activity, or, even worse, encourages the pursuit of self-interest. Its defenders would concede that it assumes
the continuance of certain traditional values to provide a framework of trust and honesty. The other version – that of Brian
Griffiths and others like him – seems to depend on a revival of
Christian moral values throughout society. The official church
study groups and commissions call for more justice, but make
few specific recommendations about institutional reforms in the

absence of a revival of Christian social values and where the market continues to be dominated by those who have power and resources. Partly, this is due to a fear of being branded as politically biased, but it also stems from a dearth of technically competent Christian economists who are prepared to develop alternative economic models that take account of theological and moral arguments.

One of the few exceptions is the Oxford economist Donald Hay (1989), who argues that institutional reforms must go further than Griffiths is prepared to contemplate. On the basis of theological and moral arguments, he makes several specific recommendations. These include changing the legal and fiscal constitution of companies so that ownership and responsibility are shifted, in part if not completely, to the people who work in them. This would be one solution to the problem acknowledged by Griffiths, that the limited liability company, which gives sole control to the shareholders, is inconsistent with Christian notions of stewardship. Another suggestion is that shareholders would no longer have ownership rights, but have the status of bondholders or, alternatively, forgo limited liability. In addition to suggestions for applying Christian principles to company organization, Hay recommends regulation of capital and labour markets to restrain the unjust exercise of power.

Whereas current economic analysis of competition policy stresses economic efficiency to the virtual exclusion of everything else, a Christian economist would emphasize considerations of fair play and justice. To some extent these considerations, rather than just efficiency, have motivated the historical development of competition policy in the defence of small businesses from the power of large firms to destroy them, and in the protection of the consumer against high prices charged by monopolies and cartels. Where Hay, like Griffiths, would disagree with the secular, liberal defence of the market system is in insisting that it should not be conceived as a spontaneously ordered structure, best left alone, but that it should be consciously ordered according to moral principles. Consequently, these Christian economists argue that moral principles should be brought to the fore in economic analysis. The values of the enterprise culture have to be judged in terms of moral principles.

Conclusion

If we are to judge by the public controversy, it seems to have come as a surprise to some people that the attempt to promote a certain version of enterprise values has given rise to debates about morals and even generated religious conflict. However, the reasons for this become clearer when we examine the nature of the neo-liberal and radically individualistic version of enterprise values propagated in Britain by Thatcherism. Its importation into Britain was inspired by the success of the new Right in America, but here it has been imposed from the top, whereas in America it built on a popular grassroots movement. It should not be surprising, therefore, that this has met resistance from those institutions, such as the Church of England, which had helped to create and safeguard the traditional ideological symbiosis of individualist and communitarian values.

It remains to be seen whether neo-liberal individualism can succeed in establishing itself as an acceptable ideological source of values for the enterprise culture in Britain. The resistance to it cannot be simply dismissed as the typical response of vested interests when faced with the need to change. Much more is at stake with regard to the moral basis of economic activities and the balance between individualist and communitarian values in the national culture.

References: Chapter 15

Biggart, N. 1989. *Charismatic Capitalism.* Chicago and London: University of Chicago Press.
Bocock, R. and Thompson, K. (eds). 1985. *Religion and Ideology.* Manchester: Manchester University Press.
Changing Britain: Social Diversity and Moral Unity. 1987. A Study for the Board of Social Responsibility. London: Church House Publishing.
Dworkin, R. 1977. *Taking Rights Seriously.* Cambridge, Mass.: Harvard University Press.
Etzioni, A. 1988. *The Moral Dimension.* New York: Free Press.
Faith in the City. 1985. The Report of the Archbishop of Canterbury's Commission on Urban Priority Areas. London: Church House Publishing.
Friedman, M. 1962. *Capitalism and Freedom.* Chicago: University of Chicago Press.

Griffiths, B. 1984. *The Creation of Wealth*. London: Hodder and Stoughton.

Griffiths, B. 1989. *Morality and the Market Place*. London: Hodder and Stoughton. (First published 1982.)

Harrison, T. 1985. *The Durham Phenomenon*. London: Darton, Longman and Todd.

Hay, D. A. 1989. *Economics Today: A Christian Critique*. London: Inter-Varsity Press/Apollos.

Hayek, F. 1944. *The Road to Serfdom*. London: Routledge.

Hirschmann, A. 1981. *Essays in Trespassing: Economics to Politics and Beyond*. Cambridge: Cambridge University Press.

Krieger, J. 1987. The United Kingdom: symbiosis or division. In G. Lodge and E. Vogel (eds), *Ideology and National Competitiveness*, pp. 29–53.

Lodge, G. and Vogel, E. 1987. *Ideology and National Competitiveness: An Analysis of Nine Countries*. Boston, Mass.: Harvard University Business School Press.

MacIntyre, A. 1984. *After Virtue: A Study in Moral Theory*, 2nd edn. Notre Dame, Ind.: Notre Dame University Press.

Norman, E. R. 1976. *Church and Society in England 1770–1970*. Oxford: Clarendon Press.

Nozick, R. 1974. *Anarchy, State and Utopia*. Oxford: Oxford University Press.

Raban, J. 1989. *God, Man and Mrs Thatcher*. London: Chatto & Windus.

Rawls, J. 1971. *A Theory of Justice*. Cambridge, Mass.: Harvard University Press.

Smith, A. [1776] 1937. *The Wealth of Nations*. New York: Modern Library edn.

Tawney, R. H. [1926] 1938. *Religion and the Rise of Capitalism*. West Drayton: Penguin. (This book is based on the Holland Memorial Lectures, given by R. H. Tawney in 1922.)

Thompson, K. 1987. *Beliefs and Ideology*. London: Tavistock.

Thompson, K. 1989. Transgressing the boundary between the sacred and the secular/profane: a Durkeimian perspective on a public controversy. Paper given at the Annual Meeting of the American Sociological Association, San Francisco, August 1989.

Walzer, M. 1983. *Spheres of Justice: A Defence of Pluralism and Equality*. New York: Basic Books.

16 *Is God enterprising? Reflections on enterprise culture and religion*

PAUL MORRIS

The essence of Christianity is the freedom of choice.[1]

[The] Tory Party was in its origin the Church of England in politics . . . the old concept of a partnership between Church and State lies very near the heart of traditional Tory thinking.[2]

Socialism . . . is the realization of the Christian gospel.[3]

She is the first proper Christian as a political leader that we have had for a long time! . . . she *does* believe in the ten commandments.[4]

During the last decade or so the Conservative government, in its attempt to recast Britain as an enterprise culture, has raised the profile of religious and theological issues to the centre of the political stage. The prime minister and the leader of the opposition have duelled about biblical quotations across the House (e.g. *Hansard*, Prime Minister's question time, 14 May 1988). Traditional Christian language and arguments have been marshalled by the proponents of the enterprise culture in support of their positions, and it has been argued by some that the Christian beliefs held by Margaret Thatcher and prominent members among her cabinet and advisers have been an influential factor in the formation of enterprise policies. Others have argued that the enterprisers have merely plundered Christian language and symbols 'to dignify their shallow ideologies'.[5] The major churches, and in particular certain leading clergymen and spokesmen of the Church of England, have been engaged in directly addressing government policies in an unprecedented fashion, thus questioning the traditional role of the churches and challenging the relationship between the state and the established church.

In this chapter I shall examine the relationship between religion[6] and enterprise culture. I begin by looking at the nature of the opposition to enterprise on the part of the churches, and go on to argue (against most of the religious and secular critics of enterprise) that religion plays a fundamental rather than instrumental role in the enterprise project. I briefly examine the notion of 'civil religion' in this context, and by way of conclusion I offer a number of more general reflections on religion and enterprise.

The Church of England as the 'loyal opposition' at prayer or '*Guardian* readers talking to *Telegraph* readers'

The 1980s saw the first breaches in the long-established and mutually supportive relationship between the Church of England and the Conservative Party, a relationship that has since reached a veritable 'separation of Church and State'.[7] Although the church had a 'special' relationship with the Tories, mutual support extended to the governments of the day, both being rooted, at least since 1945, in the sharing of the fundamentals of the postwar 'welfare state' consensus, and particularly in notions of social morality and social justice. The conscious attempt on the part of the enterprisers to demolish this consensus is obviously a major factor in the breakdown. The initial issues had little to do with the enterprise culture but represented a confrontational mode which would continue, and a perception by some government figures that the Church had overstepped its accepted boundaries and had failed in its expected duties.[8] As the Church came to be seen by sectors of the public as an 'alternative' voice to the government, a number of church leaders began responding, particularly to the issues of unemployment and poverty.[9]

Although Dr Runcie had publicly voiced his criticisms of what he saw as socially divisive government policies (interview in *The Times*, 28 September 1984), it was the report of the Archbishop of Canterbury's Commission on Urban Priority Areas, *Faith in the City* (1985), that was interpreted as a full frontal attack on *specific* government enterprise policies.[10] The report, a two-year study critical of the churches as well as of the government, was condemned by leading Conservatives and labelled as 'Marxist theology' by one cabinet minister. It was also criticized by theologians both outside and within the Church (see Biggar 1987; Badham 1989; Harvey 1989). The acceptance of the report by the General Synod led to the establishment of the Church Urban Fund and provided the justification for open Synod opposition to the 'poll tax'.

Since 1985 growing numbers of Anglicans, clergy and lay, have objected to general market and specific economic and social policies on Christian ethical grounds and there have been several publications[11] attacking government enterprise policies and their perceived consequences – particularly on the need for the extensive and extended provision of welfare services and opposition to privatization. Thus, the Church has not only found itself in the political arena but also as having taken sides in current political debates, a point not lost on the opposition.[12]

The Bishop of Durham, Dr David Jenkins, in the forefront of the clerical criticism (Jenkins 1988) of the government's 'wicked' enterprise policies,[13] has more recently been joined by the Archbishop of Canterbury himself, with his contention that those rewarded under the current enterprise system – the successful – are part of an emerging self-righteous Pharisee society of self interest and intolerance.[14] Dr Runcie, addressing the York Synod (1990), criticized capitalism and argued that:

> The market relies on moral restraints to be effective . . . The market economy does not create these moral attitudes, but it can erode them. That is why we must not allow our recognition of the value of the market to lead us to imagine it is the perfect embodiment of the divine word (Dr Runcie, quoted in *The Sunday Times*, 8 July 1990).

Several prominent theologians have addressed anew the issue of the Church's role in politics.[15] The sequel to *Faith in the City, Living Faith in the Cities* (1990), although recognizing government efforts in attempting to aid the inner cities, reiterates that economic policies must be examined in the light of their effects and is just as condemnatory of enterprise policies. Opposition to the enterprise culture continues unabated, supported, albeit not universally, by the Church at all levels. The Church has contested the enterprisers' claim to represent Christian teachings and in its opposition it has become radically politicized.

The churches share the view that the application of market forces (or quasi-market forces in the case of social services and education) has real human consequences for the least empowered members of our society, in many cases entire communities. They call for government and other provision of resources to particular industries and areas, for urban renewal and immediate relief for the hardest hit. The government's commitment to the inner cities, following the 1987 election, was very much in response to the challenge of *Faith in the City*.

The churches' attacks are often held, by their opponents at least, to be naive, but they are clearly calling for a reinstatement of some form of distributist mixed economy – the old consensus still survives in the churches if not in politics. Their main ire is not directed at the market system *per se* but at the universal claims made for its applicability. They charge that the necessary losers in the market system deserve 'social justice' and that there are 'limits to the market' and the claims for the morality of the market are questionable. The market, it is contended, is a most inadequate replacement for a sense of community, and the stress on individual responsibility is out of all proportion to the required level of collective responsibility.

A more sophisticated critique is that of Plant *et al.* (Harvey 1989), where the argument is that the notion of liberty advocated by the enterprisers (see Chapter 1) is flawed and those that enter the market system with most resources tend to gain most (and vice versa).

Faith in the City (1985) called for a 'liberation theology' for the inner cities, but recent studies have returned to a more traditional consensus view. Critics within the Church have asked where the theology is in all this, and there is some truth in the contention that the 'theological sections' often appear 'tagged on' to the concrete consensus policies.

The other major churches in Britain have followed similar trajectories into the political (albeit via the media) limelight.[16]

Although it is important to note their very different traditions of political involvement, it can, however, be seen that the collapse of the postwar consensus and the need to challenge the enterprise version of Christianity have been significant factors.

Christianity and enterprise, or 'an irregular association with the Church of England'

Although there is as yet no British study comparable to *Religion on Capitol Hill* (Benson and Williams 1986), the Christian beliefs of the cabinet and advisers have played a significant role in the determination of enterprise policy.[17] There are close links between prominent government figures and the Institute for Contemporary Christianity, the Christian Association of Business Executives, and the Christian Responsibility in Public Affairs (CRPA) group, formed in association with Brian Griffiths (head of the Policy Unit at Number 10 Downing Street) and Michael Alison, the prime minister's former private secretary. The CRPA is part of an international organization that has associations with the American 'moral majority'. In 1988, a group of senior ministers and advisers, including John Gummer, Kenneth Baker and David Mellor, led by Griffiths and sponsored by the CRPA, launched a campaign to promote the relationship between the values of Christianity and the enterprise culture.

Several of these figures subscribe to what might be called 'Christian democratic capitalism' and have been much inspired by American Christian capitalists, such as Michael Novak (see, for example, Alison, in Alison and Edwards 1990: 197–216). There are growing alliances between evangelical groups and Conservatives – 'the emergence of a British equivalent of the moral majority is to be expected' (David Martin, in Kavanagh and Seldon 1989: 340). A similar Christian capitalist position is held by Lord Harris of High Cross, the founder of the (influential in advocating enterprise reforms) right-wing think-tank, the Institute of Economic Affairs (Harris, in Alison and Edwards 1990: 179–96, and his contribution to *The New Right and Christian Values*, 1985: 4–15). Some of the other right-wing think-tanks and groups have also promoted analogous 'theologies' (for example, *The Salisbury Review*, see

Martin, in Kavanagh and Seldon 1989: 338). What these positions share is a claim that the market is both more efficient than the alternatives and more moral, and that this morality is dependent upon the Christian values that underlie and sustain it. We shall return to the morality of the market later.

The position of Mrs Thatcher as prime minister represented a typical and forceful statement of this type of 'enterprise theology'. The enterprise revolution was required because the nation was 'sick' economically, morally and spiritually. Mrs Thatcher called on the support of those holding 'Christian values' and these values play a particular part in her version of the enterprise culture. She makes a clear distinction between Christian values and political philosophy, arguing that the former provide not policies but 'the standards to which political actions must, in the end, be referred' (Thatcher 1989: 63).

The underlying values of a 'free society' can come only from religion, they cannot be generated by man – a spiritual being – or by the state (interview with Mrs Thatcher, Central Television, 29 March 1983; cf. Thatcher 1989: 66). These values are not created but 'revealed' to the human world and provide the opportunity to transform it (Thatcher, 'Preface' to Alison and Edwards 1990). Such values – the acknowledgment of God; tolerance; charity; individualism; freedom from coercion; the moral basis of the law and personal moral, familial, and social responsibility – are absolutes. This transformation produces the Christian nation-state with the task of upholding the rule of law and a civilization that has been, and is, uniquely committed to individual freedom: 'The basis of the Church is the spark within the human being which is really divine. And the Church should be working to bring out this spark' (*Daily Mail*, 29 April 1988). This spark is the basis of the individual and of his enterprise. The Christian tradition is the spiritual and cultural heritage of our nation, built by individuals. The upholding of law is vital as human sinfulness has to be 'policed' by the state.

Thatcher stresses that this religious tradition values work and 'economic activity – how we earn our living [and] create wealth' – but teaches that 'money is not an end in itself but a means to an end' (Thatcher 1989: 52); 'But Christ did not condemn riches as such, only the way in which they are used and those that put their trust in them' (p. 67). Thatcher advocates a free market as the form of economy for the Christian state whose task is to ensure that that system operates effectively. The free market is contrasted to the 'socialist' planned economy based on *secular* quasi-values, which, she argues, by definition can cater only for 'material' (that is, not moral/spiritual) concerns, and is, therefore, coercive and damaging to individual liberties. She correctly notes that the end of socialism in Eastern Europe ('the revolution that we started in 1979' (*The Independent*, 14 October 1989) – the enterprise culture) is linked to the resurgence of the free market, the nation-state and Christianity (Thatcher, 'Preface' to Alison and Edwards 1990).

Thatcher insists that free enterprise is a necessary but not a sufficient condition for national economic growth and subsequent benefits for all. Morality is also required – 'industry, honesty and responsibility and justice, its people need a purpose and an ethic', as a precondition of the market's operation, to control the worst excesses of the market (greed, exploitation, and so on) and to allow for a freedom beyond the merely material – and these cannot be provided by the state but 'can only come from the teachings of faith . . . and the Church'.

The Church has duties – to preach the gospel and celebrate the sacraments – but its main task is to promote Christian values in faith. The state is bound to recognize and defend these 'spheres of authority' (Thatcher 1989: 129). It was the churches that first promoted education and the state and church are partners in supporting religious/moral education. The 're-Christianizing' of religious education and the stress on collective Christian worship under the 1988 Education Reform Act are significant in this regard: 'The study of world religions is not enough. Religious education must expose children to the possibilities of experience and faith' (Kenneth Baker, at the Conservative Women's Conference, quoted in *The Independent*, 25 May 1988).

It is on this distinction between the discrete tasks of Church and state that the Church and the Conservatives have fallen foul of each other. In the *Baptist Times* in 1989, Lord Hailsham wrote: 'Church and State operate in different, though overlapping, spheres because they deal with different sets of values' (reported in *The Daily Telegraph*, 14 January 1989; see also, Hurd 1988). The Conservative view, exemplified by the Thatcher cabinet, is that the Church be concerned exclusively with *personal* morality: 'What we desperately need from the churches is a clear, definite and repeated statement of *personal* morality' (Douglas Hurd, at a meeting chaired by Dr Runcie on morality and the Church, quoted in *The Independent*, 16 April 1988). Mrs Thatcher held 'secret' meetings at Chequers with several bishops in 1987. The bishops considered that the issue was *social morality*, whereas the prime minister was concerned about the low level of *personal* morality (see Alison and Edwards 1990: 35 ff.). Hence the frequent calls for the clergy to stress personal and family values.

Lord Hailsham and others have accused the Church of being run by 'social science' bishops (a charge that churchmen have also levied) and of proclaiming beyond their competence: 'bishops should no more pontificate about economics than the Pope should correct Galileo's physics' (John Gummer, then chairman of the Tory Party, quoted in *The Guardian*, 29 April 1985).

Mrs Thatcher's most complete statement, to date, on the relationship between the Church and politics is to be found in her address to the 1988 General Assembly of the Church of Scotland (Thatcher 1989: 250–5). She states, 'we must not profess the Christian faith and go to church simply because we want social reforms and benefits or a better standard of behaviour – but because we accept the sanctity of life, the responsibility that comes with freedom and the supreme sacrifice of Christ' (p. 251). Christ works within the Christian to bring spiritual redemption and personal responsibility. Each individual has a Christian duty to utilize his responsibility both to create wealth for his family and to use some of his wealth for the good of others – 'It is not the creation of wealth that is wrong but the love of money for its own sake.' The state has a responsibility to relieve hardship and to ensure the provision of social services and education, but not in order to undermine individual responsibility (p. 253). The Church 'can teach the life of faith' and parliament 'can legislate for the rule of law'.

The Christian spirit of personal responsibility, with its origins in revelation, and the life of faith are the basis of the enterprise culture. The argument is taken a step further by reference to the work of Brian Griffiths (Griffiths 1982, 1983, 1984, 1985, 1990). He argues that 'the new Conservatism' (= enterprise culture) lies between any form of state socialism and laissez-faire capitalism. It is distinguished from both these forms of nineteenth-century *secular* enlightenment and 'rests firmly within the Judeo-Christian tradition' (Griffiths 1990): 218).[18]

This tradition, he contends, addresses itself to individuals and the success of the market economy is that it creates 'room' for the enterprising spirit of the individual. Markets require the existence of the cultural institutions of Christian societies – themselves based on Christian teachings – (for example, private property, the rule of law and limited government to ensure just market operation and a just law) and the virtues promoted by Christianity (the enterprising spark, self-interest, trust, justice, and individual responsibility). The market is just, not in the sense of being equalitarian (for he considers the operation of the market requires a degree of inequality) but in that the rule of law operates universally. There is a two-way relationship between Christian values and the market. First, the market requires the Christian (Protestant?) virtues. Secondly, the market rewards the individual and vouchsafes his liberties, thus sustaining those same virtues.

The virtues that are required for market 'capitalism' (Griffiths is unhappy about this term) to operate arose historically only in the context of Christian culture, and he argues that only in such a culture can the market be sustained. Without Christian virtue the market would collapse. Thus Griffiths considers that capitalism, although economically efficient and less coercive than the alternatives, can neither generate the values necessary for its operation nor sustain itself. Christian values are required. Griffiths rejects the claim that wealth creation is alien to Christianity, and considers both freedom *and* prosperity to be religious values. He maintains that if only church leaders had the will to proclaim these values, enterprise would flourish.

Margaret Thatcher argues that the whole equalitarian tradition espoused by the churches might well be based on a misunderstanding of teachers, such as John Wesley (*The Sunday Telegraph*, 26 June 1987), and even goes as far as suggesting that the failure of the churches to be true to their historic and traditional task – the inculcation of Christian virtues – may well be a significant factor in the rise of the 'dependency culture' (*Woman's Own*, 31 October 1987).

The market-led enterprise culture, thus, both rests on a Christian foundation and requires Christian values in order to keep going. The Church's hostility to business[19] and commerce (denied by Dr Runcie) and to the historic spirit of salvific Christianity plays a potentially very damaging role in terms of national wealth economy. What is needed is more appropriate Christian theologies of wealth[20] and success (John Patten, *The Independent*, 14 February 1989).

Civil religion?

It is claimed that, in 1988, Margaret Thatcher undertook to read her way through the Old Testament and gave progress reports to her staff. At the same time she was apparently not a regular church attender. It is hard to make any real sense of the figures, but it is clear that although a majority believe in God and a number of the tenets of traditional faith, church attendance is in a near-terminal decline (Jacobs and Worcester 1990: 78; Martin, in Kavanagh and Seldon 1990: 331 – 'The nationalized faith slips; the free market expands').

What part can religion play today? The same survey data show that there is still widescale support on moral issues. One way of understanding religion ('the functionalist') is in terms of the binding force that holds society together. Roger Scruton sees this as an essential feature of Conservatism, with Christianity as the foundation for all public life and social institutions in Britain (Scruton 1980: 172). Is this what the enterprisers mean by religion? Certainly some of the features of religion as it relates to the enterprise culture are the very features that unify our society (trust, rule of law, faithfulness). And it might be argued that our economic system is legitimated in terms of religion. Through religious and other education we could be seen to subscribe to a set of values that underlie our social order. Can we account for Mrs Thatcher's notion of faith in this way? She stresses that you don't have to be Christian to hold to our 'national' values. But can the transformation by faith that releases the divine spark be conceived of in this way? Certainly, the enterprise education programmes delivered in schools, polytechnics and

universities, without even a whiff of Christianity, suggest a
required underlying social 'glue' of values. Are the values required
for the enterprise culture civil religion as opposed to 'pulpit'
Christianity?[21]

Is God enterprising?

Michael Novak once speculated that God's evolutionary plans were
most enterprising – so many species engaged in the struggle to
survive – and he likened God's enterprise to that of capitalism.
God created a plethora of unique individuals with unique wants
and desires, and yet these needs can be satisfied by the capitalist
market – 'Oh, the wonder of it all!' he exclaims. Until most
recently, it was assumed that underlying our economic systems
was God (Meeks 1989).

Meeks argues that 'the metaphor *Economist* is a decisive and fully
appropriate way of describing the character and Work of God' and
that the recovery of 'God the Economist' will help the Church
to overcome the difficulties of attempting to relate faith to the
seemingly evermore dominant economic sphere of our lives. He
argues that although God has apparently been removed from our
accounts of the modern economy and thus from domination too,
upon examination, we find that domination still exists *within* the
economy, supported by 'deformed God concepts' (such as 'the
invisible hand').

Meeks contends that the 'authority attributes' of God have been
taken over by man as he is understood in terms of the modern market. Many people have been led into economic dependency, which
can be as disempowering as political dependency. Both rich and
poor in our society suffer from a loss of their full humanness. He
maintains that God is properly conveyed as Economist (community
of righteousness) and offers new possibilities for a non-dependent
economy. He attempts a redefinition of economy along Biblical
lines. Meeks insists that his study is only preliminary, but the
life of faith involves the economy (production, distribution and
consumption of the necessities of life) and involves God. Studies
such as these can push us to overcome the notion of economic
systems as somehow independent, estranged from our religious

lives and to attempt to rethink and relive them from new/old perspectives.[22]

The recovery of the older non-technical meanings of 'economy' would allow us justifiably to include 'economic' concerns within the spheres of our moral and religious discourses. Further, our recognition of the legitimacy of this connection would enable us openly to debate rival versions of such inclusive 'theo-economics' as the 'New Conservatism'. Although traditional doctrines such as St Thomas Aquinas' 'commutative' justice (exchange must be of goods of equal value) represent a worldview and morality as yet untransformed by the market, there are alternatives to the 'Whiggish' notion that all exchange entails the generation of virtue[23].

Notes: Chapter 16

1 Margaret Thatcher, interviewed by David Frost, 27 January 1986.
2 Margaret Thatcher (Thatcher 1989: 63).
3 Ronald Preston, 'Introduction' to Temple (1976: 23).
4 Paul Johnson, in Murray (1978: 77).
5 Jeremy Seabrook, *The Guardian*, 26 November 1984.
6 Although the references to 'religion' by advocates of the enterprise culture are sometimes to religions other than Christianity (usually Judaism), in this chapter I use 'Christianity' and 'religion' interchangeably.
7 Dr Robert Runcie, addressing a Free Church audience in 1988: 'In the Free Churches you have a longer tradition of being a "loyal opposition". If we in the Church of England are sometimes so perceived, please help us to get used to this prophetic perception' (quoted in, Alison and Edwards 1990: 33). An article, 'Politics and the Church', by an anonymous cleric (*The Yorkshire Post*, 18 October 1983), likened the average Anglican sermon to '*Guardian* readers talking to *Telegraph* readers' (cited in Alison and Edwards 1990). A Gallup poll found that, although 73 per cent of the C of E laity did not think that the Church should take sides in political issues, only 34 per cent of the clergy concurred (*Attitudes of the Laity, Clergy and Bishops to the Church of England*. 1984. London: Social Surveys).
8 This breach might be seen to have begun with the Archbishop of Canterbury's thanksgiving service sermon, following the Falklands War, at St Paul's Cathedral in July 1982. Dr Runcie called for a sharing of the grief of the mourners of both the British and Argentinian casualties, a suggestion condemned by a number of prominent Tories. The publication of the C of E's Board of Social Responsibility

Working Party report, *The Church and the Bomb: Nuclear Weapons and Christian Conscience* (1982. London: BSR House), which advocated unilateral nuclear disarmament, although later not accepted by the BSR, provoked anger and anxiety amongst many Conservatives.

9   Kenneth Thompson (Open University) has been engaged in a research project on the Bishop of Durham's correspondence, which reveals the extent to which people have addressed their economic and other difficulties to the Church. An example of the Church's response is to be seen in the Bishop of Liverpool's *Bias to the Poor* (Sheppard 1983).

10 The report understands the Church to be under the obligation of acting as the 'conscience of the nation', and argues that the stress on 'individualism' at the expense of 'collective obligation' is an underlying cause of 'the blighting of whole districts', the specific causes being current enterprise policies. On the question of the Church's traditional concern with general policies as opposed to policy specifics, see Forrester (1989: 16–35).

11 For example, *Not Just for the Poor* (1987. London: BSR): *Changing Britain: Social Diversity and Moral Unity* (1987. London: BSR).

12 For example, Gordon Brown, the shadow chief secretary to the Treasury, sent figures showing that the gulf between rich and poor had widened (reported in *The Independent*, 25 May 1988).

13 A term Dr Jenkins used specifically to refer to the proposed changes to the laws relating to social security (cited in *The Daily Telegraph*, 4 April 1988).

14 *The Director* (October 1989).

15 See, for example, Atherton (1988) and Atherton's chapter, 'The limits of markets', in Alison and Edwards (1990: 263–84); Forrester (1989); Medhurst and Moyser (1988).

16 For example, delegates at the 1988 Methodist annual conference called for a restoration of pre-budget tax levels and countered the claim that the poor, already paying proportionately more tax than the rich, were being given incentives. One delegate contended that the government had rejected biblical ideas of justice (*The Guardian*, 28 June 1988). The following year, Dr John Vincent, president of the Methodist Conference, referred to Mrs Thatcher's policies as a 'perversion' of the Christian tradition, that claimed to represent Christian values but did not (cited in *The Sunday Times*, 25 June 1989). The Church of Scotland has joined the fray, especially since the prime minister addressed the General Assembly in May 1988. Professor James Whyte, the Moderator, argues that there is 'a great hole in the *theology* by which we are governed' (quoted in *The Sunday Times*, 13 August 1989).

17 Hugo Young has characterized Mrs Thatcher's 'personal' relationship with the Church of England as 'an irregular association' (Young 1989: 6).

18 Griffiths has taught economics at the London School of Economics, and was the Dean of the City University Business School. He has published in the field of development economics.
19 See, for example, Lord Caldecote, 'Is profit next to ungodliness?' (*The Times*, 13 March 1990); David Edwards, 'Making money and serving God' (*The Times*, 12 March 1990).
20 See the *Oxford Declaration on Christian Faith and Economics*, signed by more than one hundred theologians and economists (Oxford, 1990).
21 See Bellah's seminal article, 'Civil religion in America' (1970: 168–89).
22 For a rather different Jewish perspective, see Neusner (1989).
23 See Macpherson (1985), Chapter 1.

References: Chapter 16

Alison, M. and Edwards, D. (eds). 1990. *Christianity and Conservatism*. London: Hodder & Stoughton.
Atherton, J. 1988. *Faith in the Nation: A Christian Vision for Britain*. London: SPCK.
Badham, P. 1989. 'Some secular trends in the Church of England Today'. In P. Badham (ed.), *Religion, State, and Society in Modern Britain*. Lampeter: Edwin Mellon, pp. 23–34.
Bellah, R. 1970. *Beyond Belief*. New York: Harper & Row.
Benson, P. and Williams, D. 1986. *Religion on Capitol Hill*. Oxford: Oxford University Press.
Biggar, N. 1987. *Theological Politics*. Oxford: Oxford University Press.
Faith in the City. 1985. Report of the Archbishop of Canterbury's Commission on Urban Priority Areas. London: Church House.
Forrester, D. 1989. *Beliefs, Values and Policies: Conviction Politics in a Secular Age*. Oxford: Oxford University Press.
Griffiths, B. 1982. *Morality and the Market Place*. London: Hodder & Stoughton.
Griffiths, B. 1983. *The Moral Basis of the Market Economy*. London: Conservative Political Centre.
Griffiths, B. 1984. *The Creation of Wealth*. London: Hodder & Stoughton.
Griffiths, B. 1985. *Monetarism and Morality*. London: Centre for Policy Studies.
Griffiths, B. 1990. The Conservative Quadrilateral. In M. Alison and D. Edwards (eds), *Christianity and Conservatism*, pp. 217–41.
Harvey, A. (ed.). 1989. *Theology in the City*, London: SPCK.
Hurd, D. 1988. *Rivals and Partners – Church and State 1988*. Oxford: Farmington Institute.
Jenkins, D. 1988. *God, Politics and the Future*. London: SCM.
Jacobs, E. and Worcester, R. 1990. *We British*. London: Weidenfeld & Nicolson.
Kavanagh, D. and Seldon, A. (eds). 1989. *The Thatcher Effect*. Oxford: Oxford University Press.

Living Faith in the Cities. 1990. Archbishop of Canterbury's Advisory Group on Urban Priority Areas. London: Church House.

Macpherson, C. B. 1985. *The Rise and Fall of Economic Justice*. Oxford: Oxford University Press.

Medhurst, K. and Moyser G. 1988. *Church and Politics in a Secular Age*. Oxford: Oxford University Press.

Meeks, M. 1989. *God the Economist*. Minneapolis: Fortress.

Murray, T. 1978. *Margaret Thatcher*. London: W. H. Allen.

Neusner, J. 1989. *The Economics of the Mishrah*. Chicago: Chicago University Press.

The New Right and Christian Values. 1985. Occasional Paper No. 5. Edinburgh: Edinburgh University Centre for Theology and Public Issues.

Raban, J. 1989. *God, Man and Thatcher*. London: Chatto & Windus.

Sheppard, D. 1983. *Bias to the Poor*. London: Hodder & Stoughton.

Scruton, R. 1980. *The Meaning of Conservatism*. Harmondsworth: Penguin.

Temple, W. 1976. *Christianity and the Social Order*. London: SPCK.

Thatcher, M. 1989. The revival of Britain: speeches on home and European affairs 1975–1988. In A. Cooke (ed.), London: Aurum Press

Young, H. 1989. *One of Us: A Biography of Margaret Thatcher*. London: Macmillan.

Name index

Subject index